Sexual Politics
in Cuba

Series in Political Economy
and Economic Development in Latin America

Series Editor
Andrew Zimbalist
Smith College

†Available in hardcover and paperback

Sexual Politics in Cuba

Machismo, Homosexuality, and AIDS

Marvin Leiner

Westview Press

Boulder • San Francisco • Oxford

To Anne, with love

Series in Political Economy and Economic Development in Latin America

Published in 1994 in the United States of America by Westview Press, Inc., 5500 Central Avenue, Boulder, Colorado 80301-2877, and in the United Kingdom by Westview Press, 36 Lonsdale Road, Summertown, Oxford OX2 7EW

Library of Congress Cataloging-in-Publication Data
Leiner, Marvin.
    Sexual politics in Cuba : machismo, homosexuality, and AIDS /
Marvin Leiner.
       p.   cm. — (Series in political economy and economic
development in Latin America)
    Includes bibliographical references and index.
    ISBN 0-8133-8654-3 — ISBN 0-8133-2122-0 (if published as a paperback)
    1. Sex instruction—Cuba.   2. Sex role—Cuba.   3. Gays—Cuba.
4. AIDS (Disease)—Cuba.   I. Title.   II. Series.
HQ57.6.C9L45   1994
306.7'097291—dc20   93-29166
                                                                                              CIP

Printed and bound in the United States of America

10   9   8   7   6   5   4   3   2

Contents

Tables

Preface

This work is part of an ongoing study of social and educational changes in Cuba since the Revolution of 1959. In a previous book, *Children Are the Revolution: Day Care in Cuba*,[1] I examined the care of small children in Cuba. This book initially was intended to analyze the whole system of education in Cuba, from elementary school to adult education. However, as I proceeded with my research and interviews, my interest was drawn more and more to developments in sex education, particularly as they emerged in the environment of the changing role of women and, later, in the relentless worldwide spread of AIDS. I became intrigued with the interrelated issues of gender equality, machismo, and homosexuality as they informed the progress of sex education and Cuba's response to the AIDS epidemic. That is the story I've tried to tell in this book.

In reporting what the Cubans are trying to do and what they have accomplished, I bring myself to this study as well—my own history and experiences, and the influence of people who have affected my view of Cuba and the educational process in general. John K. Fairbank, Harvard University professor emeritus and leading authority on China, has observed, "The reporter is part of the report, like the historian of his history." Thus, the reader must realize that while this report is as objective as I could make it, it is not impersonal.

No writer or observer can be purely objective. We bring our "selves" to our visits. However much responsible social scientists or reporters try to be open, fair, and honest in data collection and analyses, they still bring, both consciously and unconsciously, their own values, attitudes, and significant professional and personal experiences to the visited scene.

I grew up in the tenements of New York City, went on to become an elementary school teacher in poor neighborhoods, and later became a college professor committed to helping improve the quality of teaching in urban schools. I carry memories of many years teaching children in Brooklyn's Bushwick and Bedford Stuyvesant neighborhoods. Thus, I have appreciated and admired Cuba's genuine national commitment to education, where children from the urban and rural poor had real, new, "unheard of" educational opportunities.

Schools and psychology are my turf—the culture of the school and the people: children, teachers, parents, principals, university teacher trainers, psychologists, and others. I'm comfortable in a school setting after years of teaching at every level, of supervising and observing hundreds of classrooms. It's a world I know, a world that includes the dynamics and universals of making the most of limited resources, teacher training, power and authority, the psychology of children, teachers' unions, parent-school relations, curriculum change—realities that connect school people everywhere.

For more than twenty-five years, I have been studying educational changes in Cuba. During 1968 and 1969, my family and I lived in Havana. My three children were enrolled in Cuban schools (one in elementary, one in junior high, and one in senior high). My wife taught English at the university level, and I traveled the length and breadth of the island—observing children and classrooms; interviewing teachers, students, and administrators; and gathering materials. Since then, I have returned regularly to observe developments in education as well as Cuba's overall efforts to construct a socialist society.

During my visits sex educators, school administrators, physicians, students, and teachers patiently answered endless questions about goals and practices. I took notes, taped interviews and classes, and gathered whatever psychological and educational data were available. The fact that my family and I lived in Cuba helped generate a rapport with those interviewed; I wasn't a complete outsider.

Sections of this work are based on the conversations I had with many Cubans. These are some of the people to whom I am indebted:

Cuban Minister of Education José R. Fernández patiently helped me gain access to a wide variety of urban and rural schools and understand the structure and methods of Cuban schools.

Abel Prieto Morales, vice minister of education from 1968 until his death in 1984, not only directly and openly answered my questions about educational policies during each of my visits but also freely responded to my questions on sexuality, including policies toward homosexuals.

The Federation of Cuban Women and its leader, Vilma Espín, provided me with answers to a range of questions about day care, the role of women in Cuba, and the key linkage with education.

The top three administrators of GNTES (the National Working Group for Sex Education), Dr. Celestino Lajonchere, the first director; Dr. Monika Krause, his successor; and Dr. Stela Cerutti, the assistant director, not only gave graciously of their time but spoke frankly about the problems they confronted both in implementing programs and in changing attitudes.

Special thanks are also due to the following: Joseph Murphy, former chancellor of the City University of New York (CUNY); Iraida López, co-ordinator of the CUNY-Caribbean Exchange Program; and John Lidstone, former dean of the School of Education at Queens College of the City University, all provided vital support for my research efforts.

Virginia Thompson, Mildred Hardeman, Vicki Shives, and John Lidstone read early drafts of the manuscript and offered many valuable comments and suggestions. Carolyn Perla provided an insightful analysis regarding specific aspects of sex education.

I would like to thank Karen Wald, a leading reporter on Cuba's AIDS policy, for generously making available her interviews with residents in the Havana sanitorium for people who tested HIV-positive.

Annick Piant, Jennifer Peters, and Nan Selman were knowledgeable and diligent research assistants during various phases of this project. I am also indebted to the staff at the Center for Cuban Studies in New York City: Director Sandra Levinson, Irving Kessler, and, especially, Librarian Jerry Nichol. They always patiently responded to my persistent requests for new or more data from their Cuban collection.

This book was written with the help of research grants from the Ford Foundation, the Social Science Research Council and the American Council for Learned Societies, the Antilles Research Program at Yale University, and, more recently, from the CUNY-Caribbean Exchange Program and the Research Foundation of the City University of New York (PSC/CUNY Research Award).

I am grateful to Carolina Mancuso for her warm support from the very beginning of this project, her gifted editing skills, and her suggested revisions on various drafts; to Elaine Fuller for her insights and perspectives as a long-time Cuba watcher and friendly insistence on minimalism—her suggestions and changes have been incorporated into the text; and to Phoebe Hoss who, with her eye for coherence and clarity, helped turn a clumsy manuscript into a book.

I am especially appreciative of the strong support and encouragement from a leading scholar on Cuba, Andy Zimbalist, general editor of the Westview Press Series in Political Economy and Economic Development in Latin America, and Barbara Ellington, senior editor at Westview. Their on-target suggestions, advice, and comments strengthened the manuscript in numerous ways.

During the time I was completing this study, three important Americans who greatly influenced my views on building a socialist society died: Myles Horton, Michael Harrington, and I. F. Stone. Myles Horton founded the Highlander School in Tennessee in 1932. Over the years, he taught thousands of blacks and whites to challenge the strictures of a segregated society. Because of his close work with unions, antipoverty organizations, and civil rights leaders, he is often credited for being one of the sparks that ignited the civil rights movement in the United States. Rosa Parks and Dr. Martin Luther King, Jr., were among the adult students attending classes at Highlander. In his actions and writings as well as through our personal relationship—especially during an intensive trip in 1980 to Nicaragua to witness the Nicaraguan Literacy Campaign—Myles Horton had a strong influence on my work. He provided a key unit of analysis: How oppressed people and minorities are treated is a measure of a society. In this work, I have focused on people with AIDS and homosexuals as the measure for Cuban society. Myles's voice and vision during those late-night conversations in Nicaragua are still with me. He died in January 1990.

Mike Harrington was a friend as well as my colleague at Queens College. He was an unusual, special *mensch* with charisma, Irish wit, warmth, love of people, and brilliant intellect—the American socialist man of the twentieth century. We were both part of a group of professors that met weekly for lunch and discussion. Our themes were interdisciplinary and included discussion and argument about a path to socialism that was not authoritarian. Like Walt Whitman, John Dewey, and C. Wright Mills, Harrington believed in the "possibility of social betterment by means of creative intelligence, moral suasion, and political struggle."[2]

I. F. Stone was an independent socialist journalist and writer, a wise and special man who emphasized (as did Harrington) that socialism without democracy is a contradiction; that freedom and justice, which include the basic freedoms of assembly, speech, and press, must go together with socialism. Stone and Harrington eloquently argued in their works that if the contradiction is maintained, it will lead to horrendous abuse of power.[3] In this work I attempt to document their thesis. Both men died in 1989.

I am also indebted to François Delaporte's brilliant work on the cholera epidemic of 1832, to Michel Foucault, and to contemporary disciples in the United States such as Douglas Crimp, former editor of the journal *October*, for the theoretical underpinnings of some of the analysis of AIDS in this work.

In the final analysis, I alone am responsible for the opinions and conclusions expressed in this book.

My wife, Anne, and children—Kenny, Karen, and Danny—accompanied me through the first year of this Cuban journey and helped me with my subsequent efforts to understand the Cuban Revolution. I thank them with much love for their support and wisdom. My thanks to Kenny for sharing with me his diary and his current insights about the Cuban Revolution—an excerpt is included in this volume. Danny's careful critique, from politics to literacy, and Karen's varied assistance, from word processing to probing questions, are also much appreciated.

No words of thanks could suffice to express my gratitude to Anne for her valuable critical advice on the issues discussed in this book and for her patience with a husband who periodically got lost in research and writing on Cuba.

Marvin Leiner

Notes

1. Marvin Leiner, *Children Are the Revolution: Day Care in Cuba* (New York: Penguin Books, 1978).

2. Cornel West, "Michael Harrington, Socialist," *The Nation*, January 8–15, 1990, 59.

3. As I note in Chapter 6, almost 100 years ago Rosa Luxemburg in her debate with Lenin on democracy and socialism strongly argued what would be the Harrington/Stone position about the necessity of guaranteeing freedoms under socialism.

1

The Paradox of Cuba's Revolution

On February 11, 1988, while flying to Cuba, I read a *New York Times* op-ed piece entitled "Cuba's Callous War On AIDS," by Ernesto B. Betancourt.[1] In 1988 he was a director of Voice of America's Radio Martí, which broadcast to Cuba with the implicit aim of generating opposition to the Cuban government. Naturally, Betancourt was strongly critical of Cuba's AIDS policy, accusing it of violating the human rights of "AIDS carriers" because these people had no choice but to give up their jobs and spend the rest of their lives in a sanitorium, whether or not they were ill. This was a very disturbing accusation that required investigation. It would not be the first time that distorted and even blatantly untrue reports of Cuban life appeared in the United States.

This was also an issue close to my heart. I was coming from New York City, where AIDS was decimating many communities, where I witnessed family and friends suffering and dying, and where I joined others in criticizing a shocking, "tortoise-slow government policy" toward AIDS. In fact, the first response of New York City officials had been to deny there was a rampant disease.[2] As a psychotherapist I knew about the pain of people with AIDS as well as of those testing HIV-positive. I felt deeply hurt about this tragedy in their lives and in the lives of their families and friends.

It wasn't just that I hoped the quarantine report wasn't true. It seemed to contradict my experience of the role of education in Cuba since the Revolution. From the beginning, education had been essential to the revolutionary government's programs to radically transform Cuban society; it was "the path up from underdevelopment" as the government attacked the problems of public health, housing, land distribution, job opportunities, and economic development.[3] This meant not only achieving high levels of education but providing the opportunity for education for all citizens. One of the most dramatic and effective educational programs anywhere in the world was carried out in Cuba in the early years of the Revolution—the Literacy Campaign of 1961. Over 700,000 people

1

learned to read and write from young volunteers sent to the remote countryside to teach illiterates on a one-to-one basis.[4]

In all cultures around the world, the AIDS epidemic has brought to the fore deeply entrenched attitudes about men, women, and sex. The way in which any nation responds to a disease such as AIDS "reveals its deepest cultural, social, and moral values. These core values—patterns of judgment about what is good or bad—shape and guide human perception and action."[5]

The Cuban response to the AIDS crisis reflects both the strengths and weaknesses of the Cuban system. On the one hand, there exists a strong national commitment to providing health care—no matter what the cost—in order to serve the common good. This means free health care to all people without prejudice, including the best available treatment for AIDS patients.[6] On the other hand, under the justification of "the common good," the government has created a draconian institution—the quarantine of all people testing HIV-positive. This is a serious mark against an otherwise admirable public health system.

Those in Cuba who have questioned the quarantine policy are labeled "enemies of the Revolution," thus effectively excluding the possibility of public advocacy for the 703 people in quarantine and for their families.

Lacking an independent press and the right to independent assembly, Cubans were not able to hear and debate publicly the proposed quarantine or possible alternatives. There is no gay rights advocacy group, no *Gay Community News* or *The Advocate* (U.S. periodicals concerned with gay and lesbian issues); the Cuban government does not believe in the need for such groups in a society still "consolidating" the revolution.

Organizations such as gay rights groups are seen in terms of their potential for facilitating CIA infiltration. The argument is that the structure of party-based organizations overrides the need for a proliferation of different and overlapping interest groups. Homosexuals, for example, as students, poets, and workers can belong to the writer's union (UNEAC), the women's federation (FMC), the university students association (FEEM), or a worker's union. The concept that a socialist society could also include independent political organizations from the grass roots appears contradictory to those in power. They fail to see that "social control of the major means of production" (nationalization) is not inconsistent with a democratic socialism.[7]

A traditional Latin machismo, which includes a trio of prejudices—against women, against homosexuality, and against public sex education—has combined with historical international reactions to "plagues" to produce policies and practices that encroach on the human rights of Cuban citizens.

Although Cuba is the only nation to institute a quarantine of people testing HIV-positive, the sexual prejudices prevalent there are hardly unique to its culture. While some societies have gone further than others in beginning to overcome these prejudices, they are universal. And everywhere, including Cuba, there are those struggling against homophobia, for the equality of women, and for better sex education. This book is really about change and how difficult it is for an individual and a society to overcome sexism, machismo, and homophobia.

The difficulty is highlighted with the case of Cuba because for the past thirty-four years, government and social institutions there have claimed legitimacy precisely for making some essential breaks with the past. The AIDS epidemic has brought to the fore these deeply entrenched attitudes about gender and sexuality in cultures around the world. Understanding the Cuban experience may help generate better approaches to that epidemic.

Cuba's Successful Revolution

As context to our story some statement on the Cuban Revolution and Fidel Castro's role is necessary. The Revolution took place in one of the most culturally homogeneous nations of the world.[8] All but a few thousand Cubans spoke Spanish. The island nation did not suffer from the separatism and strife of land disputes or severe tribal and religious differences that beset other countries in Latin America, Asia, and Africa. There was, however, a large black minority and a large portion of people of mixed race in the population. While the 1953 census classified 26.9 percent of the people as black or "mixed race" the true proportion was undoubtedly much higher; mulattos consistently underreport their blackness because of extensive economic and social discrimination. "The man of dark skin was in general greatly disadvantaged in prerevolutionary Cuba. But this racial cleavage was not so complete as to constitute an enduring impediment to mobilization and cultural transformation after Castro came to power." Even today, however, at least 50 percent of the population is black or mulatto while the census reports 33 percent.[9]

There was and is no overpopulation problem in Cuba, and in climate and geography the country has no extreme conditions or natural barriers. Aggregrate measures of Cuba's economic and social conditions in the 1950s, notably gross national product per capita, placed it among the top seven Latin American countries. These measures revealed nothing, however, of vast inequalities. Large percentages of material goods, such as television sets and radios, and of services, such as those performed by doctors, were available only to the rich, the small middle class, and tourists in the large cities of Havana and Santiago. According to a 1950 study of rural Cuba, 60 percent of the island's rural families lived in dwellings with earth floors and roofs of palm leaves; two thirds lived in houses without water closets or latrines; only one in every fourteen families had electricity.[10] Rural families were also the most neglected in respect to education. Still, although 43 percent of the rural adult population could not read or write, they were, as Nelson Lowry concluded in 1950, "anxious for better educational facilities for their children."[11]

During my trips to Cuba, teachers and educational leaders often recounted the conditions in Havana before the Revolution—the commercialization of sex and the widespread control of the city by organized crime during the 1950s. Notorious corruption was prevalent in all sectors of public life. Lourdes Arguelles and B. Ruby Rich, researchers on the Cuban lesbian and gay experience, in a review of the prerevolutionary period describe an atmosphere of decadence and sexual degeneracy reflected in gambling, drugs, and prostitution, and the staggering statistic of more than two hundred thousand workers hired as petty traders, casino operators, entertainers, servants, and prostitutes.[12] At least half of these are estimated to have been women, either directly or indirectly engaged in prostitution.

In March 1952 a military coup made Fulgencia Batista the head of state. He immediately stopped the electoral process including elections for the Chamber of Deputies in which the young lawyer, Fidel Castro, was to have been a candidate. The opposition movement, eventually led by Castro and his 26th of July Movement, was not only against Batista's dictatorship but against all the corruption, crime, and poverty as well. And, above all, it was a movement of Cuban nationalism growing out of a history of colonialism and subjugation by foreign powers. "Most nations outside Europe and North America have had the course of their development shaped by imperialist domination. But few have experienced the degree of subjugation suffered by Cuba during its 400 years under formal Spanish control as a colony and its 60 years under the de facto control of the United States."[13]

On July 26, 1953, when Castro and his fellow insurgents led a daring attack on the Moncada Barracks in Santiago de Cuba, they initiated an armed struggle that had roots in almost 100 years of a national campaign for independence. The new movement's heroes were those of the late nineteenth century wars of independence—Antonio Maceo and José Martí.[14] After imprisonment and exile, Castro and 82 other rebels returned from Mexico to begin guerilla warfare in the eastern mountains, the Sierra Maestra. They gained growing support, primarily in the countryside but also in the cities.

On January 8, 1959, two years after landing on the coast of Oriente, Fidel Castro and his guerilla fighters entered Havana. They were greeted by ringing church bells, blowing factory whistles, and tens of thousands of enthusiastic Cubans.[15] That night Fidel spoke to those thousands of Cubans, the first of his long public talks on what became major themes of the Revolution. He emphasized the Rebel Army's responsibility for victory, the need for continued revolutionary unity, and the national task of achieving social justice in an independent Cuba. When he finished speaking, two white doves appeared on his shoulders. Tad Szulc, in his thorough biography of Castro, calls the march into Havana an "apotheosis, marvelously staged" and represents the climactic appearance of the doves as the beginning of a kind of deification of Castro:

> This astounding symbolism touched off an explosion of: "FIDEL . . . FIDEL . . . FIDEL!" as the night was caressed by the dawn. Cubans are a people with powerful religious and spiritistic superstitions, going back to the Afro-Cuban traditions of slavery, and that night in January confirmed their faith: The dove represents life and now Fidel had their protection. . . . The deification of Fidel Castro became a phenomenon in Cuba in the aftermath of his victory, so greatly had he touched the hearts and souls of the people.[16]

The new government provided large budgets for school construction, program development, teacher training, and national mobilization to eliminate illiteracy. This was a truly radical policy symbolized by the dramatic closing down of the schools and tapping the energy of idealistic adolescents who spent months in remote areas teaching adults to read. It was an education for everyone. It built real support for the Revolution and created a faith in education as necessary to any kind of progress. In both planning and practice, education was of the highest priority. Children became the raison-d'être and the darlings of the Revolution.

Schooling became available to all, especially to the poor in rural areas.[17] For the first time there came into existence widespread training programs for particular technical skills. Science and mathematics became favored subjects in an attempt to eradicate traditional suspicious attitudes toward modern agricultural methods and the technology of industrialization.

Education was also to be the antidote to the cesspool Havana had become under Batista in the 1950s—a city of commercial sex, gambling casinos, drugs, and organized crime. This thrust was vividly illustrated for me one afternoon in 1969, when I was observing the introduction of modern mathematics to young children at the Liberty City educational complex in Havana.[18] The teacher proudly demonstrated the use of the small plastic disks the children were moving around in little piles to solve problems. With a twinkle in her eye, the director asked whether I knew the origin of these teaching materials. I guessed Sweden, knowing that early childhood teaching materials in Cuba at that time often came from one of the Scandinavian countries.[19]

I guessed wrong. Holding up a handful of the plastic pieces and smiling, she proudly explained, "These were taken from the gambling casinos which were closed in 1959. How's that for a revolution in education? We closed down gambling casinos and transferred the chips to teach modern mathematics in first grade classrooms!"

Before the current crisis brought about by sudden changes in the former USSR, there had been an equal revolution in medicine and health care, one that puts to shame the health care of people in poor New York City neighborhoods where I have worked. In Cuba health care is linked with education. For example, nutritious and adequate food, together with proper hygienic and health standards, are primary considerations in the schools. School children continue to receive larger supplies of milk, meat, fruits, and vegetables than their parents.[20]

Indeed, Cuba's health care achievements have become the envy of other nations, especially in the third world. They are acknowledged to "rival those in the industrialized world."[21] In 1983 Cuba launched a family practice program that has received international praise. The director of the World Health Organization (WHO) in November 1988 stated that Cuba's target date of 1995 will make Cuba the first nation in the world with comprehensive family practice coverage of 100 percent of its population—"a revolution within the revolution." The previous director of WHO stated, "As for Cuba's self-reliance in health matters . . . it has become legendary." Pedro Cabal, the executive counselor of WHO in 1991, said that Cuba has "the only efficient health organization in Latin America."[22]

Free health care is a national priority; the system emphasizes prevention, primary care, and services in the community. Despite the fact that Cuba is a third world country with a $1,900-per-capita GNP (compared to about $21,000 in the United States), Cuba's health indicators have surpassed those of the United States in universal health coverage, preventive primary care, infant mortality, life span, and medical insurance.[23]

In addition, Cuba's progressive social security system enables women to retire at age fifty-five and men at age sixty. Cuba has the most advanced social security system in all of Latin America: It covers practically 100 percent of the population compared with Brazil (32 percent), Chile (70 percent), Mexico (25 percent), and Peru (36 percent).[24] Cuba's infant mortality rate has dropped from more than 60 per 1,000 live births in 1958 to 10.2 in 1992. This is the lowest in Latin America and in the history of Cuba. WHO General Director Dr. Hiroshi Nakjama at the Third International Health Care Seminar on Primary Health Care in Havana called this "truly extraordinary." In 1983 the infant mortality rate in the United States was 11.2 per 1,000 live births overall and among black Americans it was 21.1. In 1990 Cuba was one of the twenty-seven nations in the world with lower infant mortality rates than in the United States for African-American babies.[25]

By 1981, 100 percent of the rural population were receiving health services. Diseases such as diphtheria and polio had been eliminated. The United States and Cuba now have similar rates in whooping cough, tuberculosis, measles, and tetanus. In Cuba these days, as in the advanced industrialized nations, the three leading causes of death are cancer, heart disease and stroke.[26]

The most dramatic change in Cuban medical care has been the enormous increase in numbers of practicing physicians. When the guerrilla army came to power, there were 6,300 doctors in Cuba. Almost half of them left the country within five years.[27] Cuba, with a population of about 10.3 million, now has approximately 25,567 physicians, or one for every 399 inhabitants, as well as one dentist for every 1,772 persons. By the year 1999 it expects to have one physician for every 283 people. The United States expects to have one doctor for every 375 people by the year 2000. As this book goes to press the Cuban health care system has been severely affected by the economic crisis in Cuba. The scarcity of fuel and the severe shortages of food and medicine have strained the delivery of health services. Dr. Pedro Pons, director of the Policlinico Plaza de la Revolución in Havana said: "The economic situation has affected our health situation. We must admit that the crisis has helped lower the health status of the people. Medicines that were once distributed at the family level are no longer given out so freely . . . everything has been reduced." In Paris, 120 French medical professors and physicians issued a statement published in *Le Monde* calling for the lifting of the U.S. embargo on medicines to Cuba. They asked: "Must children and patients in any country fall victims to international political conflicts?"[28]

The combination of improved health and educational opportunities has literally changed the demographic landscape. With the large exodus of trained middle- and upper-class personnel after the Revolution, mostly white males, blacks, and women joined male white peasants and workers as they moved into responsible positions.[29] As a result, large numbers of blacks and women moved up the power ladder to skilled, professional, and managerial positions. The primary government project for women was to bring them into the workforce and the education system. Narrow as this policy may be in terms of women's equality, it cannot fail to have great repercussions for machismo and traditional sexual prejudices.

The Cuban Paradox

There is a paradox in Cuba. On the one hand, civil society has made such significant advances that the aspirations and expectations of the masses of people are greatly enhanced. Progress toward economic equality and the provision of basic social goods has gone far. On the other hand, the inability to increase outputs of goods and services and improve the distribution system threatens to overwhelm these outstanding advances. The one-party political unity that guaranteed survival in the early years has become, in effect, a political straitjacket.[30]

We can clearly see this paradox in the response to the AIDS epidemic. Those testing HIV-positive and those who eventually contract AIDS receive the best of medical care. Yet, the political straightjacket led to an early decision (with no public discussion) requiring permanent quarantine in sanitoriums for all persons testing HIV-positive. These people are, in effect, prisoners in a golden cage.

So dominant has Fidel Castro been in the Cuban government, in the Communist party that evolved out of the 26th of July Movement, and, indeed, in the whole Cuban culture, that even a book on machismo, sex education, and AIDS must include as background some discussion of this man and the economic and political system he leads. In some ways we might say that he is machismo at its best. There are numerous anecdotes about his presence all over the island, about his smarts, and his energy. The Nobel-prize–winning novelist Gabriel García Márquez describes him as a charismatic, brilliant orator, whose supreme assistant is his memory; a man addicted to conversation and the pursuit of ideas; a man who reads voraciously, especially in economics and historical subjects. One of the most eminent scholars on Cuba, Jorge Domínguez, stated in his 1989 study of Cuba's foreign policy that Castro combines strategic and tactical abilities rarely surpassed among world leaders.[31]

Once in the early 1970s, when I was having coffee in the cafeteria of the Hotel Habana Libre, I struck up a casual conversation with a man sitting near me. He was in the construction business, a tradition in his family. By 1970 he was in charge of building the new Havana province *"escuelas en el campo"*—a project of instituting large boarding schools for adolescent students in the countryside—a bold massive approach for meeting the needs of a growing universal education system.[32]

When I asked him about planning sites for new schools, he surprised me by responding, "Oh, Fidel tells us where they are to be built. He comes out with the team and says, 'Here! We will build a school here and there and there.'"

Fidel himself has become an institution, a leader so beloved that those who would do things differently nevertheless do not form any political opposition to him. Cubans are proud that Fidel appears to be ubiquitous and involved in all aspects of Cuban life—from economic development to public health, from education and sports to foreign affairs and international issues. Indeed, people complaining about particular bureaucratic and economic deficiencies often say something to the effect that if only Fidel knew about it, he would fix things. He has become the "good king" in opposition to bad bureaucrats.

Yet, Fidel Castro's long leadership can also be seen as a modern form of *caudillismo*. In this Latin American institution, power is completely centered in the chief (the *caudillo*) and cannot, by definition as a system of supreme power in one person, provide a democratic society.[33] Thus, his hands-on involvement—selecting a specific site for a school in the countryside or promising to get a new winch for workers at a construction site; changing the construction design of family doctor clinics; taking personal charge of breadmaking and beer distribution[34]—manifests his need for control even as it provides new material for popular folklore. But his attention to these details has not proven to be an efficient, competent, or effective route for national economic planning and administration. On the contrary, plans are often disrupted and the systemic causes of missing winches or faulty beer distribution are not addressed.

The Cuban government's one-party system rests on the Leninist rationale that strong political unity is necessary for the survival of the revolution. In the early years of Cuba's revolution, when the small island nation had to withstand military attack from the United States as well as continuing CIA-directed sabotage and repeated attempts to assassinate Castro, such political unity served the nation well. Cuban anxiety about violent sabotage was not a case of paranoia. From 1959 to 1967 there were a great many acts of sabotage, an attempted invasion, and many killings by armed guerillas—including the deaths of students and teachers in the literacy campaign. Much of this terrorism was backed by the United States government through the CIA.[35]

Cuba has successfully resisted invasion, sabotage, and assassination attempts as well as the economic blockade imposed by the United States in 1961. But its survival required political centralization and alliance with the Soviet Union.[36]

Concentration of political power was the most significant long-term effect of the American embargo. Fear of sabotage and threats of attack intensified the necessity for political loyalty and called for mobilization to achieve greater self-sufficiency. These threats also provided the rationale for political and economic quasi-war status, for controls, and a high degree of conformity to combat the influence of the United States and its "market mentality."

But after thirty-four years, the political centralization that was once necessary has become a severe constraint. The political system has not moved toward new democratic forms to match its radical social achievements. The assumption is that socialism and democracy can be achieved within a one-party structure.

Along with political centralization in the early years came economic centralization and a type of command economy seen as the only way to decisively attack the enemy of underdevelopment and extreme inequalities of wealth. The economic system that began to emerge after the 1959 Revolution was very much influenced by the thinking of Ernesto "Che" Guevara, the Argentine doctor who fought with the 26th of July movement and became Castro's first lieutenant in the guerrilla struggle in the Sierra Maestra mountains of eastern Cuba. Guevara envisioned the emergence of a "new socialist man" who is motivated not by material considerations of any kind but rather by moral values directed toward what is necessary to create a better life for all people. The "new socialist man" demonstrates a sense of solidarity and brotherhood. He finds fulfillment in work and respects it for being worthwhile in and of itself. He exhibits a strong moral character coupled with individual responsibility and intellectual curiosity.[37]

According to Che Guevara, moral incentives could guide economic production as well as other social relations. There is no need to strive for profitability and focus narrowly on cost accounting—the economy would grow and productivity would rise as all worked for the common good. Competition was seen only in its destructive aspects, not its constructive ones. It would be eliminated in a national centrally controlled economy—the whole economy operating as if it were one giant corporation producing everything the population needed and for which everyone worked.[38]

Questions of moral versus material incentives, of how centralized the economy should be, and whether markets had any role in it have been at the center of economic organization since Guevara's day in the mid-1960s. In general, there was a move toward material incentives, decentralization, and the introduction of some market exchanges. While there was marked economic growth and development throughout the 1970s and early 1980s, problems of low productivity, low quality, poor distribution, and insufficient diversification in exports persisted. The system could not withstand the effects of several international changes in the mid-1980s; economic difficulties began to worsen and required the imposition of a severe austerity program.

In response, President Castro initiated a "rectification campaign" in which he revived Che Guevara's economic approach, particularly on moral incentives and on combatting economic problems as though they were part of a war requiring heroic actions to overcome a prevalent "bourgeois mentality among workers." Behind the rectification campaign lies an important question: Is it possible to keep such a revolutionary spirit going indefinitely, especially when most workers were born or came of age after 1959? They are more than 34 years away from the heroics of the guerilla fighters.[39]

Today's austerity puts in jeopardy many of the social programs developed over the years. One significant example is the marked rise in prostitution. It has been a point of great pride that programs of education, job availability, and humane treatment practically eliminated prostitution in the early years of the revolution.[40]

The social security system, universal free education, and the guarantee of jobs for everyone, eliminated the economic base for prostitution. In recent years, however, with renewed development of the tourist industry, in a time of increasing shortages and economic hardship, prostitution has reappeared. Stores for tourists and diplomats offer electronic equipment and many other attractive items sold for dollars and not available elsewhere, encouraging both black market activity and prostitution to earn dollars. Since one needs an ID to buy in the hotel tourist store, prostitutes often ask their clients to purchase various consumer goods for them or take them on extended excursions to beaches in such beautiful resort areas as Varadero. Some reports in the Cuban press indicate that prostitution for foreign currency has become quite widespread. It is certainly in evidence around all the main hotels.[41]

Sexuality and the AIDS Crisis

There were nearly four centuries of Spanish colonial domination in Cuba. Originally, Hernán Cortés used Cuba as a base from which to assemble his troops for the conquest of Mexico and Peru. He left behind those who were not in good enough health or in possession of enough resources to follow him. Many were from the south of Spain, adding an Arabic influence to the culture. The Spaniards brutally eliminated the aboriginal population and imported slaves from Africa. For a long time, the African and Spanish population was primarily male. Colonial society was accompanied by what Cuban sex educators refer to as "anachronistic Catholicism, enemy of sexuality and the human body." The head of an American organization of married priests simply says, "The church is fundamentally a male, celibate, institution. It does not understand women or marriage."[42] The mix of all of this brought in and reinforced concepts and customs of male overvaluation; women were valued only for their reproductive capacity. This history contributed to modern practices of male superiority and the double standard.

Cuban culture has not been influenced as strongly as some other Latin

American cultures by the Catholic church's position on questions of sexuality in respect to marriage, celibacy, abortion, and women's rights. Indeed, most studies indicate that the Catholic church had little popular support among Cubans.[43] Most of the clergy were foreign, primarily from Spain, which was a major factor in the Cubans' historical indifference to Catholicism. Cubans "simply found little with which to identify." Although 90 percent of the population had been baptized, a 1954 study showed that only 5 percent were practicing Catholics. In a 1957 study of rural areas, 53 percent of those surveyed had *never* seen a priest.[44]

Nevertheless, the Church's concepts of morality and ethics left an indelible mark upon the attitudes and behavior of the people. Sex educators argue that, in a sense, because the formal religious connection itself was lost over the centuries, Catholic interpretation of sexual mores took on even greater status. It was accepted by most people as "nature." "It's much easier to change attitudes and mentalities if people are aware of the religious background; if they know that it is a rule established by the Church. It is enormously difficult to change any kind of attitude, or mentality, if people say it is determined by nature."[45]

Another key to the morality of the revolutionary years is the notion of the city as locus of immoral and criminal behavior in contrast to a pure and unspoiled countryside. This had been part of revolutionary thinking since the 1950s when Havana had become such a corrupt tourist center. Many policies and reforms of the Revolution have focused on improving life in the countryside. Unfortunately, homophobia has also found expression in this context. The myth is that one does not find homosexuals in the countryside, only in the degenerate city. Thus, Abel Prieto Morales could say in 1969: "Throughout the whole world, those preoccupied with these problems (homosexuality), who without doubt classify them as problems of psychosocial origin, claim that the true contagion takes place in big cities, in the darkness of the cabarets, the special 'meeting salons'. . . . Homosexuality is very rare in the countryside—in the same environment where the struggle to conquer nature is a daily and constant activity."[46]

I heard the myth of "no gays in the countryside" again in 1988 at a group interview of leading members of the writers and artists union (UNEAC). Although vigorous objection came from one of Cuba's outstanding writers, Miguel Barnet, the fact that the myth still circulates publicly underscores the reality that, in one serious regard, a revolution in education did not occur. As Monika Krause, former director of the National Working Group on Sex Education, has succinctly noted: "The one area revolutionaries and counter-revolutionaries have in common is homophobia."[47]

The sexual revolution of the 1960s profoundly affected attitudes towards sex, life styles, and work conditions in many parts of the world. The views of sex as "self-expression" and a measure of identity and happiness strengthened public movements for the liberation of women, men, and homosexual identity.[48] But, as Cuban writer Reynaldo González reminded me, Cuba did not live through the Sixties of the sexual revolution. Progress in women's rights in Cuba was tied not to the international feminist movement but, rather, to mobilizing women into the paid workforce: "We didn't live through the sexual revolution with all its problems, its positive aspects and also its excesses, its exaggerations too. Here, we didn't go through it. . . . In Cuba feminism is a sort of education of the female masses for work, but we have not had the theorizing that comes with this kind of work. . . . The woman's revolution in Cuba didn't have any theorizing; it lacked that."[49]

In the area of sexuality, dominant Cuban attitudes remain stubbornly prerevolutionary and betray the general faith in education. An alternative to the quarantine could rely heavily on a massive sex education campaign including the safe sex program developed and used effectively in gay communities of the United States and other countries. While AIDS is primarily a heterosexual disease in Cuba, first introduced by soldiers returning from Africa, its association with homosexuality contributed to the choice of quarantine and rejection of education.

The ideological position regards AIDS as a plague comparable to the "black death" that killed a third of Europe's population in the fourteenth century. It therefore requires the strongest methods of eradication. I do not dismiss this position lightly. After all, how should any government deal with a ravaging pandemic spreading death to so many? By early 1992, an estimated 12.9 million people worldwide had been infected with HIV (4.7 million women, 7.1 million men, and 1.1 million children). One-fifth (2.6 million) have thus far developed AIDS. Ninety percent of these (2.5 million) have died. By the year 2000, conservative estimates suggest a minimum of 38 million adults will be HIV infected. A more realistic projection is that this figure will be higher, perhaps up to 110 million.[50] In 1980 there were 100,000 known cases.

In examining the interrelated issues of sexuality, machismo, homosexuality, AIDS, and gender in Cuba, I have listened to—but also had to put aside—the authoritarian, homophobic speeches of Castro and other leaders. I have turned to the voices of the secondary school adolescents in the countryside; to day care teachers talking about their school/home double shift work day; to a school administrator telling me that gay teachers would be detrimental in the "formation of our youth"; to an animated discussion about the problems of ongoing shortages in a school staff meeting; to psychologists discussing "the problem of effeminate boys"; to young doctors in a sex education seminar talking about the treatment of frigidity and impotence; to a filmmaker seeking "to drop a bomb in every home" in his feature film on machismo and women in the revolution; to gays and lesbians in the arts talking about their lives in Havana. From those at the National Group for Sex Education, I heard voices of enlightenment in a resistant nation that includes the macho leadership at the top, including the Ministry of Education. Through these and many other witnesses, I have come to understand Cuba's sex education efforts as well as the changing role of women, homosexuality, and AIDS policy and practices.

Cuban society is not unique, of course, in practicing sexual discrimination, prejudice, and machismo. In fact, I hope this work offers not only to Cubans but to all of us, useful insights and a key to examining our own sexual prejudices. AIDS has brought to the fore deeply entrenched attitudes toward men, women, and homosexuals in cultures around the world. This look at Cuba provides clues to attitudes that, if changed, can help effectively address the disease of AIDS that threatens us all.

Notes

1. Ernesto B. Betancourt, "Cuba's Callous War on AIDS," *New York Times*, February 11, 1988, A35.

2. Bruce Lambert, "Koch's Record on AIDS: Fighting a Battle Without a Precedent," *New York Times*, August 27, 1989, 30.

3. See Marvin Leiner, *Children Are the Revolution: Day Care in Cuba* (New York: Penguin Books, 1978); Marvin Leiner, "Two Decades of Educational Change in Cuba," *Journal of Reading* 25, no. 3 (December 1981): 202–214; also see Dudley Seers, ed., *Cuba: The Economic and Social Revolution* (Chapel Hill: University of North Carolina Press, 1964); Jorge I. Domínguez, *Cuba: Order and Revolution* (Cambridge: Harvard University Press, 1978); Richard Fagen, *The Transformation of Political Culture in Cuba* (Stanford: Stanford University Press, 1969); James O'Connor, *The Origins of Socialism in Cuba* (Ithaca: Cornell University Press, 1970); Ramón Eduardo Ruíz, *Cuba: The Making of a Revolution* (Amherst: University of Massachusetts Press, 1968); Rolando E. Bonechea and Nelson P. Valdés, *Cuba in Revolution* (New York: Doubleday and Co., 1972); Carmelo Mesa-Lago, ed., *Revolutionary Change in Cuba* (Pittsburgh: University of Pittsburgh Press, 1971); Sandor Halebsky and John M. Kirk, eds., *Cuba: Twenty-Five Years of Revolution, 1959–1984* (New York: Praeger Publishers, 1985); Alfred Padula and Lois M. Smith, "The Revolutionary Transformation of Cuban Education, 1959–1987," in Edgar B.Gumbert, ed., *Making the Future: Politics and Educational Reform in the United States, England, the Soviet Union, China, and Cuba* (Atlanta: Center for Cross-cultural Education, Georgia State University, 1988).

4. See Jonathan Kozol, *Children of the Revolution: A Yankee Teacher in the Cuban Schools* (New York: Delacorte Press, 1978), 1–103; Fagen, *Political Culture*, 33–68; Marvin Leiner, "The 1961 Cuban Literacy Campaign," in Robert F. Arnove and

Harvey J. Graff, eds., *National Historical Campaigns: Historical and Comparative Perspectives* (New York: Plenum Press, 1987), 173–196; Anna Lorenzetto and Karel Neyes, *Methods and Means Utilized in Cuba to Eliminate Illiteracy (UNESCO Report)*, (Havana: Instituto del Libro, 2nd ed., 1971); Richard Jolly, "Education," in Dudley Seers, ed., *Cuba: The Economic and Social Revolution* (Chapel Hill: University of North Carolina Press, 1964), 194–195; see Abel Prieto Morales for a discussion of the integration of the political and the pedagogical in the campaign: "The Literacy Campaign in Cuba," *Harvard Educational Review* 51 (February 1981): 35–36.

5. Allan M. Brandt: "AIDS: From Social History to Social Policy," in Elizabeth Fee and Daniel M. Fox, eds., *AIDS: The Burdens of History* (Berkeley: University of California Press, 1988), 147.

6. Julie Feinsilver, "Cuba as a 'World Medical Power': The Politics of Symbolism," *Latin American Research Review* 24 (1989):1–33; Robert Ubell, "High Tech Medicine in the Carribean: 25 Years of Cuban Health Care," *New England Journal of Medicine* 309 (December 8, 1983): 1468.

7. Medea Benjamin, "Soul Searching," *NACLA Report on the Americas* (August 1990), 24.

Humor is often a clue to what people are feeling—especially in a controlled, restricted environment. Some of the jokes I've heard in Cuba have been around for some time. Sometimes the same joke surfaces several years later and the political names change—e.g. the same joke used Bush in 1990 instead of Carter or Reagan.

The Napoleon joke with a new cast is back in the 1990s. (I first heard this in the late 1970s when Jimmy Carter was the president.) Napoleon has returned to meet world leaders. He says to George Bush: "If I had your military power, I would never have lost at Waterloo." When he meets Gorbachev he says: "If I had your diplomatic skills, I never would have had to fight at Waterloo." When he meets Castro, he says: "If I had *Granma,* no one would have known I lost at Waterloo."

Medea Benjamin (a nutritionist who lived in Cuba from 1979 to 1983 as a freelance writer), after a return trip to Cuba in 1990, reported that "bitterly sarcastic underground jokes" she had not heard during the earlier four years she lived in Cuba are now making the rounds. For example: A United Nations representative is taking an international survey about opinions on the global food shortage. First he asks the Swedes. "Shortage?" they respond. He then tries the Ethiopians. "Food?" they ask. Then he turns to the Cubans and asks: "What is your opinion about the global food shortage?" "Opinion?" the Cubans answer.

8. Nelson Lowry, *Rural Cuba* (New York: Octagon Books, 1970); International Bank for Reconstruction and Development, *Report on Cuba* (Baltimore: Johns Hopkins University Press, 1961), 405, 434, 425.

9. Richard R. Fagen, *The Transformation of Political Culture in Cuba* (Stanford: Stanford University Press, 1969), 21–22; James O'Connor, *The Origins of Socialism in Cuba* (Ithaca: Cornell University Press, 1970), 58; Andrew Zimbalist, "Teetering On The Brink: Cuba's Current Economic and Political Crisis,"*Journal of Latin American Studies*, vol. 24, no. 2 (May 1992): 407–418.

10. Marvin Leiner, "Cuba: Combining Formal Schooling With Practical Experience," in Manzoor Ahmed and Philip H. Coombs, eds., *Education for Rural Development: Case Studies for Planners* (New York: Praeger Publishers, 1975), 62.

11. Lowry, *Rural Cuba*, 239.

12. Lourdes Arguelles and B. Ruby Rich, "Homosexuality, Homophobia, and Revolution: Notes Towards an Understanding of the Cuban Lesbian and Gay Male Experience, Part I," *Signs: Journal of Women in Culture and Society* 9, no. 4 (1984): 686.

13. Arthur MacEwen, *Revolution and Economic Development in Cuba* (New York: St. Martin's Press, 1981), 9.

14. In a most insightful essay on the influence of Martí on Cuban revolution, Ramón Ruiz notes that:

> In their views of Cuban society and of the United States and its economic and political policy in Cuba, both Castro and the revolutionaries of 1933 reiterated the ideas of Martí, the patriot philosopher and politican. In this respect, Castro and the revolutionaries of 1933 walked in the mainstream of Cuban thought, which had ennobled Martí as the prophet.
>
> No one occupies an analagous place in the history of the United States. It would require a composite of Washington, Jefferson, and Lincoln, supplemented by the best of Henry James, Emerson, and Twain to suggest a comparable figure.

Ramón Ruiz, *Cuba: The Making of a Revolution*, 59.

15. Tad Szulc, *Fidel: A Critical Portrait* (New York: William Morrow and Co., 1986), 464–468.

16. Ibid., 469–470.

17. Marvin Leiner, "Cuba's Schools, Ten Years Later," *Saturday Review* (October 1970), 59–61, 69–71.

18. Liberty City: After the 1959 Revolution, the Columbia army camp barracks—the same barracks where Batista carried out his coup d'état—were converted into Liberty City, a school complex that included grades kindergarten through senior high school.

19. Leiner, *Children Are the Revolution*.

20. Ibid., 121–141; Marc Cooper, "Roll Over Che Guevara," *The Village Voice*, July 16, 1991.

21. Robert Ubell, "High Tech Medicine," 1468.

22. Dr. Hiroshi Nakjama, II International Seminar on Primary Care in Havana, November 15, 1988, in Margaret Gilpin, "Cuba: On the Road to a Family Medicine Nation," *Family Medicine* 21 (November–December 1989): 405; Ubell, "High Tech Medicine," 1472; Gilpin states that by 1995 the Cubans expect the entire population will have full family physician coverage; also see Demetrius S. Iatridis, "Cuba's Health Care Policy: Prevention and Active Community Participation," *Social Work* 35 (January 1990): 30: "Cuba's health policy has produced dramatic improvements in health standards and practices. . . ;" Raúl Riveron Corteguera, M.D., et al., "Advances in Pediatrics and Child Care in Cuba, 1959–1974," *Bulletin of the Pan American Health Organization* 10 (1976):9–24; José

Gutiérrez Muñiz et al., "The Recent Worldwide Economic Crisis and the Welfare of Children: The Case of Cuba," *World Development* 12 (March 1984): 247–260.

23. D. Iatradis, "New Social Deficit: Neoconservatism's Policy," *Social Work* 33 (1988): 11; Iatridis, "Cuba's Health Care Policy," 29–30; see Andrew Zimbalist and Claes Brundenius, *The Cuban Economy: Measurement and Analysis of Socialist Performance* (Baltimore: The Johns Hopkins University Press, 1989).

24. See Carmelo Mesa-Lago, "A Model to Compare Alternative Stategies of Socio-Economic Development in Latin America," Table 3, (mimeo) University of Pittsburgh, 1978; cited in Claes Brundenius, "Growth with Equity: The Cuban Experience," *World Development* 9, no. 11 (1981): 1086.

25. "Health Notes," *Cuba Update* (Summer 1991): 25; Gilpin, "A Family Medicine Nation," 405; "Health Notes," *Cuba Update* (Summer 1990): 23; J.A. de la Osa, "Infant Mortality," *Granma Weekly Review*, February 1, 1987; Iatridis, "Cuba's Health Care Policy," 30; Ubell, "High Tech Medicine," 1468.

26. "Health Notes," (1990):23.

27. P. Orris, *The Sociology of Health and Medical Care; Citizen Involvement in Cuba: 1959–1980* (Chicago: Red Feather Institute for Advanced Studies in Sociology, 1980): 1–40 (Report no. 81).

28. Gilpin, "A Family Medicine Nation," 464; Iatridis, "Cuba's Health Care Policy," 30; Ross Danielson, "Medicine in the Community," in Halebsky and Kirk, eds., *Twenty-Five Years*; Ministerio de Salud Pública, República de Cuba, *Información Estadística, no. 4* (Havana: Ministerio de Salud Pública, 1983), 1–15; Ubell, "High Tech Medicine," 1468; Howard W. French, "Cuba's Ills Encroach on Health," *New York Times*, July 16, 1993, A3; Alisa L. Valdès, "International Medical Community Calls for Partial Lifting of Embargo," *Cuba Update* (Summer 1993): 20; Howard W. French, "Havana Journal: 43,412 Stricken Cubans, and Not a Single Answer," *New York Times*, June 15, 1993, A4.

29. Paul M. Sweezy, "Cuba: A Left U.S. View," *Monthly Review* (September 1990): 17–21; Claes Brundenius, *Revolutionary Cuba: The Challenge of Economic Growth with Equity* (Boulder: Westview Press, 1984).

30. Sweezy, "A Left U.S. View," 20; also see Brundenius, *Growth With Equity*. Paul Sweezy and his co-editor Leo Huberman had written and published some of the earliest work on the Cuban revolution. See Leo Huberman and Paul M. Sweezy, *Socialism in Cuba* (New York: Monthly Review Press, 1969). In his 1990 comments on the changes in race relations in Cuba since 1959 and in his early writings on Cuba, Sweezy notes that the military picture of black and white Cubans has also significantly changed:

This (the changed demographic picture of blacks in power positions—ML) has been especially true of the military, which, with Cuba constantly facing the constant threat of U.S. invasion has steadily grown in importance. . . . Moreover, within the military the weight of blacks has increased more than proportionately with Cuba's succcessful assumption of a major role in protecting liberated Angola from South African counterrevolutionary aggression.

Sweezy, "Left U.S. View," 18–19.

31. Gabriel García Márquez, "Plying the Word," *NACLA Report on the Americas* 24, no.2 (August 1990): 40–46; Jorge Domínguez, *U.S./Cuban Relations in the 1990s* Jorge Domínguez and Rafael Hernández, eds., (Boulder: Westview Press, 1989).

32. I have written elsewhere about this new development in secondary education where junior and senior high schools in Cuba were built in the countryside in the 1970s in a bold, massive, creative approach to meet the expansion needs of the growth of universal education. See Leiner, "Cuba: Combining Formal Schooling with Practical Experience," 95–96.

The first school-in-the-countryside was built in 1971. There are 502 junior high and 97 senior high schools of this type. Each *escuela-en-el-campo* costs approximately \$1.7 million to build and houses 500 to 600 students with equal numbers of boys and girls. Each new rural school offers not only classrooms, laboratories, library, and recreational areas for students and teachers, but also has its own dormitories, a dining room, and a kitchen.

From 1975 to 1980, enrollment in junior high countryside schools increased from 277,000 to 478,000, an extraordinary jump. The annual cost of maintaining each school is reported to be approximately \$572,000.

The schools set aside one half of the day for academics and one half for work. The early evening, from 5:30 to 7:30 P.M., is devoted to individual and group study time. Students attending a school of this type work on the school farm (citrus, tobacco, or other cash crops) and in this way contribute about 600,000 pesos per year to support school development and maintenance. All schools-in-the-countryside are boarding schools; both students and faculty sleep in dormitories. Transportation to and from home on weekends and for summer vacation is provided by the school. In the late 1980s the program was modified, using the countryside schools for the senior high schools and keeping the junior high schools as neighborhood schools.

Also see Kozol, *Children of the Revolution*, 155–183; Rolland J, Paulston, "Cuban Rural Education: A Strategy for Rural Development," *World Yearbook of Education*, 1974, 249–250; Abascal López Jesús, "Interview with José R. Fernández, Vice Council of the Council of Ministers and Minister of Education," *Weekly Granma*, November 16, 1980, 2, 4; Alfred Padula and Lois M. Smith, "Transformation of Cuban Education," 1988, 127–128.

33. Sweezy, "U.S. Left View," 19; Marifeli Pérez-Stable, "In Pursuit of Cuba Libre," *NACLA Report on the Americas* 24 (August 1990): 32–39; Domínguez, *Order and Revolution*.

34. "The Uncompromising Revolution," a film by Saul Landau; Gilpin, "A Family Medicine Nation," 404, 464; García Márquez, "Plying the Word," 46.

35. Under both John F. Kennedy and Dwight Eisenhower, the CIA attempted several times to assassinate Castro. In 1975 a Senate committee disclosed that the Mafia and the ITT had cooperated with the CIA in this endeavor. There were as many as thirty attempts on Castro's life using guns, bombs, and poison.

The closest call came in 1964. The CIA had discovered that Fidel Castro was a chocoholic at that time and had a habit of stopping by the Habana Libre Hotel cafeteria for a milkshake. They enlisted a cafeteria worker to try to slip a cyanide capsule into the milkshake. On Castro's next visit to the cafeteria, the employee took the capsule out of the freezer where he had kept it to place it into the drink. In an interview in 1985, Ramiro Valdés, who had been the interior minister at that time, remembered: "The capsule was frozen and it broke, and the man couldn't slip it into the milkshake. It seemed he was very nervous. And, you know, cyanide is lethal poison; it would have instantly killed Fidel. . . . This was the closest it ever came." Szulc, *Fidel: A Critical Portrait*, 600; also see Domínguez, *Order and Revolution*, 148; U.S. Congress, Select Committee to Study Governmental Operations With Respect to Intelligence Activities, *Alleged Assassination Plots Involving Foreign Leaders: An Interim Report*, 94th Congress, 1st session (Washington, D.C.: Government Printing Office, 1975), 71–90.

Through the media and in the schools, Cubans are informed of U.S. efforts to subvert and overthrow not only their own government (they see on Cuban TV excerpts of United States media tapes of Congressional hearings where assassination plots against Castro have been presented by witnesses), but also of moves to destroy other governments in Latin America.

Cuban schools at different levels include the study of twentieth century Latin American history—including, for example, the history of CIA invovement in the overthrow of the liberal Jacobo Arbenz government in Guatemala in 1954, resulting in the murder of thousands of Guatemalans over the next twenty years. Some estimates by human rights groups are as high as 100,000. Michael Powell, "The Spies Who Came in From the Cold War," *Newsday* February 24, 1989, 3.

These are confirmed by recent revelations from former operatives of the CIA such as Phil Roettinger, now living in Mexico, who in 1989 remembered: ". . . in 1954 I was selected to go to Guatemala to overthrow a government. . . ." Covert operations included planting articles in newspapers, recruiting right-wing politicians and officers in the army, resulting in violence, torture and killings. Powell, "Spies," 3. See Ron Ridenour, "Cuba: A Talk with the Dean," *NACLA Report on the Americas* 22, no. 3 (September 1989): 6–8, for an interview with Ignecio Rodríguez-Mena Castrillón, a former baseball player for the Washington Senators and dean of Cuban moles. For twenty-one years Rodríquez-Mena was a double agent, on the payroll of the CIA while spying for Cuba. In July 1987 the Cuban government revealed that he and twenty-five other Cubans and one Italian had infiltrated the CIA on behalf of the Cuban revolution. They became the stars of an eleven-part documentary series on television showing U.S. personnel dropping off money and communication equipment and CIA attempts to spread Dengue Fever and crop diseases.

36. Domínguez, *Order and Revolution*, 148.

37. Leiner, *Children Are the Revolution*, 196; Gerassi, ed., *Venceremos!: The Speeches and Writings of Ernesto Che Guevara* (New York: Macmillan Company, 1968). The conceptual framework of Cuba's *hombre nuevo* is the humanistic ideal, and its source is Marxist ideology. In "The Economic and Philosophical Manuscripts of 1844," Marx offers the view that man is essentially a free creative spirit with powers that enable him to produce for the sheer pleasure of doing so. See Karl Marx, "Economic and Philosophical Manuscripts," in Erich Fromm, *Marx's Concept of Man* (New York: Frederick Ungar Publishing Company, 1961).

38. See Bertram Silverman, *Man and Socialism in Cuba: The Great Debate* (New York: Atheneum Publishers, 1971).

39. Two of every five Cubans were born after the Revolution. Raimundo Rodríguez, "11 Million Cubans in 1995," *Weekly Granma,* January 13, 1991, 6.

40. Fidel Castro, "Fidel's Meeting with the Christian Base Communities in Brazil," *Weekly Granma,* April 8, 1990, 9. When Castro opened the National Assembly in July 1992 he said: "Our hookers don't do it out of obligation, of necessity. Here prostitution doesn't occur for that reason but because somehow they like it." Associated Press, "Hookers Not Havana Blast," *Daily News,* September 27, 1992, 14.

41. See Judith Van de Vere, "Risqué Business: Prostitution Returns to Haunt the Island," *The Pacific,* (Spring–Summer 1992): 19,25; Jorge Socarras, photographs by David LaChapelle, "Quba Libre: A Near Queer Havana," *NYQ,* December 8, 1991, 44–46, 68; also see Jacobo Timerman, *Cuba: A Journey,* trans. Toby Talbot (New York: Alfred A. Knopf, 1990), 50–51, 88–89, 92–93; Benjamin, "Things Fall Apart," 21; Benjamin, "Soul Searching," 23–31; Isel Rivero y Méndez, "Cuban Women: Back to the Future?" *Ms.* May/June 1993, 15–17.

On July 15, 1993, the Cuban government announced that Cubans will be permitted to deposit dollars in special bank accounts and make withdrawals in the form of coupons that can be spent in government hard-currency stores. Castro explained in a radio broadcast: "We have serious problems, and we have to solve them to survive." "Cuba: Castro Picks up a Capitalist Tool," *Newsweek,* August 2, 1993, 31; Associated Press, "Havana to Ease Restrictions on Currency and Investments," July 16, 1993, A3.

42. Christine Brandt, "The New York Newsday Interview with Anthony Padovano; 'Pelvic Issues Preoccupy the Church,'" *Newsday,* November 1990, 89.

43. John M. Kirk, "From Counterrevolution to Modus Vivendi: The Church in Cuba, 1959–84" in Sandor Halebsky and John M. Kirk, eds., *Cuba: Twenty-Five Years of Revolution, 1959–1984* (New York: Praeger Publishers, 1985); 94; Aldo J. Buntig, "The Church in Cuba: Toward a New Frontier," in Alice L. Hagerman and Philip E. Wheaton, eds., *Religion in Cuba Today: A New Church in a New Society* (New York: Association Press, 1971), 116; Margaret Crahan, "Salvation Through Christ or Marx: Religion in Revolutionary Cuba," *Journal of Interamerican Studies and World Affairs* 21, no. 1 (February 1979): 162.

44. Kirk, "From Counterrevolution to Modus Vivendi," 94.

45. Interview with Monika Krause Peters, Havana, 1988.

46. Abel Prieto, "Homosexuality," *Bohemia,* 1969, 109.

47. Monika Krause Peters interview, 1988.

48. Martin Baumi Duberman, "Past Experience," *The Nation,* May 14, 1988, 684–685.

49. Interview with Reynaldo González, Havana, 1988.

50. Jonathan Mann, Daniel J. M. Tarantola, and Thomas W. Netter, eds., *AIDS in the World 1992* (Cambridge: Harvard University Press, 1992), 2–3,5; also see: Jonathan Mann, "Detecting the Next Pandemic," *Scientific American,* March 1991.

2

The Homosexual in the Revolution

You have to consider Cuban traditions and beliefs, the nation's idiosyncrasy. If we consider the homosexuality issue with the same criteria as in Europe and New York, we will not understand the full and real problem.

The Cuban idiosyncrasy is very complex; it includes Spanish and African traditions. In a macho culture as ours, homosexuals are not respected; they have no prestige. The majority of our people will not see homosexuals as full people with full dignity.

—Juan Escalona

In the United States, one of the most publicized issues of postrevolutionary life in Cuba has been the treatment of homosexuals, and to it Americans have responded with a gamut of reactions, from disappointment to rage. From people on the right, who would never support gay rights in this country, has come outrage over Cuba's mistreatment of homosexuals. On the other hand, this issue alone has caused many on the left to turn away from support of Cuba. And, it has further alienated those in the middle who might at least have advocated a tolerant neutrality. These antagonisms are even more curious when we consider that only in small pockets in the United States, and there only recently, have gay men and lesbians been truly accepted, able to be public about their sexual orientation, and still be granted their full human rights.

Within the Cuban culture of machismo, the whole issue of homosexuality appears as one of male identity. The Cuban ethnologist Alberto Pedro notes the importance of *"hombría"* (manliness) in the value system of Latin America and in Cuba, in particular, its expression in the Abakuá secret society:

"Hombría" implies honor, dignity, chivalry, and is part of the continent's Iberian heritage, of values shared by both men and women. Poverty and ignorance have led to the distortion of the concept among the most backward sectors of our nations, but the consequent brutal forms of behavior do not represent our true values as Latin Americans or Cubans.[1]

21

In Cuba the Abakuá society was formed in the nineteenth century by men influenced by black slaves from the Calabar in Nigeria where there had been numerous societies for "men only." That African form of organization was reproduced in Cuba, but the concept of *"hombría"* was of Spanish origin, especially from nineteenth-century Andalusia.[2]

> The new phenomenon was neither Spanish nor African but Cuban. 'To be Abakuá you must be a man' and to be initiated into the society the man had to prove he was a good son, a good father, and good friend. But the grinding struggle for survival faced by people of this level in society in prerevolutionary Cuba made such standards impossible to live up to. The Abakuá ideal in effect reduced to "not being a homosexual."[3]

To have sex with another man is not what identifies one as homosexual. For many Cubans, a man is homosexual only if he takes the passive receiving role.[4] And a man is suspected of being homosexual only if his behavior is not macho: if he does not show interest in rough games, or is not physically strong and muscular; if he is gentle or quiet or perhaps has a nurturing sensibility to other people's feelings; if he does not care to control others or to posture and aggressively compete with his fellows. Then his behavior is seen as inferior, inadequate, and deficient: that is, it is labeled effeminate, the behavior of inferior secondary people. Nowhere in the literature or in my own interviews did I ever come across the notion that men who behave and appear strong, virile, and aggressive could possibly be gay—except from gay men themselves, of course. For example, Abel Prieto told this story in 1969:

> A few weeks ago a young man demobilized from compulsory military service came to our office (at the Ministry of Education) to complain that he had been rejected by the investigating Provincial Commission for the job of junior high school teacher. I asked him, "Did they explain why?" "It seems to be a problem from my past." "What kind of problem?" He lowered his head and answered, "A moral problem." Without any preamble: "A homosexual experience?" He said no more. His silence was the answer. Nothing indicated outwardly that the young man was a homosexual. No manifestation of mannerisms, no extravagant clothing, no suspicious behavior. He had all the requirements as far as professional preparation, but at the same time we recognized that we had to find another job for him.[5]

In the same year, I interviewed Dr. Luís Allyon, who was convinced that there were no homosexuals among *campesinos* but only in the city. Even there, their numbers had been greatly reduced, he said, since the Revolution. "I know more than ten cases of homosexuals who entered the militia and by the end of the military experience left it behind and started to act normally. . . . Yes, it makes them change; you know why? Because it was the army of the period. It was the militia, not the army— but the army of the people. The activities of the militia took many people away from homosexuality. I know four who went on to get married and have families. They became normal."[6]

The popular literature of a nation reflects prevailing attitudes toward sex and homosexuality. Lourdes Casal, who was an outstanding and gifted commentator on Cuban life, did a study of the images of Cuban society as reflected in 104 novels. She analyzed the impact of revolutionary change on popular literature and found attitudes toward homosexuals to be invariably negative. "To launch an accusation of homosexuality against a political enemy was one of the most terrible insults. To call a man a queer was a way of calling him a woman, a direct attack on his masculinity, on his value as a macho. It was a way of calling him weak and unworthy of holding power. Rejection of homosexuality led to rejection of anything soft, feminine, in men's fashions, e.g., 'He didn't like the new fashion of uncreased pants; they seemed to him somewhat effeminate'."[7]

The relegation of women as secondary, lesser "others" is also apparent in the almost total absence of lesbianism from official and social concern over homosexuality. In Lourdes Casal's study of pre- and postrevolutionary literature lesbians as a group do not exist. She found only two subtle references to them. Not even in mystery novels or short stories was there any reference to lesbians.[8] From the machismo point of view, lesbianism simply does not matter much. It does not seriously challenge machismo as long as women have no acceptable social choices other than marrying men. In many societies, including Cuba and the United States, lesbians often remain in heterosexual marriages for much of their lives. Often marriage is the only way to remain respectable and to manage economically.[9]

During the fourteen years between the end of World War II and Castro's triumphal entry into Havana, that city became a capital of vice and corruption. Tourism had, from prewar days, been an important economic activity. Tourists came mostly from the United States. Havana was a favorite place for honeymooners from all over the country and for shopping trips from nearby Florida. It became the place to go for gambling, prostitution, drugs, and a never-ending night life. In the 1950s, U.S. organized crime moved in, and the city's reputation as a sordid cesspool of sin took hold.

As a large city, Havana offered a large degree of freedom to gay people seeking to express their sexual preference. As in all parts of the world, homosexuals in rural areas, where deviance from a patriarchal culture was not easy to sustain, left for the big city.[10] Thus, Havana became the center for gay men and lesbians seeking employment and hoping for greater freedom to lead their own lives. They often became enmeshed in Havana's underworld. Lourdes Arguelles and B. Ruby Rich have examined the economics of the tourist trade in prerevolution Havana and how homosexuals fitted into it. They describe Havana's economy of the 1950s: "The only occupational sector showing substantial growth was that connected to tourism, drug distribution, gambling, and prostitution. This sector was mostly controlled by American organized crime and members of an indigenous bourgeoisie directly linked to Batista's political apparatus. It employed more than two hundred thousand workers as petty traders, casino operators, entertainers, servants, and prostitutes."[11]

During this period of severe sexual repression in advanced capitalist nations,

> homosexual desire was often channeled into illegal and lucrative offshore markets like the Havana underworld. Not surprisingly, then, Cuban homosexuals had preferential hiring treatment in the Havana tourist sector in order to meet the demands of American visitors and servicemen for homoerotic experiences. Other buyers of homosexual desire were the fathers and sons of the Cuban bourgeoisie, who felt free to partake of homoerotic practices without being considered homosexual as long as they did not take the passive, so-called female role in sexual relations. Yet another common practice for Cuban heterosexual men was the procurement of a lesbian prostitute's favors for a night.
>
> Apart from employment realities, social pressures made thousands of prerevolutionary homosexuals part of this underworld. Even homosexuals such as students ... were integrated into this subculture through the bars that they frequented: the St. Michel, the Dirty Dick, *El Gato Tuerto*. Then (as is still today the case in the United States) most of these bars were owned and operated by organized crime. Given the sharply stratified nature of prerevolutionary Cuba, working-class heterosexual men in order to make a living were also drawn into this underworld or alternatively into a homosexual underground dominated by the Cuban homosexual bourgeoisie.[12]

The underworld culture was isolated from the mainstream of social life. And being centered on the commercialization of sex, it never generated a gay culture or pride but only varying degrees of guilt and self-hatred among its gay denizens. The rare use of legal sanctions and official harassment against the "gay community" was only due to commercial considerations. In the larger society gay people were not tolerated nor was there much in the way of self-defined gay identities.[13]

The "New Man" of the 1960s and 1970s

No homosexual represents the Revolution, which is a matter for men; of fists and not of feathers; of courage, not trembling; of certainty, not intrigue; of creative valor and not of sweet surprises.

—Samuel Feijoó

As much as anything else, one of the Revolution's goals was to cleanse the city of the decadent and immoral tourist trade characterized as the worst of capitalist bourgeois decadence. First the casinos closed down, and the drugs disappeared. Eventually reeducated prostitutes and servants learned new trades and found new jobs. Organized crime looked elsewhere for business. The relatively few years necessary for these changes and the further elimination of the worst miseries of poverty inspired great hope around the world. It showed what could be done when a better life for poor people was the most important goal of those in positions of authority.

As the ideology of Marxism-Leninism began to take on greater importance within the governing party, another aspect of the campaign against "bourgeois decadence" emerged. Within Marxism-Leninism a certain puritanism and social rigidity had long since become the norm.[14] Not only was the corruption of prostitution condemned, but also any notion of sexual freedom or changes that endangered the traditional family institution, except for bringing women into the workforce. Thus, homosexuality was considered antithetical to a socialist society. It is the journalist Allen Young's contention that in Cuba these repressive attitudes found expression through the existing homophobia of machismo to the point that it became institutionalized into a political program.

> There was indeed suffering in prerevolutionary Cuba: beggars roaming the streets, decaying stinking slums, sexual exploitation—mostly for the benefit of wealthy and middle-class North Americans. In cleaning up Havana, however, the revolutionary regime has acted harshly, especially where homosexuals were concerned. While prejudice against homosexuals coexisted with the sexual openness of prerevolutionary Havana, that prejudice was institutionalized and reinforced in postrevolutionary Cuba as part of the political program of the nation, as a measure of its "progress" and "freedom."[15]

Indeed, discussions in the 1960s on what it meant to be a revolutionary often implied that male homosexuals could not, by their nature, achieve that status. Samuel Feijoó's above statement is one writer's blunt expression of that sentiment. While extreme, this statement did express the prevailing sentiment that male homosexuals are effeminate and that being feminine means to lack courage and valor. Fidel Castro at this time gave a more reasoned expression of anti-gay sentiments in response to an explicit question about whether one can be both homosexual and revolutionary.

Nothing prevents a homosexual from professing revolutionary ideology and, consequently, exhibiting a correct political position. In this case, he should not be considered politically negative. And yet we would never come to believe that a homosexual could embody the conditions and requirements of conduct that would enable us to consider him a true revolutionary, a true Communist militant. A deviation of that nature clashes with the concept we have of what a militant Communist should be. But above all, I do not believe that anybody has a definitive answer as to what causes homosexuality. I think the problem must be studied very carefully. But I will be frank and say that homosexuals should not be allowed in positions where they are able to exert influence upon young people. In the conditions under which we live, because of the problems which our country is facing, we must inculcate our youth with the spirit of discipline, of struggle, of work. In my opinion, everything that tends to promote in our youth the strongest possible spirit, activities related in some way with the defense of the country, such as sports, must be promoted. This attitude may or may not be correct, but it is our honest feeling. It may be in some cases a person is homosexual for pathological reasons. It would indeed be arbitrary if such a person were maltreated for something over which he has no control. You can only ask yourself, when assigning a person to a position of responsibility, what are the factors which might help that person do his job well, and what are those that might hinder him?[16]

The social prejudice against male homosexuality shown in Fidel Castro's narrow-minded response does not cancel out all the ideals embodied in the phrase "being a true Communist" or in the more common expression at that time, "the new socialist man." To strive to be a "new socialist man" meant becoming humanistic and altruistic: "In a communist society, man will have succeeded in achieving just as much understanding, closeness, and brotherhood as he has on occasion achieved within the narrow circle of his own family. To live in a communist society is to live without selfishness, to live among the people, as if every one of our fellow citizens were really our dearest brother."[17]

The new Cuban man would be a healthy individual with a new attitude toward work. He would identify work with the pleasure of creation and social duty rather than with a salary. He would be a man without selfish feelings, a generous man with a sense of the collective and of his social duties; a man capable of joining in solidarity with all men who suffer exploitation, regardless of where they were born; a man who will arrive at these convictions through his own reasoning and can adjust to discipline for identical reasons; a man capable of defending his beliefs at all costs and ready to fulfill every task with responsibility.[18]

One can respect such high idealism while also recognizing the exclusionary male character of the language. Of course women could live by such ideals, but the macho/socialist amalgam questioned whether male homosexuals could. Homosexuality was also condemned through association with the previous degenerate and corrupt world of Havana.

Indeed, an exodus of gay people began immediately after the Revolution. For those who stayed, life changed drastically.

> Some veterans of the old underworld enclave joined counterrevolutionary activites or were pushed into them by the CIA. Other homosexuals, especially those from working-class backgrounds or students from petty-bourgeois families, worked themselves into the revolution. For the majority this meant going into a more guarded and, it was hoped, temporary closet. For these homosexuals, class and class interests were perceived as more elemental aspects of their identity than homosexual behavior. And the revolution spoke to these interests and this identity.[19]

The 1960s were tense years, concerned with security and "holding on" in order to maintain the Revolution. The U.S. invasion at the Bay of Pigs in 1961, the killing of young literacy brigade tutors by counterrevolutionaries,[20] and attacks by CIA-supported groups led to an atmosphere of mistrust and fear. People who were different were suspect. Homosexual bars and cruising areas were viewed as centers of counterrevolutionary activities. In some cases they were, since available social outlets for gay men often still centered on the declining underworld life of Havana: "Not a few of the progressive homosexuals became implicated by default in counterrevolutionary activities and were even jailed. Young homosexuals seeking contact with "the community" in the bars and famous cruising areas of *La Rampa* were thus introduced to counterrevolutionary ideology and practice."[21]

For example, Rolando Cubela was a student leader who had fought in the revolutionary army. Later, owing to his homosexuality, he did not receive a high-level post. He was so angry that he let the CIA enlist him to assassinate Fidel Castro.

The Cuban government successfully organized resistance to large and small acts of U.S. aggression toward Cuba. A strong sense of nationalism forged a unity even amid differing views on many social and economic issues. But within the emerging Marxist-Leninist mentality of the revolutionary party, unity to maintain independence against a former colonial power merged with an ideology requiring unity in all social and individual endeavors. Homosexuals not only suffered from traditional homophobia and prejudice; for a time they were considered enemies of the state because they could not fit into this ideological social unity.

Allen Ginsberg experienced the narrowness of this ideological outlook on a visit to Cuba in 1965. He suggested to Haydée Santamaria (an early woman leader of the Revolution and member of the Central Committee of the Communist party) that the Beatles be invited to give concerts in Cuba. She objected, saying that the Beatles "have no ideology; we are trying to build a revolution with an ideology." Ginsberg was not unsympathetic either to that ideology or to the revolution. He had friends in Cuba, had been invited as a government guest, and took part as a judge in a literary contest. But he was, as ever, anti-authoritarian and could not abide that all facets of social life should come under the sway of "police bureaucrat Party hacks" whom he likened to "Mayor Daley ward-heelers: flag-waving, fat-assed square types."[22] Ginsberg saw that these types, who were

> not at all spiritually communist, were getting control of the police and em-
> igration bureaucracies and setting themselves at odds against the people
> who screw with their eyes open, listen to the Beatles and read interesting
> books like Genet, and *fought* at the Bay of Pigs against the Americans. Even
> people who had been up in the mountains with Castro were very secretive
> about smoking grass. The press was monolithically controlled and boring,
> and the newspaper reporters for the press reminded me very much of the
> self-righteous newspaper reporters from the *Daily News* as far as their
> opinionation (sic) and argumentativeness.[23]

Ginsberg challenged the official position on homosexuality and ended up wondering "what was the ideology they were proposing? A police bureaucracy that persecutes fairies? I mean, they're wasting enormous energies on that. Some of those 'fairies' were the best revolutionaries— people that fought at the Bay of Pigs, Playa Girón."[24]

The results of this marriage of traditional homophobia and Marxist-Leninist ideology were the UMAP camps organized by the army and, in the school system, the Yellow Brigades.

The UMAP Camps

In 1965, homophobia reached a level of organized repression. The military set up Military Units to Aid Production (UMAP) camps as they came to be called. At this time, homosexuals were not only being publicly and politically denounced as perverted and decadent, but viewed as social deviants. Many were interned in these rehabilitation work camps for those "whose behavior was not in accordance with the public definition of good citizenship."[25] Early UMAP draftees were treated so inhumanely that the officers responsible were courtmartialed and replaced with leaders assigned to bring order to the camps. They continued to exist, however, until national and international pressure forced their closing in 1967. The Cuban Union of Writers and Artists (UNEAC), in particular, protested the treatment of intellectuals in the camps; UNEAC was joined by Europeans, including such prestigious persons as Graham Greene, the Italian leftist publisher GianGiacomo Geltrinelli, and Jean-Paul Sartre.[26]

These camps were the epitome of organized repression against male homosexuality. Although social prejudice and legal discrimination certainly continued afterward, the closing of the camps initiated a much less oppressive environment for gay people in Cuba. In 1984 Juan Escalona, Cuban minister of justice, discussed those days in an interview. Escalona came from a Communist family. His father had been jailed for organizing the national strike in March 1953. Escalona became a defense lawyer for revolutionaries in Batista's courts, then joined the rebel army as a teacher and political commissar. He continued to serve in the Cuban military until 1983, as Raúl Castro's first assistant, as head of the Army staff, and as general and as Vice Minister of the armed forces. He became Minister of Justice in 1983. In 1989 he was the head prosecutor in the televised drug smuggling trial of Gen. Amalda Ochoa Sánchez and Antonio de la Font. Until February 1993 he was the president of the National Assembly. In the 1984 interview, he talked about homosexuals as being "disabled" and asserted that they could certainly never hold party membership given this fundamental personality flaw.

UMAP, he explained, had first been set up to deal with young men who were neither studying nor working. "We intended to make these people productive." Escalona considered those recruited for UMAP camps to be bums. According to him, camps solely for gay men were then set up to separate the "girls" from the boys.

These units were created after careful consideration. They were required by the Revolution and the new society; we had to get rid of the bums and among them were homosexuals who were vagrants. You must consider that homosexuality is not a crime in Cuba. So we decided that homosexuals should work on floraculture. Thus (laughs) these special units were really cute and neat because every day you could see these people sowing seeds and picking flowers, and from a far distance you could notice their camps because of the peculiar garments you saw hanging to dry: (laughs) girdles, bras, etc. I was working for the army during those years and I visited those units. Well, this experiment lasted until around 1965. What is important to note here is that homosexuals are neither constrained nor persecuted. Anyone who says otherwise is not only lying, but is an enemy of the Revolution. [Authors note: The UMAP camps were phased out after the Harvest of 1967.][27]

Escalona considered gay manners and clothing very amusing; he was repulsed by the thought of gay lovers unless they were famous as the artist Portocarrero. René Portocarrero (1912–1985) had become an internationally known painter by the time of the Revolution. In more recent years, he became best known for his flora paintings—various versions of a woman whose hair is a tangle of flowers, vines, and birds. From the early 1940s, he lived openly with his companion, artist Raúl Milián, in Havana where they continued to live until Portocarrero's death. His prestige was such that no one dared voice public objection.[28]

In 1966 the writer José Yglesias, a Cuban-American, visited Cuba and spent some time in the small rural town of Mayarí. He later described what he had heard about UMAP.

> These Military Units for Aid to Production were begun to take care of young men of military age whose incorporation into the Army for military training was considered unfeasible. Young men known to avoid work and study were candidates; so were known counterrevolutionaries; and also immoralists, a category that included homosexuals. How the recruitment worked was difficult to define: some were unexpectedly picked up and shipped to a camp, others were notified to report, and others were called in and warned and given a chance to defend themselves. Who denounced them? The secret police, their colleagues at their study or work center, and mainly, the local Committees for the Defense of the Revolution.
>
> It should have been predictable that the recruits would not, in practice, be limited to young men of military age, that the categories of qualification would be blurred, and that their internment would not be educational but brutally punitive.[29]

In talking to the townspeople in 1966, Ygelsias was surprised to find that while the intellectuals in Havana were against the UMAP, most people he met in Oriente thought it a good idea. "It's good for them to work," said one passenger on a bus trip to Mayarí reflecting typical scorn many Cubans feel for homosexuals. Scorn also was reflected in the answer of a rural official, Mella Sorel, when Yglesias asked him about the UMAP camps: "'I am afraid I am very intransigent about that,' Mella said, not angrily but with a smile—everything about homosexuals struck him as funny. "'A man is biologically born a man, so why can he not function as a man? What is to keep him from it but vice? Artists, especially dancers, almost have to be homosexuals, I understand that, but why cannot they keep it to themselves? . . . Anyway, what do homosexuals do for production?—they become shop assistants and interior decorators!'"[30]

On the other hand, two boys from Mayarí, who had numerous complaints about the Revolution, offered the following to Yglesias about a truckload of UMAP men in their blue uniforms: "Well, one of those sitting at the back suddenly jumped down and ran past the truck carrying them and threw himself in front of it. He wanted to kill himself. That is how desperate he was, and no one can deny it, for I was one of the ones who took him to the hospital at El Ciego de Ávila. He was fortunate—he tore up an eyebrow, scraped his face and lost a four-tooth plate. He was out of his mind with desperation!"[31]

Even during this period of the camps and public arrests, the major concern, as it had always been, was with the public display of homosexuality. Gay people did not fear punishment or other government interference with their private life. Raids or public sweeps, however, especially in the 1960s, were a common police method of rounding up "antisocial" elements who congregated in certain areas such as *La Rampa* in Havana. Those whose dress and hair styles were deemed inappropriate, or whose mannerisms were effeminate, were the victims of these raids, especially in 1968, as Ernesto Cardenal, the Nicaraguan poet, has reported.[32]

During this period several writers were attacked as being gay, and some of them eventually felt compelled to leave Cuba. The *El Puente* literary group and publishing house was one target. Within it were young, creative writers who published poetry, short stories, and plays—often rejecting traditional literary approaches and building on an earlier movement called the *Orígenes*. After some members of the group were accused of being both gay and politically unreliable, the *El Puente* group broke up. Several members went into exile (José Mario, Mercedes Cortázar, and Isel Rivero) but others such as Nancy Morejón, Belka Cuza Malé, and Miguel Barnet, are productive writers in Cuba today.[33]

Fidel Castro finally opposed the military and supported a decision to disband the camps. This marked a political crossroads. In spite of the military's protests, the use of the armed forces as a socially corrective agency, operating repressive, rehabilitative "education camps," came to an end. In demonstrating his power on the question of the camps, Fidel Castro also showed that there were limits to the potential expansion of the military.[34]

Although the UMAP camps were completely phased out by 1969, and public arrests of gay men no longer took place, coming out of the closet could be extremely disadvantageous. Even to be accused of effeminate behavior could carry the same stigma. My son, Kenny, witnessed such an example of institutionalized prejudice and discrimination in 1969 when he was a member of the Followers of Camilo and Che. This was a brigade of young volunteers who worked in agriculture. During the summer of that year, the brigade leaders held a special open meeting to discuss the question of Luís whom another brigade member, Enano, had accused of possibly being a homosexual or at least of exhibiting "effeminate" behavior. The accusation came two months after the specific events in question, which were, apparently, that Luís had touched Enano's penis on at least two occasions on the same day.

The leadership considered this to warrant a special meeting. What was at stake was Luís's continued membership in the Brigade and the Young Communist League, which were honors. Although everyone agreed that Luís was a very hard worker with a good revolutionary attitude, if he were "effeminate," he would have to go. This was the real question, since several at the meeting said that it was common for the guys to fool around in a playful way, and that touching each other rather intimately in those circumstances was of no consequence.

The meeting was democratic. Luís and Enano were present; everyone had his say, and at the end, a vote was taken that allowed Luís to remain a member of the Brigade. The message of this vote, however, was that men with behavior deemed effeminate had no place in Cuban society. Kenny himself felt this prejudice in repeated attempts to cut his long hair. Long hair on a man was one of those effeminate attributes as well as an expression of "bourgeois decadence." As Kenny recorded in his diary from the brigade days:

> Machismo is perhaps the most obvious thing here. Every other word is about sex, faggots, strength, tough talking; one of the funniest things a person can do is to make a motion like a bird with his hands and point to another person. Generally it's talking—kidding around—there are only men here—talking about another guy being a fairy and talking tough about fighting; a lot of talking . . . Tonight in the guard house (which also serves as the barbershop) there was a big discussion between some "militants" and me about long hair and things like tight pants.
>
> Whenever they tried to convince me to get a haircut—when all my arguments fell on deaf ears I then argued that I'm in "The Followers of Camilo and Che brigade"—that both Camilo and Che had long hair and they set the example. Maybe because I was a visitor—they did leave me alone—at least until the next time they tried to persuade me to abandon my long hair and take a haircut.[35]

A couple of years later, the Education and Cultural Congress of 1971 officially condemned long hair on men as an example of individualism that should be discouraged. In an interview with me in 1971, Vice Minister of Education Abel Prieto, one of Cuba's leading educators, made a distinction between "manifestations of extravagance" in Cuba and the United States.

> Extravagance means excess. It (the Congress) came out against exhibitionism and individualism. In Cuba this has traditionally been frowned upon: the tendency for some to dress outlandishly, in poor taste; an example

might be ultra-tight pants, and so forth. We also had what might be called hippies, groups which were traditionally pro-U.S. and always went to extremes in trying to imitate their concept of North America. It seems to me that this is another example of individualism in our society. In another society such as yours these manifestations mean something else; they signify rebellion.

Now let's look at Cuba. We view fashion as dictated by a market. Our society cannot be dictated by this consumer market. Our society cannot be an extension of the neo-colonial fashion parade. This is another demonstration of colonialism. We don't want our people to be "calendar conscious." We will not be slaves to the consumer market. How can we be economically free if we are ideologically dependent on them? When our magazines show the latest Paris fashions, this is an example of colonial slavery.

For that reason, we have come out against certain extravagances because extravagance is a form of dependence also.[36]

The Yellow Brigades

A 1965 Ministry of Health report concluded that there were no known biological causes of homosexuality; no "convincing somatic, genetic and hormonal causes" and no "effective biological treatment." The report then developed the thesis that homosexuality is *learned,* and that since the oedipal stage is crucial for sexual identification, "research as well as prevention must start very early in order to influence the mechanisms of this learning process."[37] In the 1960s, prevention included assigning "effeminate" boys to special schools for children with behavior problems. In an interview, one of the supervisors of the Center for Special Education made the following comments to me about boys with "homosexual tendencies": "Those with certain feminine characteristics, but who have never carried out any kind of homosexual act, are almost always those boys who have been raised by the mother alone, where there has not been a male figure present. But we think we can overcome this.

When the boy has a marked tendency toward homosexuality, or perhaps has engaged in some homosexual activity, then yes, we take him out of school because we believe that he can infect others."[38]

When I asked for further reasons for taking a child out of a regular school environment, she continued:

The psychiatrists of the world haven't yet come to any conclusions about what to do with a homosexual child, and for that reason we take them out of school. It's like a disease that no one knows how to cure, nor even what treatment to follow. When they have discovered a method of treatment, we will see that it is done. We call the parents and present the problem to them directly. And we tell them that a boarding school situation isn't good for the child. We believe that the boy can function better in a national school, that is, a day school where the child goes four hours in the morning and four hours in the afternoon. The director and the staff will be able to keep an eye on the child all the time. It is suggested that the youngster visit a psychiatrist who might put him in treatment.[39]

Children at such a school were divided into groups according to five categories of behavior problems: hyperactive and aggressive children, anxious and withdrawn children, boys with effeminate tendencies, bed wetters, and children with eating problems.[40] Each group or "brigade" was then identified with a color. The effeminate boys were in the Yellow Brigade. The brigade's purpose was to instill in these boys, who were "encountering difficulties in accepting their masculine role," an enjoyment of masculine games so they would give up "feminine games."

They are taught to use baseball gloves and balls, pistols, and swords, to practice self-defense and to eliminate the fear of being hurt: to enjoy constructive activities, in conclusion. Naturally, in these cases it is necessary to achieve a closer relationship between child and the male parent; this is achieved through parental meetings. . . . Sometimes we organize special parent groups; for example, we hold separate meetings of the fathers of boys with feminine tendencies so we can ask for their direct suppport in becoming closer to their sons.[41]

The effort to toughen up effeminate boys with pistols and swords was tied both to a psychological-pedagogical rationale and to the macho rhetoric of the "new man." The "new man" was to be not only a person of high morals but a strong and virile revolutionary, in contrast to the "weak" homosexual. It appears that at no time did social scientists or educators consider homosexuality as anything other than "feminine" behavior by males, in accordance with the common cultural stereotype.[42] One gay Cuban told me: "My parents would not believe it if I told them that those macho-looking friends of mine are all gay!"

Here we come to an underlying issue: homophobia and the oppression of gays in Cuba and elsewhere is closely tied to the devaluation of women. For if the country's strength is tied to masculine virility (the Revolution "is a matter for men; of fists and not of feathers"), and homosexuals are identified with women, the logical conclusion founded on this devaluation of women is that male homosexuals are seen as subversive.[43] The children's "Yellow Brigades," which focused during the UMAP period on toughening up "effeminate" boys, was an educational form of "aversion therapy." These techniques were also suggested by anti-gay commentators and psychotherapists in other countries.[44]

A truly new person of the twenty-first century will have a genuine respect for women and the choices in their lives. This will be a matter not of whether one is gay or straight or plays "rough and tumble games" or advocates "baby dolls for boys," but of being free to accept, tolerate, and love oneself and others who are similar or different. The struggle to understand and accept homosexuality—lesbians and gays—is intrinsic to the struggle to understand and accept the two sexual sides of animal/human nature. If people are still grappling with, or not even aware of, their base assumptions and presumptions about whether women are truly equals of men (i.e. two aspects of human wholeness) how can they possibly deal with an open approach to gayness?[45]

Making Homosexuals Second-Class Citizens

It was inevitable that homosexuality would receive attention at the 1971 National Congress of Education and Culture. The Congress met in Havana, April 23–30, with nearly 1,800 delegates from all over the country. The press gave it full coverage, including television broadcast of panels where experts from the Ministry of Education and the Congress discussed the sessions. For teachers and educational administrators, there were opportunities to discuss curriculum issues, the use of educational media, the teacher shortage, and problems such as the scarcity of materials and textbooks.

During the months before the Congress, more than 116,000 educational workers attended 2,599 sessions at the municipal, regional, and provincial level to discuss seven major themes: (1) formation of the student; (2) the educational worker and his or her role in education; (3) the objectives and content of education; (4) methods, means, and evaluation of teaching; (5) school organization and administration; (6) influence of the social environment on education; and (7) popular agencies of education.[46] At the same time, the Congress had a forceful ideological thrust, which urged tighter control of culture and publishing in Cuba and denounced the "deviant behavior" of homosexuals.

In fact, the official statement of the Declaration of the 1971 First Congress on Education and Culture supported an integration of extensive coeducation and sex education into the general teaching syllabus and, at the same time, advocated studies on the best method of barring homosexuals from the educational system, the mass media, and cultural activites—that is, preventing their influence on youth. Furthermore, the Congress offically recognized the social pathological character of homosexuality and resolved that all "manifestations of homosexual deviations are to be firmly rejected and prevented from spreading."[47] These recommendations became law in 1974. The new law banned homosexuals from positions of influence on children because "homosexualism . . . may have a negative effect on the education and conscience . . . of children and young persons."[48]

Although the labor law of 1978 did not continue the ban, I have found during my visits in the 1980s that an unwritten guideline still exists and is maintained by administrators in the Ministry of Education and other agencies. Many jobs in the field of medicine, for example, became closed to gay people since physical intimacy was possible. The army, as in many other countries, does not permit known gays to serve. In addition, as Juan Escalona explained in a 1981 interview, "as soon as we discover that a party member is a homosexual, we dismiss him."

In that same interview, more than ten years after the Educational Congress, Juan Escalona expressed the attitudes that had resulted in the 1971 statement:

Now the 1971 events. Well, you are not allowed to be a member of the Party if you are homosexual. Why? It is not possible. To be a member of the Party, you have to have a number of personal characteristics and go through a selection process. It is not easy to join the Party.

Of course, there might be homosexual members of the Party, but their sexual behavior must not show, although some people may be suspicious of them. It is not possible to have a Party member who lives openly with a boyfriend. We haven't achieved in this issue the tolerance that, let's say, Great Britain shows.

You say that our bark is bigger than our bite. We do not harass homosexuals. But as soon as we discover that a Party member is a homosexual we dismiss him.

Of course, the most important issue for us is whether the person is a true revolutionary. He has made a choice; he is a revolutionary, but he cannot be a Party member.

Think about Portocarrero, for instance, the greatest living Cuban painter. He's never been a Party member; he publicly leads a homosexual life; he lives with his boyfriend and the government shows great respect for him and his work; he receives awards, etc., but he is *disabled* (Italics mine)—this is my personal belief, because there is something missing—or rather something spared (laughs). . . . In a macho culture as ours, homosexuals are not respected; they have no prestige. The majority of our people will not see homosexuals as full people with full dignity.

This might change, of course, but getting back to our point; a Party member should be prestigious. I would like to tell you a story that happened back in the years of the revolutionary war. Actually, this happened about 15 days after the war was over at the Moncada Military headquarters. I was working as an assistant to the head of that unit, Piñeiro.

A scandal broke out. A sergeant who had fought at Sahua, Guantanamo, a brave soldier, had been found having sexual intercourse with a private of Batista's army.

Do you know what our men in the unit wanted to do with him? They wanted to execute him because, besides being a homosexual, he had had an affair with one of our enemies. Above all, you have to understand the people's attitude. Our people don't understand.

So homosexuals are barred from the army. Although we know that if war comes—let's say with the U.S.—homosexuals will join the militia. But they cannot enroll in the regular army. Who knows if this may not change in the next twenty years.[49]

Medical-Psychological Rationale

The rationale used by the Education Congress for its stand on homosexuality came from the psychological-medical community. There, the entire focus had been on finding environmental, psychological, nongenetic causes of male homosexuality and then responding with an appropriate cure. In general, homosexuality was understood as a remnant of capitalist society because of its association with prerevolutionary criminal activity, especially gambling, prostitution, and drug addiction.

Many debates in human science have evolved around the question of social or biological causes. Studies of human behavior offer ample evidence that human reality is some combination of the two but then the question becomes, which is more dominant, and how does articulation between the two take place? Even so, there are still those with a propensity to view questions of human development in an absolutist manner. Causes are found either in genetic factors or in environmental social factors. It is difficult for these polarized positions to escape political interpretation. If genetics is the sole cause, social programs cannot be the cure.

If environment is the sole cause, there is the danger of a too simplistic and deterministic approach to solutions: find the one correct change in social conditions, and the problem will disappear. This approach was dominant within the Cuban medical/psychological establishment in the 1960s with respect to the question of male homosexuality. The scientific community at that time considered male homosexuality to be a pathological disorder. In this, they were no different from their colleagues in the United States and most other countries. Female homosexuality was simply not considered of interest to scientific inquiry. Most probably this is a reflection of machismo rather than an ignorance of lesbian existence. Physicians and psychologists, however, seemed to be unaware of homosexuality in rural areas and perpetuated the myth of the "purity of the countryside."

The general psychiatric explanation of male homosexuality centered on family influence on young boys and the possibilities of seduction by adult homosexuals. Young boys who grew up in the presence of women in a family where adult males were either absent or weak were likely to become homosexual. Such families, in which the father had little to do with child rearing or other household matters, were common. Homosexuality was discussed entirely in terms of boys who demonstrated "effeminate" manners and other behavior. Young boys, susceptible because of this type of family life, were then in danger of being seduced by homosexual men they might encounter as teachers or doctors. Then it was too late. There was no effective treatment to cure them, to make them "normal" men again. Thus, prevention, through changes in family life and legal prohibition against possible contact with seducers, was the only answer.[50]

When I questioned Abel Prieto Morales in 1971 about homosexuality and Cuba's "official" views, he responded with a psychosocial rationale and cited several European sources. He went on to say:

> Within our Revolution, homosexuals have played a relevant role, but at no time a leadership role because they were a bad example for young people. Nor did they represent Cuba abroad at any time.
>
> This is a measure we have taken, but it is not part of our machismo. We are not about to harm homosexuals because they are homosexuals, but we will take strong measures against those who pervert our youth.
>
> There should be an understanding throughout the world about the phenomena of homosexuality. We in Cuba are trying to understand the problem from a psychosociological point of view; it is a social problem and, as such, we are proposing that it be treated as a social ill.
>
> Therefore, we cannot put homosexuals in positions of leadership. This is what is being stated at the recent Congress; homosexuals: no position of leadership and no contact with young people. Early contact with homosexuality has destructive effects according to Freudian theory.[51]

For Cubans in the 1960s and early 1970s, homosexuality was "treatable." Thus, in 1969 in the popular magazine *Bohemia*, Prieto argued that "homosexuality cannot be understood unless it is classified as a neurotic state." Citing a French source on homosexuality, he concluded that "neurosis applies to these conditions since at the origins of homosexuality is a fixation or a regression to an infantile state."[52]

With the very few social research studies being undertaken in Cuba during the 1960s, it is striking that several concerned an examination of homosexual tendencies in children. It seemed to denote perhaps an ubiquitous preoccupation with homosexuality.

In 1965, J. Pérez Villar and six other colleagues in the Child Psychiatric Services of the Hospital General Calixto García in Havana, became interested in the subject after encountering "a large number of effeminate boys" in their clinic. They noted that prior to 1965 Cuban psychiatric literature had touched little on this theme.[53] Villar attempted to determine the factors that contributed to effeminacy in the fifty cases he and his associates had under study. He compared these boys with fifty other boys. His theoretical position is of great interest because it offered the philosophical basis on which teachers and psychologists were trained in Cuba for the next ten years.

Villar concluded his study with a view on appropriate sex roles for children that revealed Cuban attitudes toward the nature-nurture debate. He noted that their findings contradict studies of identical twins, which attribute the "determining role exclusively to the genetic factor." Nevertheless, he made no claim for himself and his colleagues as strict environmentalists: "That would not be in harmony with the modern genetical concepts which understand all illness to have both genetical and environmental factors."

The Villar study reveals that the mothers of effeminate boys noted "differences," usually at two to three years of age:

> Often mothers, or other relatives of effeminate boys, say to us that they noticed their child was "different" very early. One mother noted this difference to have begun at six or seven months of age; and at no time during our prolonged contact with her could we shake this certainty. Others, the majority, cite the observation of the difference to be in the second or third year.
>
> What does the difference consist of? The expressions of the mothers are like the following: "he was very soft . . . he was very noble from the time he was born . . . he never gave me any trouble . . . he was quieter than the other children . . . he remained quietly in the crib or playpen without protesting . . . he was very pretty, and had a very delicate appearance," and so forth.
>
> From all of these expressions, and many more similar ones, we have abstracted the following data: The effeminate boy demonstrates less motor activity, greater psychological ductility for education, and is physically prettier and more delicate than the average boy. It is also certain that an effeminate boy is rarely corpulent and muscular.
>
> These characteristics seem to be constitutional and congenital; but it does not seem that this alone is enough. Rather, we believe that those who possess them are "effeminable," and that this happens when the propitious conditions are present, those possibly being the ones mentioned.
>
> If he does not come in contact with these factors, we feel that the boy of this type will develop a normal masculine identification and make a choice of a heterosexual type. Clearly we see many boys with these motor characteristics, with characterological ductility, and with physical beauty and delicacy among our neurotic and our normal boys.[54]

According to Villar, those significant conditions were the influence of male homosexual role models and the lack of "real men" in the boy's life:

"There is a set of interrelated factors which is observed clinically in effeminate boys. . . . This complex is composed of (1) physical and/or emotional absence of the father, (2) predominance of women in the child's everyday environment, and (3) overprotection of the child and his being restricted to the home."[55]

Thus, the practice of banning gay people from any jobs that would bring them close to male children seemed to be grounded in scientific study. It is not unlike prevailing attitudes toward homosexuality at that time in the United States and other countries.

Villar and his colleagues believed their work provided a clearer understanding of the causes of male effeminacy, but also pointed to early identification and thus prevention of the "problem."

> An implication extracted from the extremely early beginnings of so many of our cases is the necessity of the prevention of early disturbances. *This type of prevention that is necessarily directed towards the family, can only be done through the organs and mechanisms of education at the disposition of the State, which reach the family and widen the psychological comprehension, and which reach the institutions related to children and increase the preparation of the personnel. This would be the way to attempt prevention and early discovery of these cases.*[56] [Italics mine]

In my studies of the education process during the 1970s, it became apparent that Cuban educators were clearly drawing upon Villar's studies and statements in their work with children. They were primarily concerned with possible detrimental effects on child development of two factors in Cuban life: a family tradition in which many fathers did not actively participate in their children's care, education, recreation, and general child-raising; and the involvement of many fathers in the Revolution with the consequent "effects of separation on their children."

The child psychiatrist Elsa Pradere studied one hundred fathers and their relationships with their children.[57] After summarizing the importance of the father's role in the healthy development of the child, she reports:

> At present there is a critical situation of lack of paternal participation in the bringing up of children. This is reflected daily in the emotional problems of children who are seen in the psychology clinics.
>
> The father in our environment frequently plays a limited part in a child's education. This phenomenon of the cultural order is summarized in a popular saying: "The woman is of the house, the man of the street."
>
> Generally the father believes that he has fulfilled his responsibilities by giving the mother the means for her support and occasionally serving as the punitive figure in the child's discipline.

There are cases in which the father is physically absent because of divorce or death or away from the country or home for other reasons. But more often you find the father who is constantly at work or at other related activities which keep him from maintaining good and normal relations with his children.[58]

This analysis of family life need not have anything to do with homosexuality. It might just as well be an explanation of how psychological problems in children are caused by the perverted nature of gender roles that requires the father to be absent from his children, to refrain from showing emotions to them, to act only as a disciplinarian while the mother has no choice but to take complete care of them and be the servant of the household. It was used, however, as a description of conditions that give rise to male homosexuality.

Freudian Theory

Citing Freud is like citing the scriptures to support or dispute arguments. In J. Pérez Villar's 1967 *Etapas del Desarrollo y Trastornos Emocionales en el Niño* (Stages of Development and Emotional Disturbances in the Child) (a text for teachers in teacher-training programs) of twenty-two citations in the bibliography, two were Cuban and one Spanish. The rest were Sigmund Freud, Jean Piaget, and seventeen American citations, including David Rapaport, Margaret Mead, J. McVicker Hunt, Erik Erikson, Arnold Gesell, Silvano Arieti, Charles Brenner, and Otto Fenichel (a distinguished psychoanalyst who, because he was a Jew, was forced to leave Germany for the United States in the 1930s). These are a roll call of some of America's most well-known anthropologists, psychologists, and psychiatrists in the 1940s and 1950s, reflecting the influence of the United States on the training of those like Villar who were educated before the 1959 revolution.

In discussions of homosexuality in the 1960s, the Cubans emphasized the importance of the oedipal period and the pivotal role of father identification. Without citing Freud, Cuban researchers also emphasized Freud's thesis of "too much love from the mother" and "the absence of the father." Seventy years before, Freud had written what Villar and the Public Health Report in the 1960s echoed: "In all our male homosexual cases the subjects had had a very intense erotic attachment to a female person, as a rule their mother, during the first period of childhood . . . ; this attachment was evoked or encouraged by too much tenderness on the part of the mother herself, and further reinforced by the small part played by the father during their childhood."[59]

But Freud never offered a full theory on the nature of homosexuality, and some of his views on homosexuality have contradictory implications and can be cited by different camps to support their views on gays and lesbians. For example, in 1935, he took a position closer to the one taken in the 1980s by the sex education movement in Cuba. To the mother of a homosexual he wrote:

> Homosexuality is assuredly no advantage, but it is nothing to be ashamed of, no vice, no degradation, it cannot be classified as an illness; we consider it to be a variation of the sexual function produced by a certain arrest of sexual development. Many highly respectable individuals of ancient and modern times have been homosexuals, several of the greatest men among them (Plato, Michelangelo, Leonardo da Vinci, etc.). It is a great injustice to persecute homosexuality as a crime, and a cruelty too. If you do not believe me, read the books of Havelock Ellis.
>
> By asking me if I can help, you mean, I suppose, if I can abolish homosexuality and make normal heterosexuality take its place. The answer is, in a general way, we cannot promise to achieve it. In a certain number of cases we succeed in developing the blighted germs of heterosexual tendencies which are present in every homosexual, in the majority of cases it is no more possible. It is a question of the quality and the age of the individual. The result of treatment cannot be predicted.
>
> What analysis can do for your son runs in a different line. If he is unhappy, neurotic, torn by conflicts, inhibited in his social life, analysis may bring him harmony, peace of mind, full efficiency whether he remains a homosexual or gets changed.[60]

In short, Freud viewed homosexuality as stemming from constitutional factors. There was no hope, therefore, of curing such a condition through therapy. Homosexuality was a "perversion"—the sexual drives were being "acted out"—and therefore not treatable. According to Freudian psychoanalytical theory, neurosis (in which sexual drives are inhibited or repressed) is treatable, and can be cured through the talking treatment of psychoanalysis.[61]

The Cuban educators and psychologists I interviewed expressed none of the psychoanalytic Freudian views of castration and the development of homosexuality.[62] A movement away from psychoanalytic approaches began soon after the Revolution, when different advocates in the Cuban Psychiatric Society championed their particular orientation toward mental health treatment.

> There had been ongoing heated debate within the Society among the Freudians, Horneyites, the Sullivanites, and the Marxists concerning the role psychiatrists could or should play in the revolutionary changes that were occurring in social and medical practice. . . . All groups were willing to evaluate how the Revolution was affecting mental health and illness, but there was sharp disagreement that the changing social con-

dition would lead to cure and/or prevention of certain mental disorders. Debate continued as to the validity of the instinct theory and infantile sexuality as significant factors in human development, the Marxists maintaining that social experience was the prime determinant of the human condition. The majority gravitated to the non-Freudian eclectic approach.[63]

By 1978 the chief of the National Group of Mental Health of the Ministry of Health and professor of Psychiatry of the Havana Medical School, Dr. Guillermo Barrientos, was telling an interviewer that psychiatric training at the medical school had moved away from "an eclectic approach." While schools of psychiatric thought such as Freud, Adler, Horney, Sullivan, Fromm, and Erikson, are studied in medical school by psychiatrists in training, Marxist evaluations are made, and "what is considered valuable is abstracted." The current theoretical approach is "now firmly based on the dialectical approach to science and the historical materialist approach to society. . . . In simple terms it is a Marxist-Leninist outlook."[64]

The Slow Process of Change: The Attempt to Eradicate Prejudice

The Penal Code of 1979 did not change laws discriminating against homosexuals. Manifestations of homosexual behavior in the public sphere remained illegal; there were three- to nine-month fines for anyone who:

1. scandalously dedicates himself to practicing homosexual acts or makes public ostentation of this conduct or importunes others with the requirements of this nature;
2. performs homosexual acts in public or private places in such a way that they may be involuntarily observed by other persons.[65]

For pederasty, punishment was increased: Homosexual conduct with a minor under the age of sixteen carries a five- to twenty-year prison term or the death sentence. The 1979 penal code also contains the law of "social dangerousness" (*ley de peligrosidad*),[66] that vague statute that allows great scope for prejudiced interpretation. Under this law, homosexuals and others considered to have antisocial attitudes or to be "exercising socially disapproved vices" can be detained for one to four years for therapy or re-education.[67]

Yet the Party no longer considered homosexuality itself to be in fundamental contradiction with revolutionary society. It was no longer a crime. It became a medical and psychological problem requiring further study to find a cure. Although this change in itself did not end the suffering of gay people who were victims of prejudice, it was a significant move toward more liberal attitudes that allowed a challenge to homophobia to take root.

In the middle of the decade, nationwide discussions of a proposed Family Code brought some legitimacy to voices for change in traditional male and female roles within the home, and to some extent, in society as a whole. The influence of that ongoing debate provided a small opening for questioning the popular support given homophobia. But even within the progressive National Task Force for Sexual Education, set up in the mid-1970s, attitudes toward homosexuality at first reflected the social norm. As one of of its directors, Dr. Monika Krause, explained to me: "I thought homosexuals were so because of bad education, because of problems between father and mother, because of antisocial environment, and so forth. Or that maybe it was a disease. But, little by little, studying all the literature of the experiences in other countries, I got enough information to revise completely my own attitude. The same happened to Professor Lajonchere, and we studied very carefully everything we could find on the problem."[68]

The forbidden subject became a hot news item in the fall of 1979 when the Task Force published its first in a series of sex education texts. One of them, *Man and Woman in Intimacy* by Siegfried Schnabl, a book on sexual behavior and physiology as well as sex education, carried an explosive last chapter—a mere ten pages entitled "Homosexuality in Man and Woman." The scientific-technical publishing agency of the Ministry of Culture allotted it a limited run of 27,000 hardback copies. To make sure these reached their intended audience, the first 15,000 copies were sold to people presenting a coupon that had been distributed among doctors, advanced students, and clinical psychologists who worked for the Ministry of Public Health. Since the price was only five pesos, crowds appeared in front of bookstores long before they opened for business, and the whole edition sold out immediately. Current rumor had it that advance news of the scandalous subject of chapter ten was the reason for selling the book in such a selective fashion. It became a "word-of-mouth best seller," the hottest book in Cuba. People were passing rare copies back and forth among friends.

It may well be that those in the publishing house who made the decision for such a limited edition did so out of distaste for the chapter on homosexuality and thus desired to limit its possible influence. (For whatever reasons, the following books in the series had runs of 150,000 copies.) If so, the endeavor backfired. No doubt far more than 27,000 people read the famous chapter ten and, to most of them, it offered a radically new way of thinking about homosexuality. Probably most found it unacceptable at the time, but it was a beginning. That book and the continuing educational work of the National Working Group for Sex Education have made an important contribution toward the prospect of a society where gay people may more easily live without needing closets.

In chapter ten of *Man and Woman in Intimacy*, Schnabl condemned his society (East Germany) for practicing the kind of hurting ridicule and denigration that can "break a person's soul." He offered as proof the fact that in the German Democratic Republic in the mid-1970s, the suicide rate among homosexuals between the ages of eighteen and twenty-two was three times higher than among heterosexuals in the same age group.[69] The German sexologist sought to refute common misconceptions about homosexuals.

> Homosexuality cannot be classified as a sickness; rather, it must be seen as a variant of sexuality. Homosexuals do not "suffer" from homosexuality; they suffer from the difficulties that their condition causes them in society. Very few homosexuals would like to change; when they do, it is generally for reasons of social prestige.[70]
>
> ... It is often thought that homosexuals are very sensitive, that they are easily offended, are irritable, unbalanced, easy to influence, emotionally unstable, and even neurotic. But frequently these qualities develop as a result of conflicts between a person's sexuality and society.[71]
>
> ... Aside from their sexual orientations, homosexuals differ very little, if at all from persons who are considered normal. Scientists have tried to discover physical and psychological characteristics specific to homosexuals, but have been unsuccessful. The "typical homosexual" does not exist.[72]

The Effect of Sex Education

The leaders of the National Working Group on Sex Education (GNTES) have discarded any notion of homosexuality as "an arrest of sexual development" and also rejected the Freudian theory of "unconscious homosexuality" in heterosexuals.[73] Indeed, the Cubans have accepted the current official orientation of much of the mental health community in the western world. GNTES, through Krause and Lajonchere, has not only taken the position that sexual orientation is very resistant to change, but also that it must not be pushed to change because homosexuality is part of human sexuality, neither an illness nor an abnormality. They define homosexuality as the American Psychiatric Association now defines it: "sexual orientation of the same sex. Not a psychiatric disorder as such."[74]

As we know from our own society, rooting out deeply entrenched prejudices is slow work, even with highly organized massive efforts. Nine years after publication of *Man and Woman in Intimacy*, I discussed this problem with Monika Krause in Havana. While being homosexual is no longer a crime, it can still be interpreted as improper conduct under the law if the authorities so choose or if the people of a district so demand. Although not frequent, there were reports in the 1980s of "street sweeps"—the rounding up of obvious queens and other street people prior to major public events. As Krause explained, the designation of what is improper conduct "depends on the interpretation of others, and that's the weak point in the legal system."

When I asked about discrimination against gay people in the workplace, she replied that it exists in medicine, psychology, education, the army, and among political leaders. Such policies are not written down "but sometimes, this is stronger than the written law. This is similar to what I mentioned when we were talking about the extramarital activities of our male population (as being acceptable for men but not for women). It is the celebration of the male condition. The celebration of their maleness. The same situation exists about homosexuality. There's no law that forbids a person because of his or her sexual preference to study this or that, but it happens; the discrimination exists."[75]

In addition to her position as director of GNTES, Monika Krause was also professor of human sexuality in the Victoria Girón Medical School where she directed the teaching of sex education classes. She utilized a variety of teaching techniques, including class lectures, current films on sexuality (including a number from universities in the United States), and such participatory methods as dramatization and role playing. For the first time in Cuban history, sex education has been mandated in the medical curriculum, and Krause has led classes as part of a required postgraduate program for family doctors. These doctors are in the midst of a three-year residency program in internal medicine. By the time they attended her lecture on homosexuality, they had usually heard that the subject is not talked about in the customary manner.

Then I say: "I need you, from this moment on, to be capable of repressing your aversion, your hatred, because I need you to listen. You're doctors. You are not anybody from the street: you are doctors."

I try to teach this class with a lot of participation, and, sometimes, depending on the group, I also introduce skits. I tell the doctors that I need a volunteer. If nobody raises his or her hand, I continue: "You are my doctor; I am an adolescent boy." (That needs a lot of imagination.)

So I'm role-playing the boy, and I say to the young doctor: "You are the family doctor, and I am asking you what to do because I'm homosexual. I have a lot of problems, and I don't know what it is, and I want to change because I want to live in accordance with the ethical and moral rules of society. I don't want to be an outsider. Well, doctor, what shall I do? I need your help."

The members of the class don't know what to do. They are asking the same questions of me, calling on me for help. Well, then I say, "Tell me, every one of you, what are the main characteristics of a homosexual?" And

I write their answers in big letters on the chalkboard: "a disease, a plague." They continue, and I put all the words on the board: weak character, anti-social, faggot, corrupt, deviant, degenerate, unnatural. All the familiar, terrible phrases.[76]

Through role-playing, Krause creates an environment where the doctors are not just listening to a teacher but also watching the drama of a young person unfold. She elicits from them their own view of homosexuality, forcing them to confront the stereotype and bigotry.

I say, "Well, now is the moment to repress your aversion, your hatred, your distaste. Listen carefully and look carefully; it's like this (motioning with a giant X across the chalkboard). Now we are going to analyze why—why it is not a disease; why it is not the result of bad education; why it is not an aberration; why it is not corruption; why it is not an antisocial condition a priori. There are many who are antisocial, but it is because we convert them into antisocial beings, because we are members of a homophobic society, of a society that only allows a normal life to heterosexuals."

Several times when I am talking, they jump and shout, and I have to say, "Are you a doctor? Or are you illiterate?" When they ask for further clarification, I explain that we do not yet know the real essence of homosexuality. But neither do we know the real essence of heterosexuality. Only nobody is asking about that; everybody is asking about homosexuality. Our view was always that homosexuality is something bad, evil, something terrible, unnatural. I say, "We know a lot about what homosexuality is not. We have enough arguments to say that it is not what is on the board; of that I assure you." And we have no possibilities of carrying out research because our homosexuals in Cuba are still under obligation, if they respect themselves, to hide their condition. Not to do so would bring about the end of his or her life as an accepted human being.

And I always read a letter written by a young homosexual. It is such a terrible letter. It tells how he can't find any help. Nobody is able to give him an explanation. He is being blackmailed by his stepfather, the only one in the family who has found out and is trying to deprive him of his right to live at home (he has a room in the apartment). The whole situation of all homosexuals is really concentrated in this letter and it is written in such a powerful way. And at the same time, there is no exaggeration of any kind.[77]

Often when I teach this class, the doctors will interrupt me—shouting, getting very agitated and losing their control. Sometimes they feel very ashamed when I have to calm them down. "Control yourself! You are doctors! You cannot behave this way in front of a patient; you can't. Even if you hate homosexuals, you cannot manifest the same behavior and attitude you just have with me."

And then I say, "Of course, I do not expect that you will change your attitude from today to tomorrow. I know what many of you are thinking:

She is one of them because otherwise, she wouldn't say that. She is perverted; she is a lesbian; she is a feminist; she is a this or a that and so on. And I assure you, I was thinking the same ten or fifteen years ago. But we have to be consistent with our humanistic conception of society. In a socialist society, there is no place for discrimination. What any two people do in intimacy is no one else's business, whether it is Juan and Juana, Juan and Juan, or Juana and Juana. You have to change your attitudes, and you can only change your attitudes if you repress your aversion, your repression, your hatred, and if you start to get information, because the first problem of our calamity in this respect is the lack of information, the lack of education, the lack of culture. We are still behaving like people in the Middle Ages, or like people who represent the Catholic Church."

And then I tell them an anecdote. I attended the Latin American Congress on Sexuality and Sex Education in Venezuela two years ago. The representative of the Catholic Church, Bishop Monsignor Leoni from Caracas, gave a speech. He was condemning so many things, so many things. Delegates from the Congress asked him: "What is the position of the Catholic Church concerning homosexuality?" And the monsignor answered, "A homosexual can never be a good Catholic. The Catholic Church and homosexuality are antagonistic." People asked why. He answered, "Because it is so." "Why can't a homosexual be a good Catholic?" He replied, "Because he cannot."

Then I say to the class: "You are *not allowed* to answer as did the Bishop Monsignor Leoni of Caracas."[78]

Krause advises doctors to tell a young person to accept his or her homosexuality, and she counsels them on problems they encounter.

For example, a doctor may say, "I know he's homosexual, but if I say so, he will have problems in his school. His family will make his life impossible if they know." And I tell them, "You cannot tell his family. You have to give him or her whatever elements will strengthen self-esteem so he or she can live in our still very homophobic society. The fact that a person can talk with you, a medical doctor, without being hit with manifestations of hatred and aversion, is of tremendous therapeutic value. You have this obligation. You cannot be a factor in anyone's suicide. You have no right to contribute to worsening the quality of life for anybody. Consider a homosexual as a normal human being with the same rights and obligations as anybody. We are evaluating attitudes toward society, the disposition to contribute knowledge, talents, and capacities to the development of this society. Anything concerning sexual preferences, when there is no harm to others, whatever he or she is doing in intimacy, is no one else's business. That is our main principle."[79]

A good example of the kind of prejudice the GNTES is fighting is seen in 1981 Ministry of Education curriculum guidelines for teachers on sex education. It was given to me by a biology teacher in a training program for elementary school teachers. The same attitudes prevail in many school districts in the United States as well. According to these guidelines,

> You know that some homosexuals call attention to themselves with scandalous antisocial behavior. Others are not so obvious, but on many occasions try to use children and adolescents. They approach them using various tricks to satisfy their homosexual activities. Children and adolescents must be warned against that kind of manipulation. As a rule, an adolescent who has been victimized once by one of these corruptors is not going to become homosexual in turn, but it is essential to come to his/her assistance as soon as it is known that something like that happened. These abnormal and degrading practices, if repeated because of the child's ingenuity and ignorance, can cause serious psychological traumas, which may lead, in some instances, to homosexual conduct.
>
> Our society is concerned with helping children in all cases, and with adequately training parents and educators in order to make them useful to our society.
>
> The contrary occurs in capitalist societies where, for money, one can acquire or satisfy any vice; where sex, in its most degrading forms becomes a commodity; where the exploitation of sex goes from prostitution to pornography, from homosexuality to the sale of girls and boys as sex objects. This is part of the process of moral decomposition of the capitalist societies which have reached new levels of corruption.[80]

Homosexuals in Cuba Today

By all accounts, life for gay people in Cuba had improved considerably by the mid- and late 1980s. In 1984 Lourdes Arguelles and Ruby Rich wrote:

> Today, life for lesbians and gay men in Cuba is similar, in some sense, to life for gay people in the United States . . . prior to the development of the gay liberation and lesbian-feminist movements and modern identities they produced. In this, its style is not very different from that customary throughout most of Latin America and the Caribbean, where *se dice nada, se hace todo* (say nothing, do everything) is the rule. It is a closeted life but by no means a secret one. While the homosexuality of many men and women is a matter of common knowledge, it is never a matter of public record. Indeed, it is the complete absence of a public sphere that most clearly distinguishes the life of homosexuals in Cuba from any corresponding life-style in the United States or Western European urban centers.[81]

In February 1988, the National Lawyers Guild reported that:

The catch-all provision for unspecified conduct which is "socially danger-ous" permitting authorities to detain persons for re-education has been substantially limited. . . . no provision remains which could be used to punish consensual, private homosexual conduct. Some offenses specifical-ly regarding homosexual conduct remain; for example, Article 303 pro-hibits inducing a minor under 16 years to engage in homosexual conduct or prostitution.

There is substantial evidence that the situation of homosexuals in Cuba vastly improved in the 1980s. Official discrimination no longer exists, and acceptance is slowly being gained in a once fiercely homophobic society. One can find homosexuals in a wide variety of professions and even among party members. Many homosexuals interviewed on various occa-sions over the past four years confirm that the situation has improved markedly. They are not fearful of being identified as homosexual, and have many more opportunities for employment. Continued homophobia is blamed on societal values and not on official policy.[82]

In 1988 a young Latin-American woman from Texas attended classes at the film school in Havana.[83] For her project she made a short film of interviews about lesbians and gays in Cuba entitled "Not Because Fidel Says So." As a lesbian living in Texas, she knew first-hand the pain of social rejection and prejudice. Knowing that "homophobia is a world-wide disease," she wanted to explore its presence in Cuba. She inter-viewed straights and lesbians and gays, men and women, some ar-ranged, some at random—people she happened to meet in the streets of Havana, or in an ice cream parlor, or on the beach. Among heterosexuals she heard all the usual prejudice but also acceptance. She easily found the public gathering places for lesbians and gay people. Several of those in-terviewed there frankly stated, "I am gay." A young man at the beach put his arms around his friends; smiling warmly and openly, he talked about the freedom he had. He said that the government did not bother them at all although he admitted that when he and his lover wanted to go beyond the limit of acting just as friends, "we don't have a place to go, a house where we can go to make love"—a testament to the housing shortage as much as to sexual prejudice.[84] The film implies that UMAP is ancient his-tory for these young people—if they even know it occurred.

There appears to be a new level of self-acceptance, which can come only as attitudes of oppression change in respect to a group. Being gay is, for the laughing young men, simply a given, and so what if individuals may give them a hard time? It is not a film of sunlight and roses, how-ever. Sitting alone in a dark room, one lesbian discussed what it was like to be cut off from her family and from most of society because she is lesbian.

To choose being openly homosexual, without repressing one's self, is definitely a problem, because society doesn't permit it. In general, it's not accepted by your parents, your friends, your classmates, the people you work with. So all of this forms part of the repression that the homosexual feels within himself or herself, and outside as well. It's a type of repression that manifests itself both internally and externally. Internally, because you realize that you can't express yourself the way you are, that you have to lead a sort of double life—your private life, and the exterior that you show to others.[85]

Another woman spoke of job discrimination—"not because Fidel Castro says so, but because the society, the people, don't have that kind of sexual education, so they discriminate against us." And a plea from a young man interviewed in front of a cinema: "Well, it's a very delicate thing. But since you're giving me the chance to talk about it, I'd say I can't feel good if everyone knows all about me, because we are repudiated by other people. People don't help us. If they could help us and work with us, the society could benefit from us."[86]

Although this short film was shown at the Public Theatre in New York in May 1989, it was not shown publicly in Havana. Nor was "The Kiss of the Spiderwoman," a Hollywood film dealing with homosexuality, distributed in Cuba. There is never the slightest problem obtaining copies of other Hollywood films for Cuban distribution. Clearly, the appropriate government agency decided that this film, though politically quite acceptable, should not be shown.

Other interviews during the 1980s—in schools, in homes, at beaches, along *La Rampa*; with writers, artists, musicians, and film makers—indicate a general feeling that existing discrimination stems from individual social values and attitudes, not from official policies. These days, groups of gay people gathering openly in Havana experience little harassment and no violence against them.[87]

How then are we to understand the 1984 French documentary film made by two Cuban exiles about the Cuban government's repression of gay men? (The film has little to say about lesbians.) The film, *Improper Conduct*, by the late well-known cinematographer Nestor Almendros and the director Orlando Jimenez-Leal, received great publicity and was shown in major North American cities and abroad and on public television. And, of course, it created controversy.

The core of the film consists of interviews with twenty-eight Cuban exiles who testify primarily about the brutality of the UMAP camps and the kind of discrimination that encouraged many homosexuals to join the exodus from the port of Mariel to Miami in the spring of 1980. In this respect, these interviews are important as oral history protesting the institutionalization of homophobia. But there is something very static about the film as a whole. It focuses on an aspect of human rights in which significant improvement has taken place, yet the film tells us nothing of these changes and implies that conditions of twenty to twenty-five years ago are the conditions of today.

One should not read this to mean there is no discrimination and oppression of homosexuals in today's Cuba. Far from it. But it is not as described in this film. It is, in general, the kind of discrimination and oppression that would be found in most parts of the United States and in most of Latin America, notwithstanding different cultures and laws. To the extent that there have been improvements for gay people in the United States, these have grown out of the active struggles of gay people, beginning with Stonewall on a hot June night in 1969. Until the patrons of that Greenwich Village gay bar fought back rather than meekly accepting yet another police raid, gay rights organizations in the United States were small and usually met in an atmosphere of secrecy. The "illegal bars"of gay life symbolized the dominant society's view of homosexuality as criminal perversion, a degrading sin or, at best, an illness from which one should be cured.[88]

Those at the Stonewall that night, and those from the neighborhood who joined them, lit a match to dry grass. There are now several hundred gay liberation organizations with varying agendas throughout the United States. By 1989 there were gay rights laws in almost every major city. New York City finally made it illegal to discriminate according to sexual orientation in employment, housing, and public accommodation. Twenty-five states have repealed old sodomy laws.

There have been other advances and setbacks as well. The struggle continues. In no country is prejudice overturned in an instant by political revolution, legislation, or even an education program. It is rather a lengthy process—a process that, in both the United States and Cuba, has been affected by the AIDS crisis.

In spite of improvements for gay people in the Cuban social climate,[89] they do not have a gay rights movement. Such a movement cannot happen in Cuba today—a fact crucial to any attempt to understand, as I describe in chapter five, how a policy of quarantining people who test HIV positive could take place in a modern twentieth century country.

Notes

1. Esther Mosak, "Helping Machismo Out," *Cuba International*, (March 1989): 43.
2. Ibid.
3. Ibid.

4. Roger Lancaster, "Comment on Arguelles and Rich's 'Homosexuality, Homophobia, and Revolution: Notes Toward an Understanding of the Cuban Lesbian and Gay Male Experience, Part II'," *Signs: Journal of Women in Culture and Society* 12, no. 1 (1986): 188–192 and B. Ruby Rich and Lourdes Arguelles, "Reply to Lancaster," *Signs* 12, no. 1 (1986): 192–194.

5. Abel Prieto Morales, "Homosexualismo," *Bohemia*, February 21, 1969, 108.

6. Interview with Dr. Luís Allyon, Havana, 1969.

7. Lourdes Casals, "Images of Cuban Society Among Pre- and Post-Revolutionary Novelists," (Ph.D. Dissertation, New School for Social Research, 1975), 260; cited in Salas, 169.

8. Ibid.

9. In a letter to an early lesbian publication, *Ladder*, playwright Lorraine Hansberry expressed a reality that would still apply to Cuba and to most other countries:

I suspect that the problem of the married woman who would prefer emotional-physical relationships with other women is proportionally much higher than a similiar statistic for men. (A statistic surely no one will ever really have.) This, because the estate of woman being what it is, how could we ever begin to guess the numbers of women who are not prepared to risk a life alien to what they have been taught all their lives to believe was their "natural" destiny—and—their only expectation for economic security. It seems to be that this is why the question has an immensity that it does not have for male homosexuals. . . . A woman of strength and honesty may, if she chooses, sever her marriage and marry a new male mate and society will be upset that the divorce rate is rising so—but there are few places in the United States, in any event, where she will be anything remotely akin to an "outcast." Obviously this is not true for a woman who would end her marriage to take up life with another woman.

Lorraine Hansberry, cited in Adrienne Rich, "Compulsory Heterosexuality and Lesbian Existence," in Ann Snitnow, et al., *Powers of Desire: The Politics of Sexuality* (New York: Monthly Review Press, 1983), 197.

10. Mirta de la Torre Mulhare, "Sexual Ideology in Pre-Castro Cuba: A Cultural Analysis," Ph.D dissertation, University of Pittsburgh, 1969.

11. Lourdes Arguelles and B. Ruby Rich, "Homosexuality, Homophobia, and Revolution: Notes Toward an Understanding of the Cuban Lesbian and Gay Experience, Part 1," *Signs: Journal of Women in Culture and Society* 9 (4):686–687. Arguelles and Rich interviewed Cuban homosexual men and lesbians from 1979 to 1983 both in Cuba and abroad.

12. Arguelles and Rich, "Homosexuality, Part 1," 686–687.

13. Ibid.

14. In the Soviet Union under Stalin, homosexuals were viewed as criminals. This included a press campaign against gays as a sign of "degeneracy of the fascist bourgeoisie." In January 1934 mass arrests of homosexuals were carried out in Moscow, Leningrad, and Odessa. Among those arrested were a great many actors, musicians, and other artists. In March 1934 a statute was enacted that included a maximum penalty of five years for consensual male homosexuality. Lesbianism was not included.

In this atmosphere of oppression, many gays in the USSR hid their homosexuality and in contemporary Russia also avoid testing for the HIV virus. On October 28, 1992, Russian President Boris Yeltsin proposed a new penal code that would repeal Article 121–1 of the Russian Criminal Code that prohibited sex among men. "Yeltsin Lifts Stalin's Ban on Gays," *New York Post*, October 29, 1992, 5.

See John Lauritsen and David Thorstad, *The Early Homosexual Rights Movement (1864–1935)* (New York: Times Change Press, 1974), 68–70. Also see David F. Greenberg, *The Construction of Homosexuality* (Chicago: University of Chicago Press, 1988), 440–443; Mikhail Stern, *Sex in the USSR*, trans. Mark Howson and Carl Ryan (New York: Times Books, 1979), 214, 218–219; Ben de Jong, "'An Intolerable Kind of Moral Degeneration': Homosexuality in the Soviet Union," *Pink Book 1985* (Amsterdam: COC, 1985), 76–88; Jurgen Lemke, *Gay Voices from East Germany*, English-language version edited and with an introduction by John Borneman (Bloomington: Indiana University Press, 1991); John Cabral, "There's A Gay Life in China: "I . . . Very . . . Fear," *Christopher Street*, Issue 62, 27–32; Nicholas D. Christof, "China Using Electrodes to 'Cure' Homosexuals," *New York Times*, January 29, 1991, A2.

15. Allen Young, *Gays Under the Cuban Revolution* (San Francisco: Grey Fox Press, 1981); also see Henk van den Boogard and Kathelijne van Kammen, " 'We Cannot Jump Over Our Shadow,': On Cuban Actions Against Homosexuals and Against Antihomosexuality," *IGA Pink Book 1985* (Amsterdam: COC, 1985), 29–41.

16. Lee Lockwood, *Castro's Cuba, Cuba's Fidel* (New York: Vintage Books, 1967).

17. Fidel Castro, Speech at Las Villas on the 15th anniversary of the attack on the Moncada, *Granma Weekly Review,* July 26, 1968, 3–5.

18. See Marta Salander and Consuelo Miranda, "Círculos Infantiles: La Educación en la Edad Temprana," in Seminario Interdisciplinario de Educación Permanante, Mimeographed, 1970, 4; Marvin Leiner, *Children Are the Revolution: Day Care in Cuba* (New York: Penguin Books, 1978), 18.

19. Arguelles and Rich, "Homosexuality Part 1," 689.

20. See Richard Fagen, *The Transformation of Political Culture in Cuba* (Stanford: Stanford University Press, 1969), 42, 52–53; Jorge Domínguez, *Cuba: Order And Revolution* (Cambridge: Harvard University Press, 1978), 148, 209, 345.

21. Arguelles and Rich, 689. Also see Warren Hinkle and William Turner, *The Fish is Red: The Story of the Secret War Against Castro* (New York: Harper & Row, 1981), 191–192.

22. Allen Young, interview with Allen Ginsberg in *Gay Sunshine Interview,* 1974, 25–27, reprinted in Allen Young, *Gays Under the Cuban Revolution* (San Francisco: Gray Fox Press, 1981), 20.

23. Ibid.

24. Ibid.

25. Jorge I. Domínguez, *Cuba: Order and Revolution* (Cambridge: Harvard University Press, 1978), 357.

26. See Domínguez, *Cuba;* Lourdes Casals, "Literature and Society," in Carmelo Mesa-Lago, ed., *Revolutionary Change in Cuba* (Pittsburgh: University of

Pittsburgh Press, 1971); Luís Salas, *Social Control and Deviance in Cuba* (New York: Praeger Publishers, 1979).

27. Juan Escalona, Interview with Minister of Justice, 1984, Center for Cuban Studies.

28. In 1970 when Portocarrero met with the Nicaraguan writer, Ernesto Cardenal, he showed him a photograph of his large abstract ceramic mural in the presidential palace. In his diary of the Cuban trip, Cardenal reports that Portocarrero "told me that some delegates from Russia or one of the Eastern European countries at a reception asked Fidel, with a certain tone of sarcasm, 'And what does that mean?' (meaning 'and what does that have to do with the Revolution?'). Fidel replied, 'Nothing, it doesn't mean anything. It's just some crazy thing painted by a crazy person who was commissioned by the crazy men who made this Revolution'."

Ernesto Cardenal, *En Cuba*, (Mexico City: Ediciónes Era, 1968), 164; For a discussion of cultural politics in Cuba, see Michael Chanan, *The Cuban Image: Cinema and Cultural Politics in Cuba*, (London: BFI Publishing, 1985), 134.

29. José Yglesias, *In the Fist of the Revolution* (New York: Pantheon Books, 1968), 275–276.

30. Ibid., 277.

31. Ibid., 278.

32. Salas, *Deviance in Cuba*, 155; also see Wilfredo Rivera Roldán, "Vida, Pasión, y Muerte del Señor Bar," *Verde Olivo*, April 14, 1968, 26.

33. Domínguez, *Order and Revolution*, 393; See Casals, "Literature and Society," 448, 450.

34. Domínguez, *Order and Revolution*, 357.

35. Kenny Leiner's diary, 1968–1969.

36. Interview with Abel Prieto Morales, Havana, 1971.

37. Abel Prieto, Ministry of Health Report as quoted in Abel Prieto, *Bohemia*, 108–9.

38. Interview with Graciela Figueroa, Center for Special Education, Havana, 1968.

39. Ibid.

40. René Vega-Vega, "El Centro Infantil de Conducta de la JUCEI de la Habana," Universidad de la Habana, no. 186/187/188 (July–December, 1967), 119–124.

41. Ibid., 122.

42. Salas, *Deviance in Cuba*, 165, 171.

43. See Susan Sontag cited in George DeStefano, "Improper Conduct," *The Nation*, 287 (April 28, 1984): 524.

44. See work by G. A. Rekers and colleagues in both professional literature and popular books for parents on "how to shape a child's sexual identity" and help them "grow up straight.": A. Rekers, et al, "Child Gender Disturbances: A Clinical Rationale for Intervention," *Psychotherapy: Theory, Research and Practice*, 1977, 14:2–11; G. A. Rekers and O. I. Lovaas, "Behavioral Treatment of Deviant Sex-Role Behaviors in a Male Child," *Journal of Applied Behavior Analysis*, 1974, 7:173–190; G. A. Rekers, *Shaping Your Child's Sexual Identity* (Grand Rapids:

Baker Book House, 1982); G. A. Rekers, *Growing Up Straight: What Every Family Should Know About Homosexuality* (Chicago: Moody Press, 1982).

45. I'm indebted to Carolina Mancuso and other single mothers (both heterosexual and lesbian women) who are raising sons, for sharing with me their struggle to help their boys develop a genuine respect for women.

46. UNESCO, XXXIII International Conference on Public Instruction, OIE-UNESCO, September 15–23, 1971; Report of Cuba; Organization of Education, 1970–71 (UN Doc. OIE/ Q/70/3), 14. Also, for additional information on the Congress' effect on early childhood education, see Marvin Leiner, *Children Are the Revolution* 181–186.

47. "Declaration by the First National Congress on Education and Culture," *Granma Weekly Review*, May 9, 1971, 4–5; also see Casals, "Literature and Society," 462.

48. Ley no. 1267, *Gaceta Oficial de la República de Cuba*, March 12, 1974, 117–118.

49. Escalona interview.

50. Salas, *Deviance in Cuba*, 164.

51. Prieto interview, 1971.

52. Abel Prieto Morales, "Homosexualismo," *Bohemia*, 61 (February 1969): 108.

53. José P. Villar "El Afeminamiento en El Niño," *Psicología y Educación* (October–December 1965): 55–69.

54. Ibid., 63–64.

55. Ibid., 69.

56. Ibid., 64.

57. Elsa Pradere, "El Papel del Padre en la Educación de Sus Hijos," *Psicología y Educación* (October–December 1965): 42–54.

58. Ibid., 54. Pradere reports that 55 percent of the fathers never taught their children even the simplest games, and did not have anything to do with school affairs or with the discipline of their children.

59. Sigmund Freud, *Leonardo da Vinci and a Memory of His Childhood*, trans. Allan Tyson, ed. James Stachey (New York: W.W. Norton and Company, 1964), 54.

60. Sigmund Freud, "Letter to an American Mother," reprinted in Paul Friedman, "Sexual Deviations," in Silvano Arieti, ed., *American Handbook of Psychiatry*, vol. 1 (New York: Basic Books, 1959), 606–7. In Vienna at that time (1935) the Austrian fascists were rapidly gaining strength and promoting policies that linked gays and Jews as inferior beings unworthy of an Aryan society. Once part of Greater Germany, Austria advocated extermination of those groups.

61. Robert E. Gould, "What We Don't Know About Homosexuality," *New York Times Magazine*, February 24, 1974, 51; for a comprehensive synthesis of neurobiological research on homosexuality see Chandler Burr, "Homosexuality and Biology," *The Atlantic*, March 1993, 47–65. Chandler concludes his review of major research studies: "Five decades of psychiatric evidence demonstrates that homosexuality is immutable and nonpathological, and a growing body of more recent evidence implicates biology in the development of sexual orientation."

62. Some of Freud's earlier writings tried to offer psychoanalytic rationale for

a person becoming gay by emphasizing that homosexuality was a response to castration anxiety in the oedipal period. The castration anxiety may make the young boy remove himself from rivalry with the father by denying and renouncing all women. According to the theory, a boy who fears that his father will punish him because he has incestuous feelings for his mother may try to distract and placate his father by taking on feminine characteristics—"denying his heterosexuality and his love for his mother. He thus becomes a passive, effeminate homosexual." David F. Greenberg, *The Construction of Homosexuality*, 30.

63. Irving J. Crain, M.D., "Psychiatry in Cuba," Paper presented at the N.Y. Medical College, Dept. of Psychiatry, (September 28, 1978), 2.

Dr. Crain is assistant professor of psychiatry at New York Medical College. The above report was based on his first visit to Cuba in July 1969 and Dr. Crain's interview with Dr. Leopoldo E. Araujo, Professor of Psychiatry at the Havana Medical School. Dr. Araujo was president of the Cuban Psychiatric society in 1959–1960.

64. Ibid., 11. In 1985 the official government attitude towards psychonalysis changed. This was a direct result of the influence of Marie Langer [1910–1987], a psychoanalyst who was a clandestine Communist in the 1930s in Vienna and served as a medical volunteer in the Spanish Civil War. She was forced into exile in Argentina and later in Mexico. In those countries she became an influential psychoanalyst, lecturing and writing about the need to integrate psychonalysis with the insights of feminism and Marxism. She also worked as a group-therapy organizer in Sandinista Nicaragua before her death in 1987.

After meetings with Fidel Castro in December 1985 at a conference of Latin American intellectuals in Havana she was invited to present a lecture on her work. Titled "Psicoanálasis sin Divan" (Psychoanalysis without the couch] she criticized the view in the USSR and in Cuba that psychoanalysis was bourgeois and decadent; she argued that psychonalysis was part of the intellectual movement for Latin American independence. Her talk was followed by a call for the First Congress of Latin American psychoanalysts and Marxist psychologists. Castro told Dr. Langer, "We are going to bring in pschoanalysis. Yes, let's have this congress." It was held in Havana in February, 1988. See Marie Langer, *From Vienna to Managua: Journey of a Psychoanalyst* (London: Free Association Books, 1989), 229–231, 1–21.

65. Ley no. 21, *Gaceta Oficial de la República de Cuba*, Article 359, March 1, 1979.

66. Ibid., articles 76 and 77.

67. Salas, *Deviance in Cuba*, 153; Arguelles and Rich, "Homosexuality, Part 1," 694; Young, *Gays Under the Cuban Revolution*, 52; "Criminal Justice in Cuba: A Report of the National Lawyers Guild," New York, National Lawyers Guild, 1988, 8.

68. Interview with Monika Krause Peters, 1986.

69. Siegfried Schnabl, *El Hombre y La Mujer en La Intimidad* (Habana: Editorial Científico-Técnica, 1979), 328–337.

70. Ibid., 333; also see Stephen J. Risch and Randolph E. Wills, "From Cuba and GDR: Positive Views of Gays," *The Gay Insurgent*,(Summer 1990): 4–10 for

discusssion and translation of Siegfried Schnabl's chapter 10, "Homosexuality in Man and Woman."

71. Ibid., 329.

72. Ibid.

73. Erich Fromm, *Greatness and Limitations of Freud's Thoughts* (New York: Harper and Row, 1980), 20.

74. Shervert H. Frazier, et al., eds., *A Psychiatric Glossary: The Meaning of Terms Frequently Used in Psychiatry*, 4th Edition (Washington, D.C.: American Psychiatric Association, 1975), 6; Gould, "What We Don't Know About Homosexuality," 13.

In late 1973, the thirteen-member board of the American Psychiatric Association voted unanimously to remove homosexuality from the list of diagnostic categories of mental disorders in a belated acknowledgment that homosexuality is not related to pathology, to mental illness. The decision was a benchmark diagnostic change from the prevailing view of the psychiatric community during most of the twentieth century. Robert Gould, a psychiatrist who works extensively on psychosocial problems such as deviancy and changing sex roles of men and women, said soon after the APA's vote that "the significance of this act will reverberate in the homosexual and psychiatric worlds—and in the heterosexual world—for years to come." (Robert Gould, "What We Don't Know About Homosexuality," 13).

75. Krause Peters interview, 1986.

76. Ibid.

77. In a 1969 visit to Cuba, Michael Frayn, an English writer, interviewed a boy who, believing he was a homosexual, said that he wished that he died at birth since in Cuba "homosexuals are regarded worse than beasts." Michael Frayn, *Observer*, January 12, 1969, cited in Hugh Thomas, 1435.

78. Krause Peters interview, 1986.

79. Ibid.

80. "Proposal on Sex Education by the Task Force on Sex Education," 1981 Ministry of Education Guidelines.

81. Arguelles and Rich, 695–696.

82. National Lawyers Guild, "Criminal Justice in Cuba, a Preliminary Report of the National Lawyers Guild" (February 1988): 8.

83. "The International School of Film and TV, also known as the School for the Third World" is a boarding school located in San Antonio de los Baños about 25 miles from Havana. García Márquez, winner of the Nobel Prize for Literature and president of the Foundation of Latin American Cinema, is one of the prime financial supporters of this school for young filmmakers from Latin America and the Caribbean, Africa, and Asia. See Jacobo Timerman, *Cuba: A Journey* (New York: Alfred A. Knopf, 1990), 42–46.

84. This is an indirect reference to the *posadas* which are not available for use by gays. As noted in Chapter 5, the *posada* is a small hotel where a man and a woman can rent a room for several hours. There is no stigma attached to this private time for a couple during a very serious housing shortage.

85. Graciela Sánchez, "Not Because Fidel Says So," 1988.

86. Ibid.

87. See Jorge Socarras, photographs by David LaChapelle, "Quba Libre: A Near Queer Havana," *NYQ*, December 8, 1991, 43–46, 68.

88. The Stonewall rebellion in Greenwich Village, New York, on June 27, 1969, is viewed as a benchmark date for rebellion against the oppression of gays in the USA and a reminder of the current struggle for gay rights. Some obervers see that June evening day at the Stonewall Inn as the birth date of the gay liberation movement. The next night and afterwards, the Stonewall rebellion graffiti started appearing: "legalize gay bars" and "support gay power." The politicalization of gays increased. Vito Russo, film critic and author, remembered: "It took me a few months to see there was something political about being gay . . . I had never considered that gay was something you could fight for. I just accepted that a lot of people didn't like homosexuals."

Vito Russo in *Newsday*, June 8, 1989, pt. 2, 15; see also John D'Emilio and Estelle Freedman, *Intimate Matters: A History of Sexuality in America* (New York: Harper and Row, 1988), 318–319, 321; see memories of Ed Murphy, recorded by the Sage History Project, an organization of elderly gay people, *Newsday*, June 8, 1989, pt. 2, 14; "Stonewall: Then and Now: Gay Power Comes to Sheridan Square," by Lucian K. Truscott IV, *The Village Voice*, June 13, 1989, 31–32 (a reprint of the original article that appeared the week of Stonewall).

89. Recent public statements by government leaders reflect some of the changes in the Cuban social climate towards gays and lesbians. At the Young Communist League (UJC) held in Havana in April 1992, Vilma Espín, head of the Federation of Cuban Women "challenged a psychiatrist's homophobic comments, emphasizing that oppression against gays and lesbians must be stopped and gay and lesbian youth must be respected and welcomed." "Gay Organization in Support of Cuba," *Center for Cuban Studies Newsletter*," November 1992, 12; also see Sonja de Vries, "Thoughts in Flight," *Cuba Update*, (February/March 1993): 19–20.

In an interview with Tomás Borge in late 1992, Fidel Castro stated: "I am absolutely opposed to all forms of oppression, contempt, scorn, or discrimination with regard to homosexuals." Fidel Castro, *Un Grupo de Maíz: Conversación con Tomás Borge*, (Havana: Oficina de Publicaciónes del Consejo de Estado, 1992), 238.

These statements by officials—indicating some public movement towards Communist Party change in attitudes towards homosexuality—has also opened at least one possibility for the positive portrayal of gays and lesbians in Cuban films. In 1992 Tomás Gutiérrez Alea, one of Cuba's leading film directors, was working on a film version of a play about the friendship between a gay man and a straight Communist activist based on the story, "El Lobo, el Bosque, y el Hombre Nuevo," by Senel Paz. For two months, in early 1992, the play was sold out to mixed straight and gay audiences in Havana. "Gay Organization in Support of Cuba," *Newsletter*, 12.

3

Changing the Role of Women and Breaking the Taboo: Initiating Sex Education

Sex education as we conceive of it in the broad sense of the term, should be oriented toward preparing new generations for the purpose of developing stable, enduring and happy partnerships; thus we educate our children in the principles of our socialist society.

There is no other sphere of human life where prejudice, taboo, ignorance, the bourgeois double standard and other left-overs of class society persist with such strength and have grown such deep roots.

—Monika Krause Peters

Women's participation in the Revolution is a revolution within a revolution. And if we are asked what is the most revolutionary thing that the revolution is doing, we would answer that it is precisely this: the revolution that is occurring among the women of our country.

—Fidel Castro

In the Cuba of the mid-1970s, there were those in the new generation of education activists who were calling for something very new and very radical—sex education. Resistance was enormous, and the fact that the effort has gotten as far as it has is a great testament to the perseverance of a few key people. It should not come as a surprise that the sex education program sprang from the women's organization, the Federation of Cuban Women (FMC), which itself is representative of the changing situation of women in Cuban society since 1959. An outline of the changes is relevant for the process of sex education.

Out of the House and into the Workforce

Dramatic changes for women came about as a result of the government's program to encourage women to enter the paid workforce, including new and broader opportunities for women to get the kind of education

61

necessary to enter professions previously closed to them. Necessary as this was, it did not in itself establish social equality for women. That was not part of the government's agenda. It did work toward modifying patriarchal traditions. However, the struggle against those traditions has had to operate in an environment in which the mass organization for women (FMC) has not been able to take strong stands independent of the central government.

To administer and direct programs for women in coordination with other government policies, in 1960 the revolutionary leaders created the Federation of Cuban Women with Vilma Espín, Raúl Castro's wife, as its president (an office she continues to hold). From a membership of 17,000 in 1961, close to 3 million women now belong to the FMC—about 85 percent of all women over the age of fourteen. The FMC's immediate tasks were enormous—to organize adult education programs and encourage women to find jobs outside the home. Of particular concern was giving former prostitutes and domestic servants the skills and the opportunity for other work. There were also programs especially for women in remote rural areas.

Thus, the FMC challenged the traditional concept, accepted by both women and men, that a woman's place is in the home while men should be out there in *la calle* ("the street"). One of the early FMC organizers described the difficulty of getting women to enter into the workforce:

> I can remember going house to house, and explaining to housewives why they should join the workforce—why the Revolution needed their intelligence and capabilities, and why they themselves needed economic independence. It was difficult!! It was difficult because women were bound by many prejudices—from their families, from men, prejudices rooted even in the women themselves. Religion also educated women to believe that their place was in the home. She wasn't allowed in many cases to go out by herself at night. And so women who finally went out to work at night were considered prostitutes.[1]

According to the 1953 census, women accounted for only 17 percent of the Cuban labor force and, of these working women, one fourth were employed in homes as domestics. Women's participation in the labor force climbed steadily during the 1960s and at a faster rate during the 1970s. It reached 31.4 percent of the labor force in 1980 and just over 38 percent in 1988.

To bring so many women into the workforce, traditional child care, by female relatives in the home, had to be greatly supplemented with public day care. None existed before the Revolution. Clemintina Serra, an early member of the Central Committee of the Communist Party who headed up the creation of the system of day care centers (*círculos infantiles*), stated that the *círculos* were established "to take care of the children of working mothers, free them from responsibility while working, and offer them the guarantee that their children will be well cared for and provided with all that is necessary for improved development." I have discussed and analyzed the dramatic support and development of day care since the Revolution in *Children Are the Revolution: Day Care in Cuba*.[2]

In general, women have been relegated to "women's jobs" even in the paid workforce. At the same time, they have found great opportunities to get a professional education, and women are growing in number in top professions and administrative positions. The number of women who hold higher education degrees in various scientific and technical fields is testimony to future changes in what traditionally have been considered men's work. Even in 1981, this included 28.5 percent of graduates in geology, mining and metallurgy; 41 percent of graduates in the field of sugar, chemicals, and food production; 18 percent in electronics and communication; 28 percent in construction; 27.8 percent in agriculture and livestock husbandry, and 37.3 percent in economics.[3]

Girls in elementary and secondary schools do not feel excluded from technical and scientific careers. They are given positive—not negative—messages about their potential in mathematics, the sciences, engineering, and mining. They are also given strong training in such subjects as mathematics, physics, biology, and chemistry. Cuban girls do not hesitate to say, "Sure! I can do that!" This freedom was evident when I had the opportunity to talk spontaneously with young students about their dreams and aspirations. Invariably girls from the fifth and sixth grades to sixteen year olds referred to career interests in the sciences, engineering, medicine, and computer sciences. They emphasized their choices with a confidence about possibilities that similar black- and brown-faced girls in the poor neighborhoods of New York City and other cities cannot know.[4]

Professional opportunities were opened for women from the beginning of the Revolution. By the mid-1980s, women made up 46 percent of the total population. In 1985 women composed 60 percent to 79 percent of incoming students in the schools of medicine and law. Medical schools, therefore, introduced special quotas to maintain a balance of men and women, with women still being enrolled in somewhat greater numbers after this preferential treatment for men.[5]

Rosario Fernández, a fifty-year-old black trade unionist and a founding member of the Federation of Cuban Women, describes the changes that have occurred in her family and Cuba since the days her mother worked as a domestic before the Revolution.

I began working when I was eleven years old. I cleaned a house that had five bedrooms, a living room, parlor, dining room, and kitchen—and all that for seven pesos a month. I wanted to study badly. I wanted to be a doctor. But I had to give up that dream; and it was only after the Revolution that I was able to go back to school, to repeat the sixth grade, and to keep going until I became a lawyer. But look how different it is now for poor people, for Black people, and for women. We have three children: one daughter is a bridge and tunnel engineer; the second daughter is a doctor; and our son graduated in law. My husband, who also was from a very poor family, was able to become a lawyer after the Revolution.[6]

By 1983, Cuba ranked twentieth of 142 countries in the world (ahead of major Latin American countries such as Argentina, Brazil, Mexico, Colombia, and Venezuela) in percentage of women enlisted in university programs. Higher education is not only tuition-free, but all students receive support in the form of lodging, board, and stipends.[7]

The change in attitudes toward women's participation in the workforce is reflected in the comment by Isabel Larguia and John Domoulin, who have studied the changes in the status of Cuban women for more than twenty years. "Whereas in 1960 a man would have felt dishonored if his wife went to work, today he is ashamed if she doesn't and tends to rationalize with explanations like these: 'She isn't well,' 'She's having trouble with her nerves,' 'She has problems,' 'She's looking for something that would suit her.'"[8]

Formal education and workforce participation for women have been, by far, the dominant goals of the Communist Party and the FMC. Clearly, they are necessary to any meaningful social equality. Consistently, in the many interviews I've conducted over the years, Cuban educators and women's leaders, including those in sex education, have cited Engels and Lenin as the basis for their thinking on the family and women's liberation. It was not at all unusual for research papers at the Pedagogy Congress of 1986 to begin by quoting Engels. In his major work on the relations of reproduction and production, *The Origin of the Family, Private Property and the State,* Engels saw a pivotal connection between the subordination of women and the emergence of privately owned means of production, whereby "domestic labor" excluded women from social productive labor, resulting in dependency upon the husband. Thus, he reasoned, women would be emancipated when they were free to participate in socially productive work outside the home.

Never Out Front: The Legacy of Patriarchy

One can easily agree with Engels who wrote well over one hundred years ago that "the emancipation of women becomes possible only when women are enabled to take part in production on a large social scale, and when domestic duties require their attention only to a minor degree."[9]

However, the causes of patriarchy and the means of women's subjugation have always been more complex than just the social division of labor and property relations. Once women have gained access to education and work outside the home, this approach becomes less able to give direction. This is not to minimize the revolution in women's social roles manifest in access to education and workforce participation; it is, in fact, through those very changes that new questions important to women's equality have been born. Often, however, leaders and educators have not wanted to give them life. They continue to subordinate women's equality to economic development as if the latter had to be fully achieved before it would become possible to give further attention to the former. The implication is that women's equality will hinder economic development.

This was brought home to me in interviews about day care. As in most cultures, young children in Cuba spend most of their time in the care of women and are denied role models of nurturing and caring men. Cuba continues the traditional view that women are the proper caretakers for young children. When I asked a leading day care center administrator whether men would be hired to work in the centers with children, she replied emphatically, "We don't need to place men in the *círculos!*"(day-care centers).

Her reasons? Children in day care receive enough attention from men in their home, and especially those who come to the center to perform such chores as gardening, plumbing, and maintenance. And perhaps more important, "there are many fronts of work in this country, and men are very much needed. There are many jobs that women can do, but many others that they can't. The man working with children would have to be a young man. But young men are working on other important things." She assumes that "men are not going to work with children when women can do it. And in any case, since children need affection and special care, it's hard to find this in a young man."[10]

The question of why there was no male staff in day care centers elicited comments by Vilma Espín on the difficulties and resistance to change that, in turn, affected FMC strategies. Lost in these answers was any sense that perhaps men working in day care centers would itself be a revolutionary change towards social equality that need not wait for some distant future.

The struggle for women's participation in the workforce often met strong resistance, however. Some administrators would not hire women because it would increase the rate of absenteeism. After all, women still had to do all the work in the home, and it was the mother who would miss work to care for sick children. The FMC did not, in the 1960s and early 1970s, challenge that double standard.

The "Double" (or "Second") Shift

Thus, while government policy was to bring women into the paid work-force, this work was to be in addition to the traditional work of women in the home—housecleaning, washing, child care, cooking and shopping, which often means a great deal of time standing in lines. That this "double shift" of work for women was natural found expression throughout the official discourse. It was offered, for example, in 1970 by the Minister of Labor, Jorge Risquet, as an explanation for why women should be exempt from a proposed anti-loafing law. "Women have the job of reproducing as well as producing. They have to take care of the house, raise the children, and do other tasks along these lines, and that is not easy. From the political point of view, our people (men) would not understand it if we were to treat women and men alike."[11]

It is exhaustion from this "double shift" that has caused such a high turnover of women workers in the workforce. Of the 700,000 women who entered the workforce between 1969 and 1974, 500,000 dropped out during the same period, leaving a net gain of 200,000.[12]

The FMC and its leaders have always made a distinction between their philosophy and feminism. They distinguish their approach from feminist organizations in other countries by arguing that first must come economic and social change, and then women's rights as part of this total transformation.[13] They reject any "separatist" approach from the national program for change. In a 1971 interview with me, Vilma Espín made a significant statement about government policy on women's rights: that "from the beginning it has been our contention that the woman must struggle alongside the man to build the Revolution as an obligation to her country, her society, *never out front.*"[Italics mine][14]

Thus, the only Cuban women's organization, the FMC, has worked within the limited structure of the Party and its official agencies. But for women in Cuba, that current political structure does not permit a grass-roots movement independent of the government and able to initiate social change. This runs counter to the dominant, controlling role of the Cuban Communist Party and the philosophy of "everything within the Revolution."

The FMC, like the unions and other mass organizations, functions as an institution for carrying out or "transmitting" formulated policies.[15] Within that frame they urge the Party and the maximum leader to pay more attention to women's issues. For example, at the FMC's March 1990 Congress, Castro responded to delegates' statements about a crisis in day care—the need for more day care centers (with a waiting list of 19,000 in Havana)—by saying, "We just built 111 new centers in the last two years. Why didn't you tell us you needed more? We would have built 300 if you had told us what you needed."[16]

In spite of being the "official" women's organization, the FMC has played a significant role in a broader movement toward women's equality. Especially in the last decade, women have called for changes and disputed existing policies. Within the Party and government structure, it was the FMC that campaigned for a national public day care system against male resistance. It was also within the FMC that the movement for sex education emerged. These two are part of what Juliet Mitchell, the British writer and academic, calls the four elements that constitute the key to analysis of the structure of women's position in any society (production, reproduction, sexuality, and the socialization of children).[17]

The Family Code of 1975

The second Congress of the FMC marked a turning point. After fifteen years of focusing primarily on incorporating women into the workforce, the central theme of the FMC's major conference became the struggle for women's equality. The immediate form the struggle took was discussion of the Communist Party's proposed Family Code, which had already been discussed extensively in schools, work centers, and meetings of the mass organizations including the FMC.[18] The FMC wanted revisions that spelled out the equal responsibilities for the family on the part of both parents. In its final form, the Family Code states that a married couple who both work outside the home must equally share in caring for their children. Even if one spouse is not working outside the home, the other spouse is obliged to help with household chores and child care. "Both partners must care for the family they have created and must cooperate with the other in the education, upbringing, and guidance of the children according to the principles of socialist morality. *They must participate, to the extent of their capacity or possibilities, in the running of the home, and cooperate so that it will develop in the best possible way.* [Italics mine]"[19]

The code is not really enforceable as law. It takes on meaning in its encouragement of a norm. As law professor Debra Evenson explains, it "has become a tool for education and change. The adoption of the Family Code and the continuing discussion it fostered has altered the way Cubans view domestic relations. Although men did not help with the laundry and cooking immediately, and many still resist, particularly among older generations, the message was clear that the correct, revolutionary thing to do is to share in housework."[20]

The FMC and the Sex Education Program

The Second National Congress of Cuban Women defined sex education as a part of the integral education of the individual, as the capacity of new generations for partnership, love, marriage, and family life in conditions of equality and equal

responsibility of man and woman concerning these aspects and requested that this work be done by the whole society, because it is a responsibility of all.
—Memories: Second Congress of the Cuban Women's Federation

The FMC Congress of 1974 was also the occasion of a demand for a national sex education project that had official backing. During the 1960s, the FMC had already been active in the field of sex education, though it was not designated as such. In the course of the literacy campaign, FMC members provided counseling to many young teachers and students; information on sexuality was a natural component. This education was limited to questions of hygiene, care of pregnant women and infants, and information on human reproduction. By the 1970s, the FMC was able to initiate an avant-garde project for disseminating information on family planning and other similarly sensitive issues through articles in the magazine *Mujeres* (Women), which members read and discussed. Growing demands for facts and advice in the course of this highly experimental stage made it clear that a far-reaching sex education program was crucial. Thus, the national program was conceived. The FMC viewed sex education not as the dissemination of technical information, but rather as part of the development of revolutionary consciousness, interwoven with the struggle for women's equal rights.

Mutual respect in the family, care for the aged and dedication to the education of children, are principles demanded by socialist morality. Family, as society, once liberated from capitalism, flourishes with socialism.

There are still vestiges of the past. Old habits weigh much in the minds of men, above all in those who were raised in the bosoms of the old bourgeois society, and it is difficult for them to abandon their moral concepts, which are no longer in effect.

There are still some people who remain behind and who in most cases call themselves revolutionaries who nevertheless let the overweight of work, implied by domestic chores, fall on the shoulders of their own wives or mothers.

The influence of the previous society also persists in those who do not desire that the women in their families develop and contribute with their work to the advance of the revolutionary process and its economy.[21]

This analysis of social problems generated by the inequality of the sexes was a call to action, one as far reaching as the challenge to spread literacy, and even more profoundly explosive. If undertaken, it required a revolution in the consciousness of the people. By placing the demand for sex education firmly in the context of women's issues—and in the capacity of the new generation for love, marriage, and family life—the FMC pinpointed the most pervasive gap in revolutionary consciousness.

With the respect and attention to women's issues that has characterized postrevolutionary Cuba, the demands and guidelines of the Second Women's Congress were confirmed the following year by the highest political organization of the country, the First Congress of the Communist Party.

The National Working Group for Sex Education

The First Congress of the Communist Party, held in 1975, examined the resolutions and theses of the FMC Congress and converted them into political directives. The final resolution of the First Congress on the "full exercise of equal rights for women" included endorsement of a national program of sex education.[22]

This was the significant first step toward social transformation in an area that for so long had been surrounded by taboo. It had to be both an attack on ignorance and on the attitudes of machismo rampant in the society. This ground-breaking and mountain-moving endeavor was deemed all the more crucial because it was to take place in the context of striving for a socialist society. Its originators viewed it as an essential step in the development of the new socialist person.

> A new morality exists, and because of it, new relations of equality between men and women have arisen. The new generation must leave behind the remainders of discrimination. The joint action of the whole society is to praise women and teach our children and youngsters the traditional chivalry of our people in its new proletarian dimensions.
>
> Adequate sex education will have a positive impact on the social relations between men and women, starting in the home, and scientifically reinforced in school, as presented in the study-plans for sex education. The Youth Organizations must steer people toward normal, sound and fraternal relations among boys and girls, stimulate the harmonious development of young people and contribute to the establishment of relations of mutual cooperation in carrying out social duties, in the home and in the education of children.[23]

This view of sex education was broad, encompassing far more than biology. It was expected that factual as well as ethical information regarding human sexuality would do much to accomplish the basic restructuring of society necessary for a social order based upon attention to and respect for human needs rather than upon economic supremacy. Thus, sex education was not only a matter of public health and social and psychological education but also as political-ideological work.[24] It was recognized, however, that in the realm of individual and family relationships, changes regarding customs, moral concepts, habits, and interpersonal behavior cannot be legislated.

Now that sex education had been established as a necessity along with equal rights for women, a national strategy was needed. Research had already begun toward that end. In 1977 a study team began to work full time on sex education programs for teachers and began to prepare illustrated texts for the entire population. The FMC sent a small commission to eastern and western Europe to see how other countries taught sex education. (The American experience was also taken into account.) The commission concluded that the German Democratic Republic was "the most advanced in the field," since it was the first developed country that was socialist and had, unlike many other countries, a high level of culture on which to draw. The commission returned with the most recent books published in the field.[25]

Thus far, the sex education team had operated under the auspices of the Health Development Institute. It was still an open question, however, which agency would ultimately become the umbrella *organismo* for sex education. In Cuba, the *organismo* is the basic structural unit of organization; that is, the agency of government or mass organization that one works for or is responsible to—for example, education, heavy industry, housing, and so forth. In the debate over which government agency would be the best place for a program on sex education, leaders of the Federation of Cuban Women and other government participants decided early on that sex education could not be the work of one *organismo* alone because its task was much wider than a single agency. The program included not only issues of public health, but culture, education, and the mass media. Nevertheless, for practical and budgetary reasons, the program had to be based within a single agency.

In 1975 the National Assembly of People's Power provided an organizational base for sex education by creating a permanent commission on infants, youth, and equal rights for women, with Vilma Espín appointed president. Subsequently, in 1977, that commission created the Grupo Nacional de Trabajo de Educación Sexual (National Working Group on Sex Education) or GNTES, with Dr. Celestino Alvarez Lajonchere as director. His associate director was Dr. Monika Krause, who has a doctorate in sex education from her native East Germany, and has been a citizen of Cuba for the past twenty-five years. Dr. Krause later succeeded Dr. Lajonchere as director.

Dr. Lajonchere had been a gynecologist for many years before the Revolution, an exceptional physician who recognized that medical care and public health had been particularly bad for most women before the Revolution. Many were treated only by *curistas* (healers or witch doctors).[26] In the countryside, where medical care in general had been largely absent, women gave birth to their babies at home, often only in a hut, and were assisted by "*recogedoras*" (gatherers) so called because they "gathered up" the newborn infant. Prenatal and natal medical care existed only for the well-to-do and, even for them, there was little hope of obtaining any kind of information on sexuality. "To get any idea of the ignorance prevalent before 1959, it is sufficient to say that no physician ever learned anything about human sexuality in school, and if some were aware of the few contraceptive methods available at the time, they gave that information for cash. . . . People had to pay for it."[27]

Even in those days, Dr. Lajonchere showed an extraordinary sensitivity to educating the community and parents to new developments in gynecology and obstetrics. For example, in 1953, after a trip to Paris, he wrote an article in *Bohemia,* one of Cuba's leading weekly magazines, describing the advantages of the Lamaze Method of "painless childbirth." This lengthy article and its dozen photographs informed both the medical community and the public at large of this new method of childbirth. It also reinforced Lajonchere's favorable attitude toward the importance of mass communications in effecting changes in attitudes.[28]

By 1959 Lajonchere was in private practice, the co-owner of the last private medical clinic built in Cuba. With the exodus of most of the medical faculty, who had resigned en masse in 1959, and without the controls of the medical establishment under Batista, Lajonchere had the opportunity to move to a position of leadership. One of the few members of the Society of Obstetrics/Gynecology to remain in Cuba after the Revolution—96 percent left—he had a strong influence on developing sex education policies.

He became a professor of medicine in obstetrics and gynecology and was also asked to organize a national network of health care for women. He notes that in 1959–1960 "there was no maternity-infant department; there was no women's health care department; there were no statistics. There was nothing."

Another gynecologist active in women's health care, Dr. Ada Carmen Ovies García (currently director of the Piti Fijardi Hospital in Guines), recounts how things began to change in public health from the beginning of the revolutionary era:

> From the first, the Revolution took care of people's health. I needed bedsheets for Guines, and they sent them. I needed medicine, and they sent it. Some became afraid and said, "This is communism!" I said, 'They send what I ask for, they give me what I need for the patients.' Fidel has many beautiful ideas, but for me the most beautiful was his idea to train doctors in every province.
>
> I agree with this principle, because a doctor must be able to work under any circumstance. Our hospital has trained fifteen gynecologist-obstetricians. This is one of the greatest joys Fidel has given me in my professional life.[29]

During the fifteen years following the Revolution, doctors such as Ovies García and Lajonchere were instrumental in the dramatic changes in women's health care. These changes included a national study of maternal mortality, as well as the development of professional work standards. Because of the shortage of personnel to undertake research, the Cubans turned to more developed nations for assistance. For example, Nevil Butler, a researcher from Bristol, England, helped with technical research skills and advice. In 1973 they had collected information on health care, but because they did not have the personnel, it took six years to complete the study. Lajonchere recalls, "Butler would say to us: 'You have a gold mine but you don't have any miners.' I was then a bit of a miner."[30]

From the beginning Dr. Monika Krause articulated with clarity the goals and nature of the struggle around sex education. There was, she said, "no other sphere of human life where prejudice, taboo, ignorance, the bourgeois double standard and other leftovers of the class society have shown such strength and such deep roots." Later she formulated the following definition of this radical education project:

> By sex education in our society, we mean preparing the younger generation for love, marriage and family. Sex education should form part of the complete education of each individual person in our socialist society which includes acquiring the knowledge and ability which family life requires of each human being: managing domestic affairs; education and care of children; social, legal, biological, psychological and other knowledge related to the married couple and family according to our principles of moral socialism based on the disappearance of exploitation of one human being by another, on full respect among people, on the principle of equality of rights and duties between men and women.
>
> Therefore, sex education is more than merely imparting knowledge about human reproduction, about anatomy and the physiology of men's and women's genitals. To impart this information is only one aspect—and not the most important—of sex education. Nor should we understand by sex education the simple transmission of a little advice to our young people when they are on the eve of getting married.[31]

The National Working Group on Sex Education is directly responsible to the National Assembly, which provides organizational and political direction. It is financed, however, by the Federation of Cuban Women. Because it is under the aegis of the National Assembly, it is able to maintain direct links and ongoing liaisons with the ministries and organizations through which its projects operate. For example, it is involved with school programs through the Ministry of Education; it arranges with the Minister of Culture for publication of thousands of books for the general public. It is responsible for preparing and publishing materials and for developing and implementing national policies regarding sex education. In addition to the Ministry of Public Health, which coordinates its scientific work, and the FMC, the Working Group includes representatives of the Ministry of Education and of youth and children's organizations, and maintains working relations with the Ministry of Culture. Lajonchere views this structure as very important: "I don't think that in any country in the world, including the socialist world, does this kind of structure exist, except here."[32]

Guidelines and Major Issues

When we speak of Family Education, we refer to the parents' ability to contribute to the total formation of the new generation, with a view to prepare them to form a stable, lasting and happy couple, based on love, equality, mutual respect and solidarity.

—Faculty Course on Sex Education, Havana

The goal of GNTES was to consolidate the ethical values of society and to provide information and education to its people. Emphasis was placed upon mutual respect, human solidarity, and women's equality. A key guideline for the task force, adopted early on, was the decision not to resort to the spectacular or the dramatic—that is, to sensationalism. Whether the information was televised, broadcast on the radio, or put in print, "the public must see it as something that has a deep foundation, that is serious and in the line of work of a revolutionary government."[33]

The guidelines for a sex education program recognized that parents generally were neither equipped nor willing to answer their children's questions regarding birth and sex. As Lajonchere stated, "There is great ignorance. The parents are ignorant; the teachers are ignorant. So therefore the children have nobody to answer their questions."[34] The program developers expanded on this point. "Their questions must be answered in true and simple form, care being taken to speak only of what they can understand and may interest them. The child should never be reprimanded in his questioning, nor misinformed or confused by false concepts or vulgar answers."[35]

Their statement acknowledged the early beginning of sexual maturity (thirteen to eighteen years) and encouraged adults not to worry about that. It also urged them not to turn sexuality into something mysterious and perverse, but to help young people understand that sexual development is a normal bodily function. Acknowledging that "the young couple in socialism constitutes the seed of the family, society's fundamental cell," the program developers articulated the objectives of GNTES.

First: To broaden the work aimed to educate youth in our society's values, thus contributing to forming the family according to principles of socialist morality. *Second:* To provide youth with all possible information about their responsibilities in the heart of the family and society, fighting male chauvinist concepts that still exist, and exalting women's role in the Revolution. *Third:* To orient the young couple through all the means available so that they may educate their children according to new concepts, teaching them from childhood to share rights and duties at home, in the family and in the society thus making it possible for them to be real comrades of the socialist woman. *Fourth:* For these purposes, to use communication media and promote debates, lectures or other activities which may contribute to youth's education. *Fifth:* To propose to the Ministry of Education to include in curricula at all levels those subjects that deal with the family's role, sexual education, the formation of new generations and a labor educational program including domestic chores, with the purpose of strengthening youth's concepts and convictions. *Sixth:* To fight the easy attitude of those who maintain the unfair position of refusing to share with their wives the overload of domestic work at the end of the working day, with the pretext that these tasks "do not belong to men."[36]

The message to teachers was clear: The Communist Party and the FMC gave important, official support to a program of sex education that encompassed community involvement, curriculum in schools, mass media attention, support by the mass organizations, and a call for parent/school cooperation. Sex education was to include a stand on new roles in the home, accenting family sharing of household chores and responsibilities. All political and mass organizations as well as state institutions linked to these tasks were expected to participate. Responsibility for sex education was not to be left to the schools alone.

The Role of the Family

The role of the family in socialism was among the most hotly debated issues at the 1974 FMC Congress, exposing the fact that many parents and educators were not able to deal with even the most basic educational and sociological questions necessary to educate children and adolescents.

The task force resolved to produce materials, both scientific and pedagogical, that parents could easily comprehend to enable them to give "clear and satisfactory answers to their children, as required by the different ages and stages of their development." The information would be disseminated through lectures, pamphlets, and periodicals. These would be distributed among mass organizations, particularly the Combatant Mothers for Education. The educational programs would be directed at national, provincial, and regional levels.

The task force viewed education of parents as crucial to fostering principles of equality in rights and duties within the family.

The Struggle for Women's Equality

Sex education in Cuba has to cope with the historical legacy of colonialism and religion. The combination of Catholicism and a strong macho tradition toward the role of women is present in all sectors of Cuban society. "Our reality is the fact that machismo predominates. People who are very progressive in most areas of life ... when they touch upon aspects of the relationship of man and woman, and when they touch upon relationships of sexuality the legacy of machismo predominates."[37]

The proponents of sex education and women's rights understood these within the context of socialism, which they saw as providing the foundation for eliminating the double standard, not only in sexual mores, but in all spheres of social existence. It is incorrect to judge women differently from men. What is socially acceptable for men must be socially acceptable for women.

> We have left behind the time of economic dependence, mercantile relations, marriage based on material requirements maintained by prejudices and formality, without love or respect. Men and women must be equally free and responsible to form sexual relationships. This freedom does not imply libertinism, which upsets the balance and content of the bonds between men and women.
>
> The relationship of the couple in a socialist society rests on a different premise. It is based on equality, sincerity, and mutual respect. The couple must be aware of the responsibility involved with sex, since sex is the origin of the life of the new generation.[38]

The official position, then, emphasizes that radical social change toward women's rights grows out of the Revolution itself as class relations change. Thus, Cubans are reluctant to use terms such as *feminist* or *feminism;* they consider these as appropriate perhaps for those peoples struggling in capitalist societies where there has been no revolutionary transformation of society. They do, however, accept the term "liberation of women," which is more in keeping with their ideas of social liberation.

Sex education is viewed by professionals in that field as part of the struggle for women's equality. They face many challenges: the high rate of teenage pregnancies, inadequate participation of teachers in the sex education program, the high divorce rate, insufficient communication between parents and children, and society's traditional overvaluation of males in respect to females. As Lajonchere explained: "We must educate the parents before the child is born. In Cuba—and we aren't exclusive in this, not to any extent—the fathers prefer having males, even when daughters are born. Girls consequently feel rejected from birth. This must not occur—that a girl by virtue of her sex is rejected by her own father. Thus, we must educate, from the sexual point of view, before the child is born. Also, the child must be educated from the first moment."[39]

Stela Cerutti, a Uruguayan feminist, joined Lajonchere and Krause at GNTES, both in shaping sex education policy and practice and in providing a feminist orientation in the inner councils of the sex education movement in Cuba. Dr. Cerutti, a gyneco-obstetrician, comes from a family of educators. She worked as a teacher in Uruguay while studying to be a doctor. During ten years of military dictatorship, through 1986, she lived with her three children in Cuba, where she worked as a leading consultant for GNTES helping to implement goals and develop the biological teaching staff.

When Cerutti joined the sex education group in Cuba in 1978, they began studying women's issues through the Marxist classics, including Lenin and especially August Bebel, author of *Woman and Socialism* (an 1879 work which states that even before slavery woman was the first slave). Thus, the sex education philosophy emphasizes its ties with turn-of-the-century Marxism. In consistently citing Lenin, Bebel, Engels, and Marx, sex educational literature takes the position that, in spite of eliminating economic exploitation and establishing a new socialist society, customs and habits associated with prior relations of production are difficult to change. As a fundamental theme for establishing moral values to govern intimate relations in a socialist society, they cite Lenin's argument against the "socialist theory" of his day that satisfying the sexual urge should have the same moral standing as taking a glass of water when thirsty.[40]

Many describe their position (as it currently exists) as "revolutionary" and "communist." They sincerely think that it is so. . . . The so-called "new sexual life" of the youth and often of adults seems to me to frequently be a purely bourgeois life. . . . None of this has anything in common with free love as communists understand it. You know the famous theory that, in a communist society, to satisfy sexual desire and anxieties about love is as simple a thing and of as little importance as drinking a glass of water.

On account of this theory of the "glass of water" our youth—and we might add, our adults as well—have lost their heads; they have simply lost their heads. . . . Their partisans affirm it is a Marxist theory. . . . I think that the famous theory of the "glass of water" has nothing to do with Marxism and what's more, is antisocial.

. . . Naturally, thirst has to be satisfied. Moreover, in the case of a normal person, under normal circumstances—would he drink out of a muddy puddle in the middle of the street? Or from a glass whose rim had been pressed against dozens of lips? But most important of all is the social aspect. To drink water is really an individual thing but with love, two participate and a third comes forth, a new life. Here, now, appears a social interest, the responsibility of society arises.[41]

Cerutti, a member of the Uruguayan Communist Party, sees herself as a feminist-socialist and a "militant." She believes that real equality for women will occur only under socialism and that, in Cuba, much work is required to overcome a whole series of situations arising from the ideology of the previous regime. This analysis contradicts earlier statements that machismo arises from precapitalist conditions.

Cerutti frankly recognized in a 1986 interview that the sex education staff itself was not

> free of prejudices nor free of taboos. This work on human sexuality is long-time work. In these eight years that I have been on the project, I have substantially changed my way of focusing on a whole series of problems. The greatest work is not only that of information, but in the changing of attitudes.
>
> I now believe that the best position, the most positive one, is to truly accept another person. To accept sexuality as something important in the life of an individual—developed along with the other aspects of his/her personality—not to try to apply directives to people, but instead to help them to accept themselves. . . . (and to see that their happiness should not cause) the suffering of another person. It is not easy and surely I must have a few taboos myself.[42]

Premarital Sex and Teenage Pregnancy

The main focus of sex education in Cuba is the nature of a couple's relationship—values, ethics, love, intimacy, and responsibility. It is not a question of encouraging or prohibiting premarital sex. A flavor of this orientation is captured very well in a response to a letter from a sixteen-year-old girl appearing in a Cuban newspaper in 1986. It was part of a long—and continuing—series of open discussions on issues of human sexuality. The letter was simple and to the point:

> I am 16 years old, I'm in love. We've known each other for a week. I was happy, but last night we wanted to make love, and suddenly, I couldn't, I felt nothing for him. Is it normal? What is happening to me? Write to me,
>
> Yamila.

The long response spoke to all young women facing the same concerns. The following are excerpts:

You say that you are sixteen and that you've known your boyfriend for a week. Do you believe, Yamila, that you've really had enough time to know the young man with whom you've formed this relationship, to make love with him?

First of all, you must be aware of the difference between love and sexual impulse. Love is not only a profound sentiment, it's also a talent. It is a manifestation not only of nature but also of culture (Lenin). We acquire culture with education and training. Nevertheless, the sexual impulse is inherent to every human being and manifests itself with great vigor in adolescence—the very stage of development you're going through, Yamila. Your evident attraction to your boyfriend is one of the various characteristic manifestations of human sexuality.

There is no training on how to satisfy this impulse that young people (and adults) experience, but some necessary conditions must be there. There are people who can have sexual relations without knowing their partner, without privacy or intimacy, with no other premise than mere biology.

These people have sex simply to reach a goal, have a long list of "conquests," measure their "virility," or to get rid of "tensions" and give rein to the impulse.

Such a relationship—although those involved say that "they're making love"—has nothing to do with love as we understand it. We think that a love relation must be based on attraction, affection, respect, solidarity, support. It must inspire the desire to be happy and make the other one happy, to give love and not only receive it. It's a relationship that does not tolerate selfishness, and in which it is illicit to use the other as an object, to consider him/her one's property. In love, it is immoral merely to satisfy one's desires without taking the other one's into account; love is also a relationship based on the equality of women's rights and duties.

I think, Yamila, that all I have already told you will show you that your feelings for your boyfriend are merely physical attraction, and that you two are not yet ready to start an intimate relationship based on love. You see now that you must feel all the things I mentioned earlier to be sure it's love. You don't know one another well. You did not go through the process, a process that, I repeat, takes a long time (one week is not enough); that allows us to notice in time whether our partner really has all the necessary qualities, whether the positive factors dominate, whether we have more in common than what we're discussing (sexual attraction). It happens that with time we come to realize that the "infatuation" was nothing more than a brief and superficial personal experience. He/she, who at first seemed to us perfect, is really not so great.

Regrettably, we see young people who start "making love" (most of the time, it's simply sex, without love), and later realize that the relationship cannot be profound and long lasting; and that can be damaging. At least one of the two suffers, often because she/he feels disappointed, frustrated, and disillusioned: he/she feels used like an object by the other one's impulse and egotism.

In your case, Yamila, it seems fortunate that you did not get involved in this relationship, which would not be happy, lacking all the necessary conditions, and anyway, apart from all this, you showed that you were able to take care of yourself. It's probable that your boyfriend exerted some pressure on you and that, as you were wishing to make love with him, you remembered what your mother told you about the risks to which young people who have sex at an inappropriate time expose themselves. Possibly you recalled that you could become pregnant; since it was the first time, maybe you felt inhibited and insecure (quite a normal reaction), since only a few girls can have satisfying sexual relations without strong feelings for their partner. Or you may have been disconcerted by the lack of privacy, afraid that others might listen to you, hear you, and you feared other possible consequences that might follow an act characterized by haste and superficiality.

Rest assured, dear Yamila, that the disappointment you suffered will turn out to be a useful experience, and that reflection and the right information (I recommend that you read *Are You Thinking of Love?*) will help you establish a true relationship based on love and will bring you happiness.[43]

Written with a tone of frankness, respect, delicacy, and gentleness, this response exemplifies the philosophy of sex education innovators in Cuba. It crashes through centuries of cultural and religious influences as well as economic abuse that deepened the inequities between men and women already seeded by machismo. Machismo is a particular form of patriarchy that has as much to do with public relations between men as between men and women. The code of machismo requires individual men to make a display of physical power and social domination, and to disdain any feminine, or supposedly feminine, traits. It inevitably contains a deep-rooted homophobia. The theorists of sex education in Cuba have endeavored to treat sexuality with a wholistic approach that removes it from sheer biology and physiology. They elevate it to the level of humanism where it belongs. In a 1986 interview, Dr. Cerutti elaborated on the GNTES thinking about premarital sex.

We know that here in Cuba, as other countries, intimate sexual relations among youths are taking place at ever more precocious ages. We do not have a criterion that there must exist an age for sexual relations. What we consider to be fundamental is the formation of youth. . . . We try to teach them the ethical criteria that correspond to this so that they can know and define for themselves the moment of when to have sexual relations and when not to. No, we are not repressive in the sense of saying, "That must not be done!" Because we know that the impulse of youth in adolescence is a very strong impulse, that there really is love, but it is also important that they have criteria first about responsibility.[44]

This orientation cannot be separated from the growing problem of teenage pregnancy, which has received a great deal of attention in the Cuban media of recent years. By the mid-1980s, it had become evident that more teenagers were having babies each year and that the age of first pregnancy was decreasing. Demographic data give some indication of why this is taking place.

After the Revolution in 1959, the birth rate increased through 1964, then began to diminish slowly. Although there was an increase for 1971, 1972 saw the beginning of a sharp decline in the birth rate. However, as a result of the high birth rate in the 1960s, there were, according to the 1981 census, more than 500,000 women between 15 and 19 years of age, and almost half a million women between 20 and 24. In short, the population of young women has increased rapidly, and at the same time teenage pregnancy rates have also increased.[45]

In 1985 Dr. Lajonchere stated, "In recent years, the birth rate for women younger than 20 has not gone down as we had hoped. There are still too many births per 1,000 women younger than 20, despite the kind of education and assistance we provide. This means that our plan is not good enough for that age group. The ideal age to give birth is between 20 and 29; in other words, the third decade of a woman's life."[46]

Monika Krause added that in addition to the baby boom of the 1960s, "A large sector of the population believes, erroneously, that the optimum age for a woman to have children is 15 to 19; these actually are the ages of most risk for mother and child."[47]

The sex educators have a strong faith that the power of education will ultimately solve the problem of teenage pregnancy. In a 1983 *Granma* article, Monika Krause stated that "teenage parenthood constitutes an obstacle to the development of our society" because teenagers were least prepared to be parents. She emphasized, however, that "teenagers can't be blamed for certain attitudes and behavior if they haven't been properly prepared, since the sexual impulse is a natural part of every human being." She called for sensitivity to pregnant teenagers and awareness of the "very delicate situation" of the teenage mother-to-be. "Any future mother deserves as much care and help as we can give her, and a teenager who is about to become a mother needs that care and help even more. Blaming and scolding her about her condition doesn't help, especially since we ourselves didn't know how to guide her properly in the first place."

"All of us," Krause concluded, "still have quite a few limitations in this endeavor since parents, teachers, and experts in the various branches of medicine, psychology and education were not properly trained to incorporate matters dealing with human sexuality into their educational and counseling work."[48] The Cubans argue that, in order to overcome those deficiencies there first must be a careful and systematic education of teachers and other professionals who work with young people so that they can prepare them for love, marriage, and family life. Knowledge is "not enough." The goal is to develop a consciousness that includes improved parent-child communication.

> We must understand that prohibitions and threats do no good and that honest discussion, free of unfounded suspicions and coercion and backed up by responsible behavior on the part of the adults, can be an effective means of helping children and teenagers to understand fully the issues involved.[49]

A 1985 pamphlet "Some Fundamental Themes On Sex Education" offered these recommendations:

1. It is not sufficient to tell adolescents not to have intimate relations. It is important to convince them that such relations are not necessary at such early ages and that they can lead to serious complications in their lives.
2. It is necessary to form young people's consciousness so they can act with responsibility in terms of love relations.
3. Adults as well as adolescents should know explicitly that even one single sexual experience can result in pregnancy.
4. Couples who don't want to have children yet or don't have it together yet to devote themselves to the important social function of being parents, should use an effective method of contraception. (Remember: Abortion is not a method of contraception; it is a risky surgical procedure. One should resort to abortion only as the ultimate means to resolve a situation that one did not know or was not able to adequately prevent with the use of contraceptive methods.)
5. Reducing the incidence of teenage pregnancy—and in that manner, the birth of unwanted children—should be of concern to everyone.
6. To contribute to our educational work so that Cuba may be a country of healthy strong and happy children.[50]

The Issue of Virginity

Male attitudes about female virginity is another example of continuing patriarchal traditions, as illustrated in a survey done in the early 1960s: "The young men were asked what they thought about their girlfriends working at a plant or office where there were men. Almost all of them said no, they did not want their girlfriends to work under such conditions. A second question was about virginity—100 percent said they wanted their wives to be virgins."[51]

More than thirty years of revolution does not mean that these attitudes have disappeared, as Lajonchere has observed.

> We do not have any illusions. Changes are not as dramatic as we would
> like. While it may not be a majority, colonial and prerevolutionary atti-
> tudes toward women and sex are prevalent in a substantial minority.
>   Also, there is always the question of the reliability of the data. I do not
> know if they are being totally honest in groups. Many times one is tempted
> to say things in groups because it works to one's advantage.
>   Nevertheless, you will find some young men who say that the woman
> who marries him *must* be a virgin. We have this recorded in film and video
> tapes—where the man strongly says no, he wants her to be a virgin or he
> will halt the marriage plans.[52]

Natividad Guerrero reported on a study conducted by the Center for
the Study of Youth. Eleventh graders were asked questions on such
themes as virginity and premarital sex.

> We asked the students if they considered immoral a girl who is no longer a
> virgin: 82.08 percent girls and 69 percent boys were in complete disagree-
> ment about that. Nevertheless, in response to an indirect question—"do
> boys prefer to marry a virgin?"—49.85 percent girls said yes while 72.42
> percent boys said yes as well.
>   These figures show a certain discrepancy between the sexes, which in-
> dicates that the concepts prevalent in the previous society are still present,
> although not as strong. This kind of prejudice, like all prejudices, cannot be
> pulled out at the root; it requires tenacious and efficient ideological work.
> Nevertheless, the fact that opinions differ is an improvement that can be
> observed in the brightest girls, those who will become influential perhaps
> because they've suffered more from the various taboos existing in the area
> of sexuality.
>   Boys have not advanced as much. As can be observed, they show pref-
> erence for a virgin as a future wife, although they don't consider immoral
> what they don't see. . . . a woman's morality must not be appraised or re-
> duced to the existence of the hymen."[53]

In a three-part article on virginity, Dr. Lajonchere stated that expectation of virginity is the most anachronistic symbol of woman's devaluation and a sign of woman's servitude. It is based on the desire of men to
secure the heritage of their offspring, who were considered their posses-
sions. To guarantee paternity, women must be prevented from having
sexual relations with other men. In addition, men wanted to be not only
the sole recipient of a woman's favors, but also the first. "In our culture,
virginity is associated with purity, innocence, and to a certain measure
with women's submission to men." Young men who demand that their

future spouse be a virgin are not accepting the principles of women's equality.

Some parents even demand a medical-legal examination of the girl to check whether she is a virgin. In most cases, this concern is not prompted by rape. "Even in the case of rape, gynecological examination of a young girl is not only humiliating, but useless; these examinations do not prove when and if the girl had sexual relations. Women have the absolute right to control their own bodies."[54]

The problem of premarital relations keeps cropping up in sex education presentations given for adolescents as well as adults. Lajonchere, for example, emphasizes that premarital sex should not be a taboo subject, but an acknowledged reality. The literature should explain why it should not occur so early, and should set out the ideal for a healthy relationship—one that describes two people getting to know each other over a period of time, caring for and being considerate of each other, then falling in love. As the relationship deepens, it eventually arrives at the moment of sexual relations—whether the couple is married or not. He stresses the reality that most people have relations before they are married. The real problem, then, is to encourage young people to postpone sexual relations and, when they don't, to use birth control to avoid early pregnancy. "Here difficulties with parents arise, since often they do not want to see that their children are having relationships, and would rather ignore what is happening. Educators must encourage parents to participate so that they can face these situations, and do so in plenty of time—before one's 'little girl,' say, is pregnant."[55]

These sentiments are reflected in magazine and newspaper articles as well as pamphlets on sex education for teenagers. The writers all insist that sex education should be part of people's general education, that it has a moral as well as medical value, and that it helps individuals become happy, which in turn profits society at large. They do not advocate teenage sex; in fact, they try to discourage it. Although they repeat that only people who are emotionally and physically mature should experiment with sex, they do acknowledge that teenage sexuality exists, and that ignoring the problem or responding with threats and punishment will not solve it.

Lajonchere and Krause consider one of the biggest problems to be ignorance of, or resistance to, use of birth control methods. One approach to this problem is education about the health risks when young girls give birth, particularly when the mother has received little or no prenatal care. Often afraid to reveal her condition, an adolescent will hide it as long as possible, presenting herself for medical care only when gestation is already very advanced. Therefore, she has not taken measures in time to assure the healthy development of the fetus.[56]

There is a marked increase in both mortality and illness for mothers under twenty and, even more so, for those under seventeen. At that age, the reproductive organs as well as the skeleton are still not developed enough for the fetus to grow sufficiently. Thus, pregnancy cannot develop without affecting the health of the fetus and may result in premature birth.

The sex education program also considers the psychological risks of early motherhood. As Krause has explained it,

> The unwanted child suffers because of the irresponsibility of its parents. In most cases, it is born when the mother is facing a critical situation, feeling frustrated, having left school or her training center, without having her own resources to take care of the child, without the knowledge or experience for the function she is inopportunely, at the same time, required to fulfill, being herself a person who needs help and guidance; a situation that is aggravated when, as happens in not a few cases, she is rejected and discriminated against by her family, friends, and teachers.
>
> Many fathers, although obligated by law to be responsible for their children—at least paying for a food allowance—evade their duty, abandoning the mother and even denying paternity.
>
> There are other young couples who, "accidentally" beginning a pregnancy, are obliged by their parents to marry in order to "save the honor" of the family. Marriages formed in this way "by the hammer blow," without a solid foundation, not based on love, respect, and mutual solidarity, are sure divorces and the worst possible solution. . . .[57]

There is still the question of which birth control method to recommend.

The Issue of Contraception

Before the Revolution, contraceptives were practically unknown in Cuba. Abortion was the only possibility for many women who did not want a child, but abortion was considered a crime. Doctors who performed abortions could be prosecuted, although those who did them for U.S. weekend tourists were left alone. Only women with financial means had access to doctors; the others had to resort to abortionists who used toxic chemicals, clothes hangers, and other dangerous methods. Many women died or were left unable to have children. After the Revolution, many gynecologists-obstetricians left for the United States. In Cuba, it was difficult to find medical equipment, medications, and contraceptives.

The Social Defense Code of those early years postulated in Article 443 that "abortions necessary to save a woman's life are legal." The penal code, drawn up in 1979, specifies that only abortions performed by specialists in hospitals are legal. A woman sixteen years or younger must obtain parental consent to be eligible for abortion, which can be performed only up to the tenth week. After ten weeks of pregnancy, the decision rests with the doctors.[58] The first hospital abortions were performed in 1965, after which the mortality rate among women began to fall. Abortion was not, however, considered as a means of birth control nor always looked upon favorably. Instead, contraceptives became more available after the mid-1960s. At the same time, the Ministry of Health (MINSAP) introduced the study of birth control into the medical curriculum as well as into the national health system. At first there was resistance and opposition from some physicians. There were also errors in judgment regarding the ease with which change could be implemented. As Lajonchere explained:

> MINSAP dealt first with the use of the diaphragm, one of the most effective birth-control methods then and now. That was a mistake on our part. Many women could not accept this method because of embarrassment and cultural biases. Proper use of a diaphragm requires a woman to be comfortable with her body and know how to insert the device. Another problem arose for women who had had multiple pregnancies; in these women, weak muscles often cause the diaphragm to shift out of place and "disappear."
>
> In July 1963, we made IUDs available in the offices of gynecologist-obstetricians (most of which were still located in hospitals). This was the first contraceptive method used massively by Cuban women. It's a contraceptive efficient enough to prevent unwanted pregnancies and has few side effects. The IUD we used was a ring of nylon, a material we first produced for fishermen, which nurses used to make by hand, giving several turns to the thread with their fingers. For many years, the (U.S.) blockade prevented us from buying manufactured products because the U.S. commercial firms had the patents. With great difficulties and at great expense, we were able to buy them not only in large quantities but also to get the ones we wanted.
>
> Roughly a decade later, inventors came up with an IUD made of metal, copper mostly, with fewer side effects, better tolerated, but more expensive.
>
> When an IUD of better quality appeared, MINSAP imported them and put them at the disposal of women. The copper device shaped like a T is well-known in Cuba.
>
> Socialist industry has developed in recent years a great variety of intrauterine devices: the DANA (Czech), the Medusa (GDR). The Medusa is small, with a more flexible plastic body than the polyethylene implement made in capitalist countries. It "winds" like a thread of silver and copper. According to reports, Medusa is the most efficient device on the market.
>
> Under consideration is the possibility of producing IUDs in Cuba, to make this method available to Cubans under any circumstances. The existence of IUDs in the socialist world is also reassuring: it means we will always have them at our disposal.[59]

The official position is that the condom is a preferred method because it not only prevents unwanted pregnancies but also provides protection against sexually transmitted diseases. Condoms are sold at drug stores in Cuba, with "strong efforts" to make them equally available to men of all ages. Condoms are also preferable, according to the sex educators, as a birth control method for young people. It is not recommended that young girls use internal contraceptives or take birth control pills for a long period of time.

In both Cuba and the United States, however, the legacy of machismo and homophobia have resulted in suppression of strong sex education programs about the use of condoms. Thus, on one of my trips to Cuba, I was surprised to hear a teacher report that on prime-time television the night before, he had seen a demonstration of "What a Condom Is." "A young woman was showing a real condom, not a drawing or some other visual aid. The girl showed how the whole thing works!"

Upon hearing of this program, Lajonchere smiled and told how several years earlier he had presented on television a drawing of an erect penis with condom; so it was progress to display an actual condom. This television program, however, was as much the exception to the rule in Cuba as a similar PBS broadcast in November 1987 had been in the United States. That program, on AIDS, included a woman teacher demonstrating the use of a condom, which created an enormous controversy.[60]

Dr. Krause still faces great resistance from the medical profession and public health officials on education about condoms, which in turn is reflected in the general resistance to using them.

At first I thought opposition to condom use in Cuba might be a reflection of education or occupational status. One physician said to me: "If you observe behavior in a pharmacy—people are uncomfortable, including men, going into a pharmacy to ask for condoms." Interviews with sex educators, teachers, and doctors (both male and female) indicate that most men do not want to use condoms and most women do not want to force the issue.

However, this oppositon is not only from the lay public. Many physicians oppose condom use. In 1989 at a workshop meeting of MINSAP officials, many doctors argued against Dr. Krause's position on the need for education about condoms. In the view of the male doctors, men and women correctly oppose condom use because the device interferes with sexual pleasure, i.e., it interrupts the sex act, reduces tactile sensitivity during intercourse, and leads to impotency in men. When Krause argued that newer condoms are thinner and do not restrict pleasure, they dismissed such claims.

Dr. Cerutti explained in 1986 that the sex education team really believed the ideal method to be the one most acceptable to each particular couple.

> I believe that all birth control methods that are not accepted by both part-
> ners in the end fail. The birth control method that the doctor or the nurse,
> or whoever, imposes, is not the most adequate because in one way or an-
> other at some moment, the couple will cease to use it.
>
> Now, within the gamut of birth control methods, it's the task of the
> doctor to orient the couple, to give them, or the woman who goes to ask
> for it, birth control information so that she has possibilities of selection and
> within that orientation the most adequate one for the specific situation.
>
> We try to educate our youth in the use of the condom. We think it is a
> very good birth control method. The condom is a birth control method that
> makes the man conscious of the birth control responsibility; it is also a pro-
> phylactic against venereal diseases and for that it is a first-line birth control
> method, especially among adolescents. And I would say among the not-
> so-adolescent as well.
>
> There are three places where young people can learn about birth control
> methods. We (that is, physicians) instruct them ourselves in the polyclinic;
> they also learn in classes given in junior high schools and in senior high
> schools.[61]

In communities, sex education was introduced into pre-wedding events. Dr. Ovies, director of Guines Hospital, established a working alliance with the Guines Palace (where couples go to get married) for a gynecologist and a psychologist to meet for a premarriage sex education meeting. In the town of Guines:

> When kids come for their turn to get married, we meet with them, talk to
> them about sex education, explain to them how to use contraceptives. I am
> assisted by a psychologist, Felix Estevez, who explains things clearly. The
> psychologist is a professional not every hospital has. But this is a job for
> them. I think that the advice given here, when the couple has decided to
> get married, comes too late. At least, we help them understand that they
> shouldn't have children right away. The girls are more receptive. Another
> sensitive subject is to teach young women how to keep track of their pe-
> riods. In the gift store, we should sell good diaries for this purpose. Some
> of the gynecologists-obstetricians complain that women don't write down
> the date of their period and, as a consequence, get the delivery date
> wrong.[62]

By the mid-1980s, Lajonchere had come to think that even abortion could play a greater role as a method of birth control. In the 1986 edition of his book *El Embarazo en la Adolescencia* he first suggested that rather "delicate" idea along with another equally radical one—that it is not always the best solution to force a pregnant teenager to marry the father of the child. Lajonchere views voluntary motherhood as inviolable; that is, a woman must have the right to regulate the number of children she wants and the time of life when she wants them.[63]

In a 1989 study of family planning, Dr. Patrica Bravo interviewed 72 women in childbearing years—15 to 45 years old, in La Lisa, a working class community in Havana. She questioned the women about their family planning methods. To increase reliability, responses were kept anonymous. She reported that the major family planning method was the IUD (50 women). Fifteen women had chosen sterilization. These were older women—30 and over—who did not want more children. Two practiced coitus interruptus, three took the pill, and one was not using protection because she wanted a second child. Only one woman reported that her husband used the condom for birth control.[64]

Dr. Bravo reports that the diaphragm is not popular in Cuba—partly because women view it as inconvenient and, since Cuba does not have a variety of diaphragm sizes, they do not want to risk pregnancy because of "a poor fit." The pill is popular with adolescents; when they go into young adulthood they usually shift to an IUD. Dr. Bravo reviewed other studies on family planning in Cuba and discovered that, in the late 1970s and early 1980s, the results of family planning interviews were similar to her study. The largest number of women used the IUD. Women in their thirties and forties had their tubes tied and preferred sterilization for prevention of pregnancies. Adolescents used the pill.

Based on interviews with patients and physicians, Dr. Bravo's data are not accidental. Even when the family doctor discusses alternatives in family planning with patients, the culture exerts pressure to perpetuate existing norms, which were previously established in large part by male physicians. As long as condoms are frowned upon, a difficult cycle remains in place. And despite the increase of women graduating from medical schools and practicing in the field, men still prevail there (including the Ministry of Health), as well as in politics and in education. Thus, Monika Krause and her allies in GNTES often walk alone on their mission, facing a sexist, macho—and uphill—battle.

Notes

1. Rosario Fernández, Trade unionist and FMC leader: in Johnetta B. Cole and Gail A. Reed, "Women in Cuba: Old Problems and New Ideas," *Urban Anthropology* 15 (3–4)(1986): 328–329.

2. Clemintina Serra, "Report on the Círculos Infantiles," typewritten (July 13, 1969), 1; also see Marvin Leiner, *Children Are the Revolution: Day Care in Cuba* (New York: Penguin Books, 1978), 49–50.

For statistics of women in the labor force in 1988 see Comité Estatal de Estadísticas, *Anuario Estadístico de Cuba,* 1988, 199.

3. Isabel Larguia and John Dumoulin, "Women's Equality and the Cuban Revolution," in June Nash and Helen Safa, eds., *Women and Change in Latin America* (South Hadley, Mass.: Bergin & Garvey Publishers, 1986), 368. This data was compiled from the 1981 census of Cuba, population over eleven years of age holding diplomas and certificates, by sex, age, and diplomas obtained.

Girls in Cuban schools, along with the rest of the population, are getting a direct message about education as the road up for Cuba. The focus on the sciences and technology is a nationalist, patriotic message that top Cuban leaders highlight constantly to teachers and students of both sexes. As Fidel Castro noted at the Pedagogy '90 Congress, national independence "isn't a matter of symbols. It is a matter of development, mastering science and technology, if we want to have a place in the modern world." Fidel Castro, "Pedagogy '90: Fidel Stresses Role of Education for Independence," *Granma Weekly Review,* February 18, 1990, 9.

4. During the years 1976–1981, the Cubans restructured their schools with the *Perfeccionamiento*—a plan for improving education. The revised national curriculum for all levels illustrates the dominant roles held by mathematics and the physical and biological sciences. All children, beginning in elementary school, are required to study biology, physics, chemistry, and mathematics. See Marvin Leiner, "Two Decades of Educational Change," *Journal of Reading,* 25, no. 3, December 1981: 202–214; for education in the cities of the United States, see Jonathan Kozol, *Savage Inequalities: Children in American Schools* (New York: Harper Collins Publishers, 1992); Marvin Leiner, ed., *Children of the Cities: Education of the Powerless* (New York: New American Library, 1974).

5. Debra Evenson, "Womens's Equality in Cuba: What Difference Does a Revolution Make?" *Law & Inequality: A Journal of Theory and Practice* 4, no. 2 (July 1986): 317.

6. Johnetta B. Cole and Gail A. Reed, "Women in Cuba: Old Problems and New Ideas," *Urban Anthropology* 15 (3–4) (1986), 328.

7. Ruth Leger Sivard, *World Military and Social Expenditures 1983: An Annual Report on World Priorities* (Washington, D.C.: World Priorities, 1983), 36.

8. Isabel Larguia and John Demoulin, "Women's Equality and the Cuban Revolution," 352.

In paired student surveys taken in 1960 and again in 1965, women felt more than men that they had opportunities to study; women were less motivated by economic improvement than the men in the sample; women also wished more than the men to become independent from their parents. A majority of women expressed concern about inadequate work opportunities when the government moved to incorporate women into the workforce. Louis Jones, Lenna Jones, and Edith Falcon, "Actitudes Vocaciónales de Estudiantes de 1960 y 1965," *Psicología y Educación* 2, no. 5 (January–March 1965): 44, 47, 50, 52.

9. Frederick Engels, *The Origin of the Family, Private Property and the State* (New York: International Publishers, 1972), 221.

10. Marvin Leiner, *Children Are the Revolution: Day Care in Cuba* (New York: Penguin Books, 1978), 50; Interview with Marta Santander, Havana, 1971.

11. *Granma,* September 9, 1970, 5 in Domínguez, *Cuba,* 268.

12. Communist Party of Cuba, "Thesis: On the Full Exercise of Women's Equality," in Elizabeth Stone, ed., *Women and the Cuban Revolution: Speeches and Documents by Fidel Castro, Vilma Espín and Others* (New York: Pathfinder Press, 1981). This thesis was approved by the First Congress of the PCC in December 1975.

13. Serra, "Círculos Infantiles," 7.

14. Interview with Vilma Espín, Havana, 1971.

15. Nichola Murray, "Socialism and Feminism: Women and the Cuban Revolution, Part 2," *Feminist Review* 2 (1979), 103.

16. Karen Wald, "Cuban Women Face the Future," *The Black Scholar,* vol. 20, no. 5 and 6: 15.

17. Juliet Mitchell, *Women's Estate* (Harmondsworth: Penguin, 1971). See Murray, "Socialism and Feminism, Part 2," 105.

18. The discussions of 1974 and 1975 also included the new constitution of February 1976 and the Family Code of 1975. About 2,196,000 people in 66,513 assemblies had discussed the draft of the Family Code by November 1974. The Family Code proposed 16 years as the minimum legal age at which boys could marry and 12 years for girls. 48,042 people proposed raising the legal age with the result that in the Code's final form the minimum marriageable age for girls was 14. See Jorge I. Domínguez, *Cuba: Order and Revolution* (Cambridge: Harvard University Press, 1978), 301.

19. "The Family Code," Article 26, in Elizabeth Stone, *Women and the Cuban Revolution* (New York: Pathfinder Press, 1981), 146.

20. Evenson, "Women's Equality in Cuba," 312.

21. *Memories: Second Congress Women's Federation* (Havana: Editorial Orbe, 1975); see *Materiales de Consultas Para Desarrollar El Curso Facultativo de Educación Sexual.*

22. Lajonchere interview, 1986.

23. "Tesis Sobre la Formación de la Niñez y la Juventud," *Materiales de Consulta para Desarrollar El Curso Facultivo de Educación Sexual* (Havana, 1981), 106. This statement was excerpted from the *Primer Congreso del Partido Comunista de Cuba* (Havana, 1976).

24. Interview with Celestino Alvarez Lajonchere, Havana, 1986.

25. Ibid.

26. Ibid.

27. Ibid.

28. C. Alvarez Lajonchere and Romilio Portuondo Cala, "La Supresión del Dolor en el Parto," *Bohemia,* September 6, 1953, 8–10, 118–119.

29. Isle Bulit, "The Doctor from Guines," *Bohemia,* May 10, 1985.

30. Lajonchere interview, 1986.

31. Monika Krause Peters, *Algunas Temas Fundamentales Sobre Educación Sexual* (Havana: Ministerio de Cultura Editorial Científica-Técnica, 1985), 10; see also Monika Krause Peters, "The Political and Ideological Character of Sex Education," *Granma,* August 22, 1982, 10.

32. Lajonchere interview, 1986.

33. Ibid.

34. Ibid.

35. *Materiales de Consulta*, 103, originally cited in Second Congress of Federation of Cuban Women; FMCII 66; Resolution, Commission no. 3, "Young Couple in Socialism" (Consulta, 102–103; FMC II, 185–186).

36. Ibid.

37. Lajonchere interview, 1986.

38. *Materiales de Consulta*, 67–79.

39. Lajonchere interview, 1986.

40. Lenin cited in Krause, *Algunas Temas Fundamentales*, 2; also see August Bebel, *La Mujer y el Socialismo* (La Habana: Editorial de Ciencias Sociales, 1979); also see José Zilberstein Toroncha and Esther Miedes Díaz, "La Educación Sexual: Parte de la Formación Político-Ideológico de las Nuevas Generaciónes," *Educación*, January/February 1990, 11–18.

41. Ibid., 3–4.

42. Interview with Stela Cerutti, Havana, 1986.

43. Monika Krause Peters, "Yamila," *Juventud Rebelde*, August 18, 1986; Heinrich Brückner, *Piensa Ya En El Amor?* (Havana: Editorial Gente Nueva, 1981) translated from the German, *Denkst Du Schon An Liebe?* (Berlin: Der Kinderbuchverlag, DDR, 1976).

44. Cerutti interview, 1986.

45. Lajonchere interview, 1986.

46. Celestino Alvarez Lajonchere, "La Educación Sexual: Algunas Antecedentes y Perspectivas en Cuba," *Bohemia*, January 4, 1985, 62–63.

47. Krause Peters, *Algunas Temas Fundamentales*.

48. Monika Krause Peters, "The Problems of Teenage Pregnancy," *Granma*, February 20, 1983.

49. Ibid.

50. Krause Peters, *Algunas Temas Fundamentales*, 29–30.

51. Prof. Ernesto Bravo, Victoria Girón Medical School, Interview, Havana, 1986.

52. Lajonchere interview, 1986.

53. Natividad Guerrero, "Virginity and Pre-Marital Sex, It Does Not Add Up," *Juventud Rebelde*, July 14, 1985.

54. Lajonchere interview, 1986.

55. Ibid.

56. Krause Peters, *Algunas Temas Fundamentales*, 7.

57. Ibid.

58. Monika Krause Peters, "Planificar La Descendencia: Un Derecho De La Mujer," *Bohemia*, November 23, 1984, 76–77.

59. Lajonchere, "La Educación Sexual," 62.

60. *AIDS: Changing the Rules: A Television Special About AIDS, How You Get It and How to Avoid It*, a transcript of a television program produced by WETA-TV (Washington, D.C.: 1987). In Cuba, when Dr. Monika Krause Peters demonstrated the effectiveness of condoms by filling one with water on television she was harassed with phone calls and letters calling her the "Queen of Condoms" (Krause Peters interview, 1986).

61. Cerutti interview.

62. Bulit, "The Doctor from Guines."

63. Celestino Alvarez Lajonchere, *El Embarazo en la Adolescensia* (La Habana: Editorial Científico-Téchnica, 1982).

64. Interview with Dr. Patricia Bravo, July, 1990.

4

The Audacious Subject:
The Sex Education Program

*Our history of educational progress is truly brilliant and a country with almost
100 percent of its children and adolescents in the school system cannot in any way
dispense with that educational instrument.*

—Celestino Lajonchere

Those who initiated sex education in Cuban society clearly saw it as a
revolutionary project within a broader educational agenda. It came to include new programs in elementary and secondary schools, changes in
science textbooks, educational material for parents and teachers as well
as children, and even a new focus for feature film makers. This herculean
task to change attitudes and behavior in the realm of relations between
men and women came up against the deeply entrenched traditions of
machismo. Changing such social attitudes is in some ways far more difficult and confusing than ousting a military dictator.

A Giant Step: Programs in the Schools
The Havana center of GNTES now has twenty staff members, including
professors, psychiatrists, psychologists, and a support staff of technicians
and secretaries. This national group structure is replicated on the provincial level.

From the beginning, those responsible for the new program had in
mind integrating sex education at appropriate places within the general
primary and secondary school curriculum. The strategy was not to prepare experts who would occasionally come to the schools, but to educate
professors and teachers to understand sexuality and become the sex educators themselves.

Teaching the Teachers
The new program was slow in developing because there were neither
materials nor trained teachers. Sex education was about moral behavior,

93

and teachers were expected to be role models; but, in fact, teachers often needed sex education as much as their students did. Also, owing to the rapid expansion of schools and educational opportunities during the 1960s, there was a shortage of teachers. To make up for this shortage, university students taught part-time, yet these young teachers were not much older than the secondary school students they were teaching.[1]

The Working Group for Sex Education received a great deal of support in many ways from East Germany. In the area of sex education, East Germans also had to deal with the problem of insufficiently prepared teachers. An East German research study showed that only 27 percent of teachers had preparation that could be considered adequate to the tasks of sex education; another 11 percent had some small degree of preparation, while 54 percent had none at all.[2] A study carried out by the Cuban Ministry of Education and the E. J. Varona Institute of Higher Education[3] in Havana from 1978 to 1981 also highlighted the inadequate preparation of Cuban teachers. Some 46.4 percent were considered inadequately prepared, and 52 percent had taught themselves.[4] Thus, improved preparation of teachers was identified as the crucial pedagogic problem for developing a sex education program. "Such importance is given to this requirement, that the principal problem at present in sex pedagogy is considered to be the education of the educators."

The strategy of the Ministry of Education was to teach the teachers first by introducing sex education in the pedagogical institutes. We planned to begin, Lajonchere explained, "at the top of the educational pyramid, educating staff. And, in a few years, the entire base of the educational pyramid—the elementary school teachers, including the day care teachers—will have good preparation to assume the task of sexual education.

We cannot responsibly assign the task to a child (the young teacher)—who has possibly not recognized nor resolved his own problems of sexuality in adolescence—the task of teaching an important area which has not been taught to him"[5] As one remedy, a *curso facultivo* was introduced at the E. J. Varona center to prepare teachers on content and methodology—"biological, psychological and social questions of sexuality and two subjects related to sex pedagogy."[6]

In the earliest sex education seminars, beginning in 1976, Cuban specialists called for further research to help understand attitudes, knowledge, and behavior regarding the sexual life of the public. Special emphasis was given to studying the attitudes of teachers in teacher training centers, since they would be doing the "educating" in the field.

A study of 239 trainees enrolled in the Enrique J. Varona Institute during 1982–1983 reveals interesting data. These 239 male and 70 female students were majoring in history and social sciences, pedagogy and psychology, mathematics, physics, chemistry, and biology. They most frequently cited adolescence as the developmental period when they first learned about sex, with boys tending to "become more knowledgeable at a younger age."[7] While 70 percent of the students stated that they had asked their parents about sex, more than half said their parents did not provide any information. Some 24 percent did not ask questions of their parents because they lacked confidence in their parents' knowledge, attitude, or ability to communicate. For example, a twenty-one-year-old woman student said, "I don't ask them; they seem to feel shame in responding." Another student said, "My parents say that the young are lost, and if I were to ask them for information, I know it would be something I'm going to reject." Parents dealt more openly and frequently with their sons about sex than with their daughters. When they did ask questions, 25 percent of the women students felt that they received unsatisfactory answers. Here is a sampling of the students' responses about their parents: "Because of their low cultural level, they saw this as something sinful." "They became nervous." "Repulsive reaction." "They say that this is something shameful that I shouldn't talk about."

The first sex education materials were introduced experimentally in 1974, but it was not until 1977 that official texts became available. One such experiment took place in Camaguey with students and alumni of the Máximo Gómez School. It was organized by Rafaela Blanca, head of the biology department, Dr. Manlio López, head of the medical school in Camaguey, and the sociologist José Ignacio López. They started with a questionnaire for eleventh and twelfth graders to assess prevailing attitudes and knowledge. It was answered by 150 students of both sexes who indicated their gender but did not identify themselves. This and another questionnaire circulated among parents showed tremendous ignorance about sex among children and parents alike.[8]

Since children asked few questions, many parents thought their children knew everything; in other cases parents could not answer their children's questions. The children were instead seeking answers from their peers or "reading inaccurate and unscientific books," thereby adding to their store of misinformation.

These findings confirmed the first-hand experience of the doctors and social workers who continually confronted problems caused by the taboos of the Spanish Catholic culture and the ignorance they created. Said José Ignacio, "Girls don't know what to do when they're pregnant, can't bring themselves to tell their parents, dare not try an abortion, are very uncertain." Manlio, head of the medical school, added: "Some of us had no idea of the level of misinformation about sex; it's really alarming. In Denmark and in the GDR, sex education is taught in primary schools."[9]

Blanca and colleagues began holding lectures once a month, followed by a question-and-answer period, and in 1977–1978, continued the program with 256 students. Although the students' parents were initially guarded, the fact that there were doctors among them who talked with their children about sex and allowed the youngsters to go to the sex education lectures eventually encouraged others to do the same. A flyer was sent to parents to explain the necessity of giving sex education to their children.[10]

The plan was developed by professionals—gynecologists, dermatologists, obstetricians and others. Reports on this pioneer plan stressed that without such collaboration the project would not have succeeded. It was necessary, however, to plan conferences around the free time of busy health workers: "They have to study, prepare for the conference, look for photos, slides, films, and so on. All this is free; they don't get a centavo for this. Some professionals were not enthusiastic about our offer and gave us evasive answers. Some refused. So we had to look for new people who could work with us, and we had to explain our objectives all over again."[11]

Of the question-and-answer period after the dialogue, Herrera said:

It's evident that girls are more forward than boys. They ask questions of everyone. The other day, during a conference, a girl came to tell me that she had wanted to ask a question at a lecture on the sexual act, but that her boyfriend who was with her didn't let her. Ah, this shows something very singular, that I have personally noticed: a certain rebirth of machismo in young couples. Boys are very aggressive this way, and this worries me. Girls who have asked certain questions to their professors on the topic have seen them turn red and start to stutter. Obviously, not everyone is ready to talk about this audacious subject.[12]

The experimental period gave Cuban educators important guidelines for teaching sex education. The most significant discovery was the necessity of learning from the children. Since everyone was learning about sex education, teachers and curriculum developers had to learn not to bring their own biases or misconceptions to the teaching or to go beyond what the children were asking at any particular moment. For the younger children—nine and ten years of age—Cuban educators hope the program will prepare them for the series of changes they are about to face in their lives: "We try to make the most of it before the changes begin—such as menstruation, first ejaculations, wet dreams; we believe they will be more secure if they understand the bodily functions they are going through at that age and the next few years."[13]

Teaching the Children

The Ministry of Education made the decision that sex education would be formally taught in grades three, four, nine, and eleven. Although it was part of the science curriculum, its focus was to be moral principles of social living as well as scientific information on reproduction. After a decade of experience, Monika Krause enunciated the set of principles that had come to guide the project's work:

1. The principle of truth. Telling lies, half-truths and giving ambiguous information will lose us the confidence of our children and students.
2. The principle of repetition and systematic continuity. We do not do sex education in one conference or chat; the information is not assimilated by hearing it only one time.
3. The principle of gearing information and the language used to the age or level of understanding of the students.
4. The principle of daily example by the educators. A parent or teacher whose attitude and actions are not consistent with their word will not train a child well. It is very important that we rid ourselves once and for all of the anachronistic idea of the bourgeois double standard. We cannot expect attitudes and conduct corresponding to socialist morality if we continue transmitting different patterns of behavior for boys and girls.[14]

As all education in Cuba is now coeducational and sex education is being introduced as part of existing curriculum, textbooks and materials on sex have had to be prepared for teaching boys and girls together. In the third grade text under the heading "Reproduction," there is a brief and simple description of the sex organs, the reproductive system, and a discussion of fertilization and birth. There is no mention of intercourse, but there is a straightforward discussion of physical changes in the reproductive organs of girls.

Children are urged to be conscious of the needs of mothers and expectant mothers, and to help them in many ways such as carrying packages or giving them a seat on the bus. This advice both instructs the child and, in turn, reminds parents about healthy practices. In some cases, the child must become the educator where parents are not informed: "When a woman is pregnant, she needs care so that the little baby being formed can grow and get the food and everything it needs. Medical attention in the polyclinic is very important for the mother; there she will receive adequate attention."[15]

The text gives advice on the importance of good hygiene and ends with the following discussion questions: "What is the importance of reproduction? What organs are in charge of the formation of the elements essential for reproduction? Where is the future baby formed and how does it receive the food it needs? How can we help pregnant women in order to help in the development of the future child? When are young people ready to form a home which will be an example for their children?"[16]

In the fourth grade, pupils study plants and animals including their reproduction. This is followed in the text with a unit on human reproduction, which gives a more detailed description of the sex organs and reproduction—from egg to embryo—and also discusses male and female development. The importance of the family is stressed. The text emphasizes that both father and mother must work outside the home to support the family and must do the domestic work as well. The child's role is to help by keeping his or her room clean, doing some of the house cleaning, setting the table, and running errands. There is advice on methods of hygiene and guidance about when one should see a doctor for treatment. More scientific terms are used, and there is a section on population growth.

There is a discussion of the bodily changes that boys and girls experience, particularly menstruation in girls, along with the social responsibilities of bearing children. It emphasizes the dangers to the fetus if child-bearing occurs too early and the concepts of social development associated with sex, marriage, and the family.[17]

By the ninth grade, a chapter entitled "Anatomy, Physiology and Hygiene of Humans," is accompanied by detailed illustrations and describes the sex organs, reproduction, pregnancy, birth, menopause, hormones, conditions necessary for fertilization, hygiene, venereal diseases and their treatment. All of this is followed with a section on the human couple, which discusses love. It distinguishes between "sloppy and unsubstantial love relationships," which do not bring "joy, happiness, and optimism," and profound, mature love that ensures a couple's "happiness and stability." All this is tied to social morality: "Our society, based on the true principles of communist morality demands from each person that sexual satisfaction does not translate into unprincipled conduct."[18] There is no mention of homosexuality in the text.

The text goes on to emphasize that human beings are not only products of nature but shapers of their environment as well. Human sexuality is determined not only by biology but also by society, which, in fact,

> ultimately plays the decisive role. Independently from reciprocal attraction which unites men and women on the biological plane, a couple's relationship primarily develops according to material conditions of existence, along the principles, norms, traditions, and other social aspects in which education, over all, plays a preponderant role.
>
> We want to emphasize that a full love life exerts a great influence on happiness, *joie de vivre*, and optimism. Nevertheless, sex must not become the center of man's life; certainly not in a socialist society where the individual has all the opportunitites to develop fully. This does not imply that sex loses its value or its inherent importance. . . .

Chaotic forms of sexual relations between people, disorderly switch of partners and the practice of what is called "free love" are phenomena that have nothing in common with the moral conception of our society and are nothing more than the signs of the decomposition level of decadent societies.[19]

Young people, with today's "immense opportunities for development" and for "different kinds of relationships," are counseled "not to make a game of sexuality, nor make the change of partner a trivial act, nor take love lightly." They are encouraged to participate in various activities together so that a deeper understanding and respect for those of the opposite sex will evolve as a sound basis for love and sex. And finally,

> The couple who truly love each other want to see their relationship consolidated in marriage, the end of which is the creation of a happy family.
> We know that through reproduction, we maintain or conserve the species; this is what gives this function its importance. The human species' biological development took a long time; the biological maturity required for production is between 18 and 20 years.
> During the first years of his/her life, man/woman needs a great deal of attention, and the couple needs more than biological maturity; for example, social maturity, or being ready to be useful, to constitute and maintain a family according to all our society's principles.[20]

In the eleventh grade, the text offers an examination of the human reproductive cycle through study of biological characteristics, the functions of the organs, and the physiology of the system. As in the earlier texts, the focus then shifts to relationships and elaborates on other aspects of sexuality, such as explaining various birth control methods and discussing the advantages and disadvantages of each. This includes abortion as a risk to health that should be avoided by use of birth control. It recommends that the couple seek further consultation with a medical specialist who can help them choose which method is best for them.

The following year, at a greater level of detail and complexity students again study the reproductive organs, including the formation of sperm and semen, the description and function of the penis and, for the first time, ejaculation and the mechanics of the sex act. In the discussion of the female organs, there is much greater detail on the changes in the cycle, including a discussion of the role of hormones.

Teaching the Doctors

Not only has sex education been mandated for elementary and secondary schools, but an important part of the whole program has been geared toward developing human sexuality programs in the medical schools. Before the activity of GNTES, medical training did not include the study of human sexuality. Contraceptives were not mentioned in the textbooks. Physicians who wanted such information had to buy special literature. Again, the approach was to work sex education into different subject areas such as urology, psychiatry, and gynecology.[21]

Strong emphasis is also put on effecting changes among medical personnel already working in the field. Postgraduate programs are being established for doctors who missed in-service training. Seminars and conferences with doctors are aimed at changing attitudes. As Dr. Cerutti points out, "We are conscious of the fact that what lies before us is to change attitudes, and that is not something that can be done with eight conferences, or ten conferences. It is a long-term project, of course. But it is necessary work."[22]

An examination of Cuban medical literature shows just how necessary. The attitudes of paternalistic sexism are deeply embedded. Just one example comes from a 1979 text on psychology for general practitioners. The subject is "sexual frigidity in women."

> Although the biologically and socially conditioned sexual passivity of the woman permits her to hide her disorder from her husband in a great many cases, it often happens that her feelings of inferiority and guilt are the primary reasons she is seeking psychiatric consultation. . . . The golden rule consists of orienting the woman toward faking her orgasm until the disorder has been overcome since otherwise many men lack the information and maturity to behave properly in this situation.[23]

I could not help but contrast the above attitude with the approach being presented by the sex education program. In 1988 I observed one group of young physicians who were in their second year as family doctors. These seventeen women and five men were in the midst of their weekly sex education workshop with Dr. Krause held at the GNTES center in Havana. Dr. Krause announced that the doctors would first view two video tapes about couples with specific sexual problems—impotency and frigidity. Afterwards, she would return to the classroom to lead a discussion.

The video tapes were produced in English by the State University of New York at Stonybrook, and the Cubans had added a Spanish overvoice. In one film, a man was having problem maintaining an erection, and in the other film a woman had vaginismis. On screen the students saw the dramatic portrayal of the distress and tensions in each couple and the unfolding helpful, sensitive treatment after they finally go to a doctor for help. The training film included home scenes, patient/doctor consultation, discussion of suggested procedures to improve sex life, and bedroom sequences where the young couples successfully utilized the techniques suggested.

In light of the respect doctors have and the willingness of people to place a great deal of confidence in them, the focus on sex education within the medical profession is a key step for Cuba. People listen to their doctor's advice.

Dr. Ada Carmen Ovies García, director of the Piti Fijardo Hospital in Guines, is a strong supporter of sex education. She explained why parents will listen to her, a doctor, about sex but are still "opposed" to sex education as such. "I am a doctor; they know me; I deliver their babies; they see me at the hospital and then they see me in the schools in the countryside at night."[24]

Sex Education Literature

While sex education was slowly evolving in the school system, the sex education task force undertook to publish books for parents, children, and professionals. Says Lajonchere, "We spent three years . . . working in silence. Nobody heard from us because the publishing houses wanted us to write books. The problem was huge, and we were too ignorant to sit and write everything we needed."[25]

It was then that the National Working Group decided to make a selection of appropriate books from the most highly developed socialist country in this area, East Germany. Texts from the German Democratic Republic were translated and technically revised in Cuba. The East German authors went to Cuba several times, offering courses and seminars. Of their importance to the sex education program, Lajonchere has said: "This ongoing relationship, coordinated between the two governments ensures continuity. . . . We can change something if we want to—write it in a different way, even a bit more liberal if necessary. In the end the 'technical revision,' the final revision, is *our version*."[26]

Translation and technical revision were facilitated by the fact that Lajonchere's co-leader, Monika Krause, is fluent in both languages.

The first book was planned for parents; the second for children. But since they were delayed, the first book off the press was *El Hombre y la Mujer en la Intimidad* (Man and woman in intimacy) by Siegfried Schnabl, published in August 1979. This volume was geared to professionals who were, in one way or another, going to help in educational work. As in the literacy movement, the sex education movement has held that many must be trained in order to teach. According to Lajonchere,

the professionals need to have access to information; above all, the health care professionals—the physician, the nurse—but especially the physician.

I felt personally guilty about the fact that doctors didn't have sufficient information. Before the Revolution, doctors graduated without having heard a word about birth control methods. When I introduced curriculum changes in the medical school to include birth control, I felt that I had done something of gigantic progress. Even then, it had not included aspects of sexuality.

The first Cuban edition of *Man and Woman in Intimacy* had a run of 27,000 copies. I believed I had a debt to parents and to physicians. We reserved 15,000 for doctors, advanced students, and clinical psychologists who worked for the Ministry of Public Health.[27]

The book sold for five pesos to the general public, but physicians received coupons for its purchase. People lined up early in front of bookstores in Havana, Santiago, and other provincial capitals, lest the supply run out before they got their copy. Bookcase cabinets were damaged and windows broken by the intensity of the crowds pushing to purchase the books.

This treasured book details the reproductive process, discusses venereal diseases, and under the section titled "Responsible Paternity," birth control methods. Although the Cuban edition did not eliminate any of the original German illustrations, it did contain several additional ones, particularly about birth control methods—for example, pictures of a condom and a diaphragm.

Man and Woman in Intimacy was organized into three parts: the first discussed human sexuality in cultural terms; the second described intimate sexual behavior; the third took up sexual problems, deviations, and variations. The last chapter was the very controversial one on homosexuality (discussed in Chapter 2 of this book.)

The following year saw the publication of Heinrich Brückner's *Cuando tu Hijo te Preguntas* (When your child asks you), and *Antes de que Nazca un Niño* (Before a child is born), each with a run of 150,000 copies. A promotional campaign with television and press coverage preceded their sale in the bookstores. It is customary in Cuba to launch a book expected to arouse interest with an opening in front of Havana's Modern Poetry, the leading bookstore in the nation. By noon on the day sales began, all 150,000 copies of *When Your Child Asks You* were sold. Lajonchere reported approaching

an old man in line waiting to buy the book [*When Your Child Asks You*]. I ask him, "Well, what do you think of the sale?" "Very good, very good," he responds.

I say, "I guess you're buying the book for a child or a grandchild."

By that moment he has moved up, and they are in the process of giving him the book. When he completes the purchase, he embraces the book like someone who had a treasure in his hands, and says to me, "Yes, it's for my grandchild, but I'm going to read it *first*."[28]

The fourth book in the series—*Piensas Ya en el Amor?* (Already thinking about love?), geared for adolescents—was published in 1981. Originally written by Heinrich Brückner, the Cuban version has minor changes, such as the placement of certain chapters and the selection of some illustrations. The inside cover design contains a reproduction of hand-written questions young people have asked at sex education lectures. For example:

- Can a girl get·pregnant without having sexual contact?
- What are the causes of homosexuality, not only under capitalism, but also under socialism?
- Is it true that masturbation causes facial skin eruptions?
- Is it considered a 'deviation' if a couple (neighbors) throw things at each other and hit each other?
- Is it true that a 15-year-old girl is more mature and more developed than a 16-year-old boy?
- In our Socialist society is it considered an immoral act to have sex before marriage?
- From what age and for how long can one take the birth control pill?
- Must one want only children from sex or something else?
- Is it normal for a boy to eject sperm during sleep?
- Is it necessary for male adolescents to satisfy their sexual impulses?
- Why is the woman's virginity still considered necessary?[29]

The book is recommended as "study material by adolescents and youth in conjunction with their parents."

In accordance with the sex education team's conviction that to change attitudes, they must begin with the parents, the emphasis of the six-book series is on the need for both parents and children to read them. The parents are urged to read them first alone and then again with their children.

All 100,000 copies of the book for parents sold out in one day; a second edition of 150,000 also sold out quickly. As a basis of comparison, 250,000 is three percent of the Cuban population; the U.S. equivalent would be a sale of 7,800,000 books (.03 times 260 million people).

Mamá, Papá y Yo, another of the six-book series, was an effort by East Germans and Cubans to offer sex education literature for parents that would help in instructing three- to seven-year-olds. The book, which contains twenty-eight pages with illustrations, covers such questions as: Why do people have navels? Where do babies come from? How does the baby get into the mother's body? Can I have a baby?

Originally written by Heinrich Brückner and titled *Mutter, Vater, Kind,* the book addresses the parent-reader:

> We beg you not to take this as a rigid recipe; you'll have to get into each idea with more details from the world your child lives in, from his or her particular familial situation, or the situation of children in your care.
>
> You must start from the premise that a child who asks a question . . . is mature enough to get an answer. The answer must be true, clear—that is, comprehensible for the child's age—and given in a friendly way. It is not a matter of teaching biology, but of giving children information about something natural, interesting, and beautiful, which they sense as such. For parents who are adequately prepared, these conversations with their children can be unforgettable personal experiences.
>
> The atmosphere in the family becomes enriched; don't deprive yourselves of that! Little by little you're setting up the foundations for human solidarity and mutual respect. This will allow you later to have uninhibited discussions with your children and become their trusted advisors when they ask particularly intimate questions.[30]

Although Brückner only uses the traditional two-parent family as a model, he offers some counseling for divorced or single parents in the book's introduction. "Please, never say anything negative about the other parent. That's exclusively an adult problem.

Moreover, you must as much as possible insulate the child from the tensions between parents when the marriage is shaky.

Children suffer enormously when adults use them to complain about people they love."[31]

The text attempts to cover a tremendous area—pregnancy, development of the fetus, the birth process, breastfeeding, the importance of love, family values, and the allaying of children's fears—all at the same time. It does so through a story-telling style already familiar to children and then incorporates images they can easily understand. A good example is the explanation of birth.

> Susana was thinking hard about what she had felt in Aunt Catalina's belly, and asked her mother: "How do the babies come out?" and her mother replied: "Through the small slot between the legs. There are three holes there: one for urinating, one for defecating, and one exit for the baby. This hole is called the vagina. Therefore, little girls are different from little boys below the belly. When the baby has grown so much that there is no room in the belly, the exit widens, the little baby opens it further with its little head and comes out. This is called birth."
>
> Mother took a turtleneck sweater from the closet and put it over Susana's head. Susana felt how the sweater's neck stretched. "Can you picture it now? After the birth, the exit becomes smaller and stays as it was before."[32]

Brückner doesn't shy away from explaining intercourse in his children's story.

> When Susana was going to the kitchen this day, her mother was washing
> the dishes; the sunlight was reflected in some water-splash. Susana re-
> membered her game with the drops of water, and she was thinking: "How
> can the father really bring the semen inside the mother, and where does the
> semen come from?"
>
> Her mother told her: "All the boys, when they become men, can be fa-
> thers at any time. They have a little tube called the penis below the belly,
> and the semen is formed in a little bag behind the penis. If a man and a
> woman wish to have a child together, they embrace very tightly and affec-
> tionately and the father introduces his penis in the mother's vagina; the
> semen moves from the father's little bag of skin through the penis into the
> mother's vagina and from here to her cavity where the baby will be
> formed. As you see, the semen enters the cavity by the same path that the
> baby follows when it's born. There is just this path from outside to inside
> and vice versa. In the cavity, a mature egg waits for the moment to join a
> particle of semen, and so a new human being is formed. The tiny dot then
> grows. The baby receives food through the umbilical cord. If it grows
> enough, it comes out. Now, you know everything. You understand, of
> course, that a man and a woman want to have a child only if they love one
> another very much." Susan nodded affirmatively.[33]

At times, these descriptions become unduly complicated and confusing, tedious even. Brückner sometimes ignores his own advice about
simplicity and accuracy. Nevertheless, to translate, publish, and promote
such a primer for children was quite a radical step for the Cuban sex education working group.

The Media and Sex Education

Cuban Newspapers and Magazines

The strategy of approaching sex education on many fronts included
the dramatic use of the media to "inform the people and consolidate the
ethical values of our society, (emphasizing) mutual respect, human solidarity and women's equality." The mass media offered their resources
and remain the main source of public information to the people.[34]

Cuban newspapers, especially *Juventud Rebelde*, disseminated information and publicity about the series of books on sex education. Many of
these reports discuss young love and answer questions from young
people. Often they end by urging teenagers to read such books as *Are You
Thinking of Love?*

Also reported in the newspapers is research data gathered by the

Center for the Study of Youth. Often this material appears in an advice column offering answers to letters from young people or parents in a tone similar to the answer to Yamila (see Chapter 3). For example, in response to a question from a thirteen-year-old girl who was being pressured to have sex with her boyfriend, the columnist Navidad Guerrero in *Juventud Rebelde* used data to support her response and to underscore the principles of the sex education program. She reported that, in 1982, 1,370 girls under the age of fifteen gave birth, as well as 50,754 young women between the ages of fifteen and nineteen.[35]

The article stressed not only the importance of accurate information and an emphasis on love and respect, but also parental awareness of what is age-appropriate for adolescents.

Also in *Juventud Rebelde*, Ofelia Bravo writes that having a child must be a decision of both partners. Young men are ignorant of their future role as father. Woman need the moral support of their mates during pregnancy.[36]

Newspapers and magazines have had numerous articles on themes of sex education; the reporters are mainly from the GNTES staff. Besides teenage pregnancy and premarital sex, other topics have been the education of parents, women's equality, the female sex drive, myths about virility, the double standard and the devaluation of women, how such notions contribute to the transmission of venereal diseases, psychological conflicts in women, the necessity of parental honesty and openness in discussing sex with children, the rationale for a sex education program, the difference between love and sexual attraction, divorce, early marriages and forced marriages, affairs with married men.[37]

When discussing sexual problems in advice columns, Cuban writers often draw upon and cite East German sources for such diverse issues as premature ejaculation[38] and breastfeeding. Articles giving information on breastfeeding accent its psychological benefits as well as the nutritional advantages. The official position, in posters, articles, and pamphlets, aims at presenting the positive benefits that come to the infant combined with warm, verbal communications from the mother—always pointing out that "mature people" are able to organize appropriate infant care, (that is, teenagers are *not* ready for "mature care"). One goal is to offset misinformation and the negative attitude of older members of the extended family who try to dissuade mothers from breastfeeding, and to give the young mother the support she needs.

Cuban Film and Women's Equality

While there are no Cuban films that in any way reference sex education per se, they have most definitely taken on issues of women's equality.

This is of great significance since Cubans love films. An enormous number of foreign films play in movie theaters throughout the year. At least 110 to 120 films from 50 countries are shown annually. Films from the United States are very popular and, in spite of the U.S. government's ban on their export to Cuba, prints are regularly secured outside regular channels. Cuba's censorship system screens out violence, drugs, pornography, and discrimination: "All those films which denigrate the human being, are pornographic, or excessively violent, or encourage the use of drugs, are banned in Cuba."[39]

Cubans are also proud of their own films and of their international recognition. The yearly International Film Festival of New Latin American Cinema, which began in 1979, is held in Havana in December each year and draws delegates from all over the world.

During the two weeks of the festival, more than 400 films are shown in eight cinemas, with thousands of people packing the theaters featuring festival films. Havana filmgoers are alive with talk of what's being shown and the availability of tickets; people stand outside those theaters displaying "sold out" signs, hoping to secure a ticket. Only the popular peak baseball matches rival films in recreational interest and conversation during festival time.

The Cuban film industry is producing more films, both documentary and fiction, than ever before. During thirty-four years of filmmaking, they have demonstrated a growing concern with issues about women, the legacy of machismo, and the double standard in the Cuban household since the Revolution. Indeed, Cuban film has played a catalytic role in challenging traditional family relationships and the role of women in society.

In 1968 in Havana, I saw *Lucía*, a Cuban classic directed by Humberto Solas and cited by Cubans as one of the international "greats;" it received the gold medal of the Moscow Film Festival in 1969. An epic story spanning most of a century, *Lucía* focuses on women and political change, specifically on three different Lucías and their involvement in three of Cuba's major struggles for independence including the Revolution of 1959.

Another film about women, *Portrait of Teresa*, made in 1979, led to dramatic public and private debate about the role of women and the continuing double standard regarding sexuality, specifically extramarital sex. Pastor Vega, director of the film, says he was inspired to do it because of an Academy of Sciences report about the impact of the Revolution on personal lives. "The investigation revealed that the fundamental problems are the tensions created between married people, the personal relationships between husband and wife. The traditional family, inherited from Spanish society, is in a state of permanent crisis at this time because the stimulus provided the Cuban women by the Revolution has made it clear that the familial structure won't work any more."[40]

"We wanted to drop a bomb inside every home," said Vega and his wife Daisy Granados, the star of the film. They did just that. The film, which could not be viewed by anyone under twelve years of age, was an overnight success. During its month of screening, it was viewed by more than one quarter of the population.

The theme concerns the revolutionary man who wants to hold on to male privileges. It is told through the story of Teresa and Ramón, a couple with three small children whose marriage is in crisis. He is a TV repairman; she is both a textile worker and a leader in the workers' dance group at her factory. The dance group is the pride of the textile workers and is competing on a national level.

Teresa is completely occupied with the tasks of wife and mother: rising in the morning to the rooster's crowing while her husband still sleeps, preparing breakfast for everybody, getting the children up for school, dressing them, combing hair, filling bottles of milk for the younger ones, preparing dinner, making the beds, washing the laundry in a pot of hot water, and hanging it on the clothesline to dry. Sometime in the midst of all this, she manages to rouse Ramón, who rises, gets only himself ready for work, enjoys the breakfast he finds on the table, and leaves for his job. Only after all her chores are done does Teresa leave for her factory job. At the end of her shift she stays to work with the choreographer and the troupe on a dance performance. Because of this, Ramón complains that Teresa is neglecting her duties as wife and mother. He objects to having to feed the children and put them to bed in the evenings. His anger and frustration lead to a physical fight with Teresa. He finally leaves and then becomes involved with another woman.

Teresa talks out her marital problems with her mother, whose advice is to back off: "Men are men and women are women ... even Fidel can't change that." But Teresa does not back off. Instead, she struggles with her right to continue paying attention to her self-fulfillment, as symbolized by the dance group.

The film ends with a meeting in the street between the couple. Ramón wants to get together again and asks Teresa to join him in a job promotion at another city. He also wants to know whether she's had an affair with the dance group choreographer. Teresa responds that it's none of his business: Hasn't he had affairs during their separation? Ramón answers, "I'm a man. It's not the same."

Teresa's final sentence is, "It's not the same?" Ramón says, "No," echoing her mother and friends, who have said that again and again throughout the film. Taking in the reality of his position, she says, "No?" and walks away, breaking away for good.

Part of the strong emotional reaction of Cubans to the film—the first feature to deal with these issues since the enactment of the Family Code of 1975—was due to its bold questioning of prevailing roles. Many Cuban men and women have been made very uneasy by the Code's endorsement of changes in their traditional way of life. It's one thing to mandate the opening of all beaches to blacks or to provide universal educational opportunity, and quite another to touch the gender scripts that have operated for generations.[41]

Even this film does not challenge the continued cultural acceptance of men's extramarital affairs as "natural" while women are generally condemned for the same thing. Although the double standard could have been addressed by showing Teresa having an affair, her ambiguous answer to Ramón's question—"It's none of your business"—evades the issue.

Other contradictions are obvious in the way she dotes and hangs over her own boys, these "men in formation." The very things she is rebelling against in Ramón, she perpetuates in them, especially the way she completely "does for" the boys in the film. One Cuban psychiatrist wrote to *Granma* that Teresa was raising "little machos" of the future.[42]

In recent years, Cuban films have come into the house, the bedroom, and the kitchen. Although no women have directed this new genre of films, sexual politics has become an ongoing theme: "The cinema that had found its first subjects on the streets and on beaches-turned-battlefields could no longer feed on heroics of the past. Cuban drama these days is in the work of transforming daily life—a heroics of housework you might say."[43]

The films produced in the mid-1980s both mirror and examine efforts to transform daily living, not only of workers and peasants but also, as in the film *Up to a Certain Point (Hasta un Cierto Punto)*, of intellectuals concerned with sexual equality in the Revolution. Winner of the Best Film and Best Actress awards of the 1984 Latin American Film Festival in Havana, this film was directed by Tomás Gutiérrez Alea, one of Cuba's leading directors. His 1968 film *Memories of Underdevelopment* received international acclaim.

Up to a Certain Point portrays Oscar, a middle-aged intellectual screenwriter working on a film about machismo among workers whom he interviews at the Port of Havana. Gutiérrez Alea chose dock workers because historically they have been among the most radical working-class groups in Cuba, and he wanted a juxtaposition between intellectuals and workers. "One of the film's objectives is to reveal, through confrontation, that these two social groups (intellectuals and workers—ML) see the Revolution from a different perspective. Ultimately both identify with the same goals, but on the surface, some contradictions manifest themselves."[44] The film within the film underlines the theme: the gap between "preaching" equality between the sexes and actual practice, strikingly portrayed by Oscar who, macho himself, is writing a film meant "to help men understand their machismo."[45]

The title of the film comes from one of the interviewed workers who replies to a question about change that he can "change 80 percent, maybe 87 percent," but most likely will never be completely accepting of the concept of a liberated woman. When asked if equality has been achieved, he says "*Hasta un Cierto Punto*"—up to a certain point.

Oscar falls in love with Lina, a dynamic, strong young woman who works on the waterfront. She is a hardworking, single parent who expresses strong positions at union meetings and represents the new Cuban woman both in a traditional male workplace and in her self-sufficient life style combined with her effort to be an effective mother. Her powerful character contrasts with Oscar's male arrogance, spoofed in this film. Oscar says, "I was criticized for being arrogant. So I admitted it. And now I'm perfect."

Gutiérrez Alea sees machismo not just as an issue between men and women but as part of a broader question of domination and authoritarianism. And he sees film as a way to promote "consciousness raising," as a way to remove society's deficiencies and "paternalistic attitudes."[46] *Up to a Certain Point* clearly points out that there is a long road yet to travel regarding the issue of equality. It also exposes the arrogance of intellectual revolutionaries who refuse to recognize how far they themselves need to travel along that road.

Thus, Cuban films, such as *Teresa*, *Up to a Certain Point*, and *Lucía*, reflect a strong, creative effort to effect changes in attitudes and question prevailing patterns. Portraying everyday life and using skilled cinematic technique, they have stirred up the psychosocial landscape and given eloquent support to the program efforts of the FMC and GNTES.

Sex Education in Cuba Today

In the process of sex education in Cuba, there have been neither miracles nor shortcuts. There are no fairy tales of magically changed attitudes or smooth adaptations. As befits the topic, controversy and conflict abound. Even given the lag-time needed for changes in human values to appear, the statistics do not inspire awe. There remains a high rate of teenage pregnancy and early marriage. Despite great gains in economic and social status, women still must fight against the oppressive and abusive posturing of men in their daily lives. And despite a strong statement of social legislation—the Family Code—one cannot legislate the deepest of values, those locked in the privacy of the human heart. In the area of homosexuality, as I discussed in Chapter 2, the bigotry that created sex-ism weighs even more heavily.

The legacy of patriarchy persists in the midst of change, however, and the young are not necessarily the carriers of antipatriarchal positions—as is clear from the following interview with a fourteen-year-old junior-high-school student, Silvita, and her mother, an activist in the Federation of Cuban Women. Silvita's maternal grandfather was killed at the Moncada Barracks attack in 1953.

Involved in a process of change—her own as well as the nation's—the mother has seen this as truly her revolution, her political and social struggle to challenge a patriarchal society. On the other hand, Silvita has grown up learning the Revolution as history; the revolutionary struggle has not really been part of her life experience, nor that of anyone else her age, boy or girl. Although she understands and articulates the position in the Family Code on changes in the relationships between men and women, and is active in her student organization, she and her friends have also quietly accepted the reality of the social change thus far: that women are still in a limited role and that they, as adolescents, had best conform to what is actually required by the culture regardless of rhetoric or good intentions. The culture, in spite of the official code or her partic-ular nonsexist parents, still teaches that the way to higher status is to get a boyfriend.

The interview gives a vivid portrait of the problems in changing "old attitudes."[47] The issue is a simple one: some of the girls in the junior high schools in the countryside are washing the boys' pants.

Silvita: It's not something that the boys demand from the girls, but the girls do it out of friendship and camaraderie among the boys and girls. You see that a lot. The girls are the ones that wash out the boys' pants, underwear, shirts . . . but it's not a problem of machismo, that the girls are obligated to do it. Of course, you see the boys in the laundry too, to wash out their own stuff. But most of the time it's the girls who wash the pants: not because they think, well, I'm a girl and I have to do it, but because they offer to do it, as a normal part of friendship, which really comes from the girls them-selves.

Interviewer: What do you think a relationship should be like at home?
Silvita: Well, sharing the housework, in everything. That's in addition to understanding each other, loving each other, and all of that. Sharing the work, a reciprocal attitude.

Interviewer: And do you think the boys of your generation see it like that?
Silvita: There's some that can get kind of dumb about it, but all of them understand it. Underneath, they understand it. As a matter of fact, there was an article in *Pioneer* magazine the other week [the Pioneers are a mass organization of Cuban youngsters], where the kids are talking about the

girls washing out the boys' clothes at school, and everybody was giving their opinion—a sort of airing of the whole question. But, in general, I'd say that the boys of my generation don't have machista characteristics.

Silvita's Mom: I don't agree with you. It's really amazing because in spite of my working at the Women's Federation, where we study these questions a lot and we talk a lot about them with the Federation members that come with concerns—now I'm really concerned myself. I never thought you might have these ideas. They say you find a wooden knife in the blacksmith's house!

I really don't agree with you, Silvita. I think this business of washing the boys' clothes is poor education, poor formation from the beginning. These are leftovers from the past—the idea that the woman has to do the washing. Without thinking, you're creating a pattern that belongs in the past. And what's more, I'd say that it's not the girls who wash better. If the boys really put their minds to it, they would wash much better in many cases because they are often stronger. I don't mean by that that men and women should reverse roles. In other words, I'm the one who has to wash my clothes because I'm the one who dirtied them, whether I'm a girl or a boy, a woman or a man. It's nothing but machismo, that when you come in from working in the countryside, you set about not only washing your own clothes but the boys' clothes too. I think you are wrong about how you see it, and your thinking has to evolve further than that. In the home, it's different. You share because you have equal obligations: to raise your children, carry out housework, etc., because you have taken on that responsibility together. But in school, you don't have this kind of reciprocal arrangement, and then there's certainly no reason that any of the girls should be washing any of the boys' clothes. Do you wash your girlfriend's clothes? No, you don't. So why do you wash the boys'? That is where the machismo is; it's undercover. But it's not about camaraderie, because if it were, then you'd wash out your girlfriend's clothes too.

Interviewer: I was thinking about what FMC President Vilma Espín said at the Fourth FMC Congress, that sometimes it's the girls or women themselves that perpetuate machismo.

Silvita: Well, after what my mom said, I'm not so sure anymore. But we really don't see it as machismo. And it wasn't a lot of extra work.

Silvita's Mom: The point is not whether the woman feels oppressed or not by machismo—women who accept machismo are happy, contented—and that's precisely the mentality we have to change. She's doing everything for her husband, waiting on him hand and foot, because it's the old mentality, that the husband is the boss, the great gentleman, that you even have to put his socks on for him. Make his dinner. Today, your husband or lover is the man at your side, to share your life with and to share the burdens too. The woman is not his slave—and this business of washing, it's a bit of that slave mentality. Because to say that women wash better is a lie. The first time I washed, nobody had shown me how, and I didn't go to college to learn.[48]

This exchange bears out my own interviews with adolescents in other schools since 1969. Many boys in both junior and senior high school readily admitted that they had *never* washed their own clothes.

In short, Cuba—like the rest of the world—has not been able to shed patriarchy with its gross as well as subtle devaluation of women.

Yet changes in attitudes and behavior have taken place in Cuba over the past years. Machismo and the equality of women are talked about, reflected on in press and cinema, and emphasized in teacher education and school curriculum. In 1993 there are many more men at the market place, at parents' meetings, and at day care centers. As Krause has pointed out, "Our task is directed to achieving the full exercise of women's equality, including the sphere of sexuality. And this doesn't mean to declare war on men, but on the contrary, to secure him as a firm ally."[49] Cerutti, describing the changes she has observed since 1976, points out that "to call a man machista in 1986 is to create in him a sense of guilt, a charge that he does not have a consciousness."

The leaders of the sex education program are convinced that sex education will positively influence relations between men and women and young people. They look to the development of a "sex pedagogy," defined "as a branch of pedagogical science that comprises everything that relates to the methods, means, forms, objectives, and tasks of sex education."[50] Lajonchere spoke of a study on sex education carried out in Boston, which found that boys and girls who have had an adequate sex education over the years begin their sexual activity later and do so with some form of contraception, and that girls who have had sex education get pregnant much later than do those who have not had it. "A very beautiful study," he said, "very beautiful."[51]

Thus, Cuba is making an honest and enlightened struggle to tackle what is the hardest to change. Undertaken with integrity and grace, such a struggle promises that social transformation, however rebellious to the dictates of time, can openly challenge taboos and advance an understanding of human existence. However slow and subject to resistance, it can be viewed as a labor of love just as surely as a campaign to teach people to read. In some areas of human life, mountains must be moved with spoons.

Notes

1. Interview with Celestino Alvarez Lajonchere, Havana, 1986.

2. Beatríz Castellanos Simons et al., "A Comparative Study of Sexuality and Personality of Students in the Institute of Pedagogy Enrique José Varona Before and After a Course in Sex Education," presented at Pedagogía/86 Congress in Havana, 1986, 4.

3. The Institute of Pedagogy Enrique José Varona offers university teacher education programs for the preparation of secondary school teachers and inservice training for experienced teachers.

4. Simons et al., "A Comparative Study," 9.

5. Lajonchere interview, 1986.

6. Simons et al., "A Comparative Study,"

7. Ibid., 8.

8. Mariano Rodríguez Herrera, "Educación Sexual En Los Escuelas: Rompiendo un Tabú," *Bohemia*, November 30, 1979, 46–49.

9. Ibid.

10. Ibid., Herrera, 46–49.

11. Ibid., 47.

12. Ibid., 48.

13. Interview with Margarita Silvestre, Ministry of Education, Havana, 1984.

14. Monika Krause Peters, *Algunos Temas Fundamentales Sobre Educación Sexual* (Havana: Ministerio de Cultura Editorial Científica-Técnica, 1985), 9.

15. Ilia S. Ferran, Daisy A. Herrera, and Celia S. Mendaro, *Ciencias Naturales 1: Tercer Grado* (Havana: Ministerio de Educación, 1977), 170–171.

16. Ibid., 171.

17. Ilia S. Ferran et al., *Ciencias Naturales 2: Cuarto Grado* (Havana: Editorial Pueblo y Educación, 1978), 188–200.

18. Manuel P. Cendon et al., *Anatomía, Fisiología, e Higiene del Hombre: Noveno Grado* (Habana: Ministerio de Educación, 1980), 200–219.

19. Ibid., 215–217.

20. Ibid., 217.

21. Lajonchere, *Bohemia*, January 4, 1987.

22. Interview with Stela Cerutti, Havana, 1986.

23. Dr. Ricardo González Menéndez, *Psicología Para Médicos Generales* (La Habana: Ministerio de Cultura, Editorial Científica, 1979), 166–167.

24. *Bohemia*, May 10, 1985.

25. Elizabeth Fee, "Sex Education in Cuba: An Interview With Dr. Celestino Alvarez Lajonchere," *International Journal of Health Services*, vol. 18, no. 2 (1988): 348.

26. Lajonchere interview, 1986.

27. Ibid.

28. Ibid..

29. Heinrich Brückner, *Piensas Ya en el Amor?* (La Habana: Editorial Gente Nueva, 1981), trans. Olga Sánchez Guevara.

30. Heinrich Brückner, *Mamá, Papá y Yo* (Habana: Editorial Gente Nueva, 1983), trans. Monika Krause Peters, 4.

31. Ibid., 4.

32. Ibid., 16.

33. Ibid., 27.

34. Celestino Alvarez Lajonchere, "La Educacion Sexual: Algunas Antecedentes y Perspectivas en Cuba," *Bohemia*, January 4, 1985, 62–63.

35. Guerrero, *Juventud Rebelde*.

36. Ofelia Bravo, *Juventud Rebelde*, November 24, 1987.

37. Celestino Alvarez Lajonchere, "Educación Sexual: El Embarazo en La Adolescencia, pt. 1," *Bohemia*, November 28, 1990. Monika Krause Peters, *Juventud Rebelde*, December 25, 1983; Lajonchere, *Juventud Rebelde*, July 21, 1985. Méndez, Ada, *Juventud Rebelde*, July 21, 1985. Krause Peters, *Juventud Rebelde*, August 18, 1985. Krause Peters, "No Habra Sido Demasiado Temprano?" *Juventud Rebelde*, August 18, 1985. Guerrero, *Juventud Rebelde*, September 22, 1985. *Juventud Rebelde*, December 29, 1985. Escobar, Milagros, *Juventud Rebelde*, February 2, 1986. Escobar, Milagros, *Juventud Rebelde*, February 16, 1987. Méndez, Ada, "Something That Should Start at Birth," *Juventud Rebelde*, September 1, 1987. Raimundo Rodríguez, "Marriage and Divorce Among Cuban Youth," *Granma International*, November 17, 1992, 2. "Sex and the Elderly," *Granma International*, November 17, 1991, 3. Sara Mas, "Sex, Lies, and Stereotypes," *Granma International*, May 31, 1992, 2.

38. Milagros Escobar, "Early Ejaculation, A Problem Easy To Solve," *Juventud Rebelde*, November 17, 1985, 46. For example, after presenting the problem of early ejaculation, the author of one of the sex advice articles cites Schnabl for clinical details, i.e., helpful techniques. Escobar refers to the relationship of early ejaculation to young men undergoing lengthy periods of abstinence. He reports that according to Dr. Siegfried Schnabl, the speed of the ejaculation is caused by four factors: individual nervous excitability; momentary level of excitement; psychic influences; and tactile sensations.

Some of the helpful procedures to eliminate premature ejaculation include: freeing oneself from tension and worries, decreasing periods of abstinence; repeating coitus immediately when the man is able, avoiding the use of condoms, using certain medicines prescribed by a specialist. It also calls upon the partner to help by not creating "a drama" of the situation and giving support.

39. Ezequiel Pérez Martin, "Films to See in Cuba," *Granma*, September 27, 1987; for a history of prerevolutionary Cuban films and for an analysis of film as a center of Cuban cultural politics since the 1959 Revolution, see Michael Chanan, *The Cuban Image: Cinema and Cultural Politics in Cuba* (Bloomington: Indiana Press, 1986).

40. Patricia Peyton and Carlos Broullon, "Portrait of Teresa: An Interview with Pastor Vega and Daisy Granados," *Cineaste* 10, no. 1 (Winter 1979–1980): 24.

41. Margaret Randall, "Portrait of Teresa: A Letter from Havana," *Cineaste* 10, no. 1 (Winter 1979–80): 26.

42. Susan Linnee, "Ambivalence over the 'New Cuban Woman,'" *Oakland Tribune*, September 4, 1979.

43. Pat Auferheide, *Sight and Sound*, 49.

44. Senel Paz, "Hasta Cierto Punto: Entrevista a Tomás Gutiérrez Alea," *Areito*, vol. 10, no. 37 (1984): 45.

45. When I saw *Up to a Certain Point* in Havana, the audience loved the realistic, humorous portrayal of Cuban life, from housing situations to the prevailing machismo on all levels of society. The housing scenes poke fun at daily life with problems familiar to all. In Oscar's house, for example, a middle-class home, the walls badly need painting and repairs. When he goes to the veranda with friends to talk about the plot of his film, it is clear his porch furniture is not in good shape. Oscar says, "Don't sit there," pointing to a chair with obviously

lopsided, broken legs. In Cuba, the audience broke into laughter at this scene. When I saw the same film in New York, the audience hardly reacted, perhaps not connecting to "in" jokes of the Cuban culture. Similarly, in Lina's tiny apartment, where she lives with her ten-year-old son, Oscar finds the refrigerator padlocked, and the audience again burst into spontaneous laughter.

46. Roxana Pollo, "Interview With Tomás Gutiérrez Alea: Working Toward Authenticity and Sincerity," *Weekly Granma*, January 17, 1988, 7.

47. Johnetta B. Cole and Gail A. Reed, "Women in Cuba: Old Problems and New Ideas," *Urban Anthropology* 15 (3–4) (1986): 340–342.

48. Ibid.

49. Monika Krause Peters, "Sex Education in Cuba," Paper presented at the Latin American Studies Association Congress, New Orleans, Louisiana, March, 1988.

50. Simons et al., "A Comparative Study," 3. Monika Krause has returned to her country of birth, Germany. The current director of sex education in Cuba is a young psychologist, Lourdes Florez, who continues to emphasize the "humanistic sex education principles" of Lajonchere and Krause. The name of the Working Group for Sex Education has been changed to the National Center for Sex Education and continues to be based in Havana. Sara Màs, "Màs Que una Edad y Tres Consejos," *Granma*, July 15, 1992, 3.

51. Lajonchere interview, 1986.

5

AIDS:
Cuba's Effort to Contain

We have the opportunity to stop the disease in our country. It would be irrespon-
sible if we didn't face the situation with courage, knowing we could stop it. We
have an epidemiologic opportunity that we are not going to lose.

—Dr. Hector Terry

In Cuba, AIDS has not become a dilemma, a social problem, a phobia, a madness,
as in the United States.

—Reynaldo González

In Cuba, the medical establishment's response to AIDS was immediate
and thorough; its goal was to prevent an epidemic by identifying, isolating, and treating, to the extent medically possible, all persons infected
with the HIV virus, whether or not they had developed AIDS. To this
end, mandatory screening for HIV infection began in 1986, and persons
testing positive were sent to a sanitorium in a Havana suburb. The first
blood tests targeted the most high-risk groups: Cubans who had traveled
abroad in various capacities since 1975; in particular, soldiers who had
served in Africa.

By April 1991, 9, 771,691 people, almost the entire population, had
been tested. Almost two years later, a cumulative total of 13 million tests
had been carried out as people in high-risk groups began to undergo repeated tests.[1] Twelve special sanitoriums are now in operation throughout the country. As of December 1, 1992, 862 positive HIV cases had been
detected. Three months later the number was up to 902. One hundred
fifty nine have developed AIDS, and, of these, 119 have died including
two children.[2]

To achieve this medical success, the primary aim has been to identify
infected persons and bring them completely under the control of the
medical establishment. Education has been relegated to a marginal role.
Although people living in a sanitorium receive (at no cost to them) the
best possible medical treatment and have comfortable living conditions,

their quarantine is obligatory. They must live isolated, nonproductive lives until they contract AIDS and are moved to a hospital, or until a miracle cure is found. Already some people have lived almost seven years in this state of limbo. It amounts to a life sentence for healthy people. Although it is difficult to know how long it will take for a person to progress from HIV infection to symptoms of AIDS, studies have shown that the median time is ten and one-half years. Some people testing HIV-positive may not develop AIDS for twenty years. Indeed, with excellent medical care and early intervention with present drugs and more powerful ones yet to be developed, researchers state that the hope is "that it will take longer and longer before symptoms occur and that some people may never become ill at all."[3] And, even with improved testing procedures, there is still some chance of false positives.

The Quarantine Policy

The sanitorium is also the most viable solution for a poor country like Cuba, so that resources can be focused efficiently in efforts to keep the disease from spreading indiscriminately. The way we see it, we must also protect the human rights of the majority of the population.

—Dr. Hector Terry

All of these reasons lead us to believe that the prevalence of the HIV among the Cuban population is really very low and that it is mainly due to the nationwide program which allows for relatively early detection and to isolation of those detected to keep it from spreading in geometric proportions.

—Editorial, *Weekly Granma*

The most controversial aspect of Cuba's program for combatting AIDS has been the creation of sanitoriums for the compulsory isolation of those Cubans who test positive for HIV antibodies. While there have been discussions in other countries about instituting such a national quarantine for those identified as infected, Cuba's is the only one of its kind in the world. People admitted to a sanitorium have the virus but do not have AIDS. People with AIDS are hospitalized.

The first sanitorium opened in Havana in April 1986 with 24 patients. It is now the largest of the twelve sanitoriums with 300 patients; another five regional sanitoriums are under construction.[4] The first director of the sanitorium, Dr. Juan Rivero Gómez, currently heads the medical department, which is made up of three wards—observation, psychiatry, and dental. In addition, there are four clinics. Every Friday, specialists see patients for whatever problems they may have.

The Sanitorium

The Havana sanitorium is located near the city in Santiago de las Vegas, a residential resort area known as Los Cocos. Visitors to the facility of forty hectares have described the residents' living quarters as apartments, which include color television, air conditioning, and kitchen facilities.[5] The most attractive part of the sanitorium is El Maranon, an area with two-story houses near the main entrance. El Maranon is the community for the most "responsible" patients—married couples or two patients of the same sex living together. Patients receive the weekly food ration, which they prepare as they wish.[6]

Upon first arrival, patients are interviewed by physicians and nurse specialists—epidemiologists. There is, according to public health officials, an emphasis on both the "personal" and the "communal."

> Once a person is diagnosed, an interview takes place at which his/her situation is set forth. "You have the AIDS virus," the person is told. It is as if a twenty-story building had fallen upon the person. The person is informed that there is no effective treatment.
>
> It is explained that there are enormous financial, human, and technological resources throughout the world dedicated to the study of the disease—dedicated to the pursuit of a vaccine that will prevent the disease, to seeking a drug or an effective pharmacological agent to treat this disease, but that at the present time none of this is available.
>
> ... The person is told that there is no way to protect the life of those who carry the virus at present other than to protect them from the aggressions of the environment. ... It is a somewhat individualistic focus ... directed to make the person understand that this measure is taken for his/her own good. It is like putting him/her in internment for a while until the solution to the problem appears, whether it be one year, two years, or longer.
>
> And the other aspect is the social aspect. If you are infected, you may infect others.[7]

The interview data gathered for each person include family history, housing, work history, and present work situation, including salary. Patients continue to receive full salary even though not working. Arrangements are made to enable university students to continue their studies.

In the sanitorium, married couples and homosexual couples live together if both have tested positive. Uninfected children then live with other family members rather than with their parents. If the children are also infected, they join their parents in the sanitorium. If only one parent tests positive, that parent lives in the sanitorium, and children continue living with the other parent; family members and friends can visit those living in the sanitorium any time they choose.

On staff, working closely with residents, are health professionals trained to work with HIV-positive people. In order to provide continuity of treatment and a personal connection to the resident, a physician is assigned to each patient (the term health officials use to denote a resident of the sanitorium). A team of psychologists, social workers, and sociologists not only work with the patients but meet with and provide counseling and psychiatric services for family members. Families are encouraged to visit as often as every day.

Residents of the sanitorium may also make trips outside. There are occasional organized recreational activities such as an evening at the cinema or the theater or an outing to the beach. Residents also return to their communities for visits and meetings—for example, of the block association or parent-teacher conferences. Those who do not live far away can spend weekends with family and friends. If they do live farther away, they can arrange four-day trips home every four to six weeks.

On most of these trips, a senior medical student or intern goes along as chaperone because, as the director of the Havana sanitorium explained, "Our responsibility doesn't end at the doors of the institution; we must see to the health of everyone."[8] Dr. Terry says, "Our objective is not to have them lead an isolated existence, but to find a way to keep them from developing the disease and from spreading it to other parts of the population."[9] He has also explained that "those hospitalized in the sanitorium continue to have sexual relations with their partners if they so desire"[10] when they go home on weekends. Presumably, these partners are considered as good as infected, since the whole point of the sanitorium and chaperoned visits is to prevent sexual contacts that could spread the virus. Married couples are allowed passes to leave the sanitorium under more liberal conditions than others and are not required to be chaperoned.[11]

The new director at the Havana facility, Dr. Jorge Pérez Avila, seeks to identify stable and responsible couples and individuals who can be trusted to return to normal life in the community without engaging in behavior that will put others at risk. Pérez reported to the "First Seminar on HIV Infection and AIDS in Cuba" (*Primer Seminario Sobre Infección Por VIH y SIDA en Cuba*) held in Havana on October 30–31, 1992 that the quarantine program is now more flexible.[12]

Thus far, a handful of people have been deemed responsible enough to return to society, and about half those residing in the Havana sanitorium may now leave on unchaperoned weekend visits. Being among these requires approval by a group of psychologists, medical personnel, and social workers who consider epidemiological records, psychiatric data, relations with family members, and the person's behavior while at the sanitorium. A person is not eligible for this "parole" until he or she has lived in the sanitorium for at least six months. Thus, the quarantine is eased for people who are HIV positive and are "responsible." But, what is "responsible" or "trustworthy?" This is an Orwellian/Catch-22 nightmare. If you're a homosexual resident in a sanitorium and put on makeup or are considered "effeminate," is this "irresponsible?" If you protest sanitorium conditions, does that mean that you will be designated "untrustworthy?" If you protest or object to the entire quarantine concept for HIV positives, is this also "untrustworthy" and "irresponsible?"

Dr. Fernando Zakarias of the Pan American Health Organization's AIDS division has visited the sanitoriums regularly. He reports that the Cubans "have psychologists who do tests and claim to be able to prove at the outset who is trustworthy. We say 'How can you do this? Unless someone is a clear sociopath, how can you tell?'" He further states that the Cubans find most homosexual residents of the sanitoriums "untrustworthy."[13]

Indeed, the process is much like that of release from a mental hospital. No doubt a few people testing HIV-positive are mentally ill, and no doubt a few are highly promiscuous with no sense of concern for their sexual partners. The process, however, seems to assume that to test HIV-positive is to be mentally unstable and irresponsible until proven otherwise through a rigorous process.

Carlos Cabrera, who reported on the sanitorium for the *Weekly Granma*, thought it would not be easy for these people to return to society because of prejudice and the lack of education about AIDS. "Reintegration into the society is also difficult because Cubans have reacted with panic to AIDS."[14]

Thus, when sanitorium residents go out on visits, people they encounter often feel endangered. One woman resident described to a North American journalist in Havana an encounter she had with an old friend who would not believe she was a sanitorium patient. "I couldn't convince her I was serious." She went on to describe an evening at the Tropicana night club:

There were two young men at the next table. One of them was telling the other, "You know, you have to be really careful on Sundays, because that's when they let the 'siderosos'[15] out." I turned around quickly and must have glared at him, because he said somewhat defensively, "Excuse me, Ma'am, but it's true. You should be careful too." I don't have to be careful, I told him, because I already have AIDS. The young man said: "Señora, you shouldn't joke about things like that."[16]

The Testing Program

Given the growing international epidemic the Cuban Ministry of Health ordered a screening process that would eventually test virtually every person on the island for the HIV infection. It began in 1986 when all blood donors were tested. At that time, 17 carriers of the virus, or .0026 percent, were found, according to Deputy Health Minister Hector Terry.[17] Among Cubans having contact with foreigners, one of the first major groups tested were troops, aid workers, and technicians returning from Angola. By 1989, this included 300,000 Cubans, among whom 82, or .0002 percent, tested HIV-positive. In addition, all Cubans returning from abroad were tested, whether they were diplomats, athletes, sailors, soldiers, or students.

Testing also began on citizens having contact with foreigners in Cuba, whether in education, tourism, or foreign relations. Hotel and restaurant workers in the tourist industry, for example, are considered a high-risk group. All foreigners who reside in Cuba for three months or longer are now tested, except for diplomats. Tourists are not tested. Anyone who tests positive is returned to his or her country of origin.[18]

Early on, the mandatory testing program expanded to include all pregnant women, all adults admitted to hospitals, people treated for sexually transmitted diseases, the sexual contacts of those testing HIV-positive, and prisoners. There has also been some screening of specific residential areas where an initial high proportion of HIV-infected people were found or where there was a high level of tourist activity. Ultimately, all members of the armed forces will be tested.

In the absence of a serious educational program on AIDS, the quarantine itself becomes a kind of collective safe sex program that requires that infected people remove themselves from society so society can remain untainted. This also explains why people rarely refuse to cooperate with the quarantine and what happens when they do. Most people accept the need to protect society, and since the quarantine policy was put into place early on by high-level authorities, it preempted consideration of other possibilities. People cannot imagine either an alternative or any way to achieve one. Some GNTES staff have indicated that, although they did not agree with the quarantine, they did not feel they could actively oppose it. And, after a while, who argues with success? Nationwide testing and quarantine have kept AIDS at a very low level.

To gain compliance from those testing positive becomes a matter of paternalistic persuasion rather than force—as is obvious in several health ministry statements in response to questions of noncompliance. In a 1988 interview, health care officials stated that there were no refusals because when one learns one is infected, one is in a fog and can be convinced to accept the painful logic of isolating oneself for the good of family and nation.[19]

Diego Franchi, a psychologist at the Havana sanitorium, explained to Carlos Cabrera of *Granma* that patients at the sanitorium go through three stages: first, denying one is sick; second, refusing to acknowledge it publicly; third, accepting one's condition and cooperating with medical staff.[20] Since most of the people he is talking about are not sick, denial is understandable even as they come to understand what it means to test positive for HIV. It is also understandable they would not want it publicly known given public attitudes about "diseased people who are such a social menace they must be put away." Finally, the third stage seems like one of defeat: there is no other place to turn. This feeling was expressed by Dr. Terry in response to a question on whether people tried to escape from the sanitorium.

> Some patients have left the sanitorium. It's easy to do since this is a health facility, not a prison, and so therefore has only the most elementary physical measures for containment that any other health facility should have. The patients who have left have gone to their homes; they did not try to evade health authorities so the term "capture" is inappropriate. All we did is locate them at their homes and convince them that in doing so, they are only harming their own health.
>
> There are some people who at first refused to go to the sanitorium. We simply kept talking to them until they were convinced of the necessity of in-patient care. There are, however, health regulations in our country that would allow health officials to take measures against anyone who was endangering the health of the general population in their community.[21]

Impediments to Alternative Policies

Why has Cuba—outstanding for its achievements in education and for its emphasis on education as the solution to many problems of underdevelopment—been almost the only country not to make education the central or dominant element in its anti-AIDS strategy? The reason lies, I think, in a convergence of five conditions:

1. The nation's successful development of a highly technical and advanced health care system providing free services to all citizens;
2. The fear generated by an epidemic that appears to be uncontrollable and feeds on public ignorance;
3. The pervasiveness of machismo and its general rejection of sex education;

4. An authoritarian political system in which voices that might advocate alternative policies are not allowed the means to organize and
   present their case;
5. The strong prejudice against homosexuality and the perception of
   AIDS as a homosexual disease.

Cuba's Advanced Health Care System

Cuba's health care system has, as I have discussed, won respect in international health communities. Death and infant mortality rates are among
the lowest in the world; indeed, infant mortality is the lowest among all
Third World countries. Several diseases common to nonindustrial countries have been eliminated. Medical care is available even in the remotest
regions of the country. Cuba's community doctor program, a doctor for
every 120 families, has earned the interest and admiration of doctors and
health workers throughout the world.[22] This small island nation has
become a medical power admired by most Third World countries for the
availability of free medical care and the development of medical technology on a par with industrialized countries.

Some American physicians and health experts have criticized "Cuba's
excessive use of doctors and the government's reliance on highly trained
physicians to perform tasks that can be done by paraprofessionals." They
fear an overemphasis on physician care that dangerously inflates the cost
of health care. "Nevertheless, the Cuban health care system has accomplished what few if any of the other 100 developing nations of the
world—and many industrialized countries—have attained."[23]

These advances made it possible to offer AIDS patients and those testing HIV-positive the best in medical care. The first steps in Cuba's anti-
AIDS strategy were taken in 1983 when blood and blood products from
countries with AIDS cases were not permitted to enter the country. The
Cubans, aware that blood concentrates needed in the treatment of hemo-
philiac bleeding are a major source of HIV infection in Latin America,
stopped importing them from the East or the West. After a visit to Cuba
in the early 1980s, Jeanne Smith and Sergio Piomelli, hematologists and
professors of medicine and pediatrics at Columbia University's College
of Physicians and Surgeons, reported that the Cubans

> started on their own to manufacture cryoprecipitate, a less purified blood
> fraction used several years ago, less efficient than the concentrates, but
> much less likely to be contaminated with HIV. This was no minor effort for
> a small country; during the night trucks still ferry the plasma from blood
> banks throughout the island to a central laboratory. Today, only four out
> of 500 hemophiliacs in Cuba are HIV carriers. By contrast, in the United
> States, the vast majority of hemophiliacs became HIV carriers in the early
> 1980s, and hundreds have died of AIDS.[24]

Ironically, the United States policy of prohibiting shipment of medical supplies and products, including blood, to Cuba unintentionally protected Cuban hemophiliacs. Officials state that Cuba is now almost completely self-sufficient in its blood supply.[25]

Because all health care for all citizens in Cuba is free, the cost of treating seriously ill people, including those with AIDS, does not become a hellish economic crisis that depletes income, is next to impossible to manage, and degrades patient, family, and friends in the process. In Cuba all hospital stays, doctor's treatment, and medication are free. For example, those who become ill with AIDS are treated in hospitals and receive medications such as AZT (at a cost of $7,000 per patient per year) at no cost to themselves. A number of asymptomatic patients at the sanitorium have been treated with Interferon; the results are encouraging but not conclusive. As Paula Treichler notes in her work on AIDS and HIV infection in the Third World: "One can certainly argue that Cuba is providing more support and resources for its infected citizens than many other countries."[26]

In Puerto Rico, on the other hand, federal records for the year ending March 31, 1990, show that it had the highest incidence of new AIDS cases of any place under U.S. government jurisdiction—47 new cases per 100,000 people. Yet the few facilities offering care do not offer AZT to patients because it is too expensive. Dr. Samuel A. Amill explained that at the nineteen-bed adult ward of the AIDS Institute, no one received AZT "because if we give it to one, we should give it to everybody, and that would consume the Institute's whole budget."[27]

The centralized structure of Cuba's health care system makes it feasible to carry out an ongoing massive national testing program. This, in itself, generates a propensity to approach the disease only in medical technological terms. Reliance on a medical approach alone is no doubt influenced also by knowledge that AIDS is a rapidly spreading worldwide epidemic. Thus, strong measures must be taken as rapidly as possible lest the disease become uncontrollable.

The Top of the International Volcano:
The Worldwide Drastic Increase of People with AIDS

At the Eighth International Conference on AIDS in Amsterdam (July 1992), health officials from all regions of the world reported that AIDS is spreading unchecked in a growing number of developing nations. Jonathan Mann, former head of World Health Organization's (WHO) Global AIDS Program and chairman of the Amsterdam Conference, reported that the epidemics in Africa, Latin America, the Caribbean, and Southeast Asia are not coming under control.[28] "In the developing countries, we are sitting on top of a volcano," said Dr. Vulimiri Ramalingaswami of the All India Institute of Medical Sciences. "I have come here to plead to this conference for a human response, a global response, to this emergency. We are facing a very major disaster." Reliable projections indicate that while AIDS came relatively late to Asia, it is now spreading so rapidly that scientists report that AIDS will kill more people in Asia than any other continent. By the end of the decade, conservative estimates report that more than one million Asians will be infected with the HIV virus each year. However, some researchers fear that the infection rate in Asia will reach three or four million a year. Mann and his colleagues predict there will be 100 million HIV-infected adults worldwide by the year 2000. This means that the number of cumulative AIDS cases by the year 2000 will exceed 25 million people.[29]

The continent hit hardest by the epidemic is also the poorest—Africa. There, at the end of 1989, medical estimates put the number of women infected by HIV at 2.5 million. In 1992 at least six million people were infected in Africa alone. The World Health Organization reports that 75 percent of people with the HIV virus worldwide were infected through heterosexual sex, especially in Third World countries. The health care systems of these countries simply cannot cope, and there seems to be little likelihood of new treatments being utilized on anywhere near the scale that is needed.[30]

In the United States, ten years after the first report (1981–1991) on a mysterious and profound immune deficiency, over 120,000 people have died of the condition while the Center for Disease Control counts more than 200,000 cases of AIDS. It took eight years for the first 100,000 cases of AIDS in the United States to be reported, but only two years for the second 100,000. The Center acknowledges, however, that these figures are underreported by ten to twenty percent. The National Commission on AIDS reports: "There are at least one million Americans silently infected with the Human Immunodeficiency Virus. Most of them will get sick during the next decade." The report estimates that in the next three years, another 200,000 people will die, and 200,000 to 600,000 new infections will occur. This spread of AIDS is compounded by the shameful fact reported in a January 1992 article in the *New England Journal of Medicine*: 29 percent of people with AIDS in the United States have no health insurance.[31]

Puerto Rico has the highest per-capita rate of new AIDS cases in the United States, more than three times the national average. Studies have indicated that Puerto Ricans on the mainland are the most severely affected ethnic group. Puerto Rico's 2,603 AIDS deaths means that AIDS is one of the leading causes of death on the island for those between twenty and forty-five.[32] In New York City, AIDS is the number one killer of all Hispanics between the ages of one and four and twenty-five to forty-four.[33]

The Cuban AIDS Screening Program

In Cuba, the testing program and necessary census procedures were carried out with the support of the mass organizations. The same organizations that had been the key to mobilization for the literacy and education campaigns and for the giant vaccination and health campaigns again helped with the screening program for AIDS.

In addition to government agencies, the Cuban Trade Unions (CTC), the Federation of Cuban Women (FMC), and the block organizations—the Committees for the Defense of the Revolution—all helped gather information for the census: for example, compiling lists of persons who had been outside of Cuba since 1975.

By October 1988, after almost two and a half years, nearly three million Cubans had been tested for the HIV virus—approximately 30 percent of the nation's population. During the following two and a half years, the rate of testing more than doubled so that an additional 6,839,442 were tested.[34] Those in high-risk groups are tested more than once.

At a 1989 meeting on AIDS in Latin America sponsored by the Pan American Health Organization, experts acknowledged that Cuba's screening was proportionally the largest in the world. The Cuban AIDS infection rate is one of the lowest in the world and the lowest in Latin America.[35]

Table 5.1 presents the infection rate within the specific groups tested for HIV as of 1989. Thus, the largest percentage of persons infected, 4.6 percent, was from the group of "sexual contacts of seropositive persons." Sexual contacts of HIV-positive Cubans are retested every three months and offered counseling services.[36] When questioned about intravenous

TABLE 5.1   1989 Infection Rate Within Specific Groups Tested for HIV in Cuban Population

Groups Tested	Percentage of Infection Within Designated Group
Foreign students	.44
Persons with hemophilia	.3
Those who have lived outside Cuba since 1975	.025
Patients with sexually transmitted diseases	.010
The general population of resort areas	.005
Pregnant women	.0037
Sexual contacts of seropositive persons	4.6
A residual category (including prisoners)	.014
1989 total seroprevalence since testing began in 1986 (N=259)	.0089

SOURCE: Francisco A. Machado Ramírez, director of the Cuban AIDS Investigations Laboratory, cited in Ronald Bayer and Cheryl Healton, "Special Report: Controlling AIDS in Cuba," *The New England Journal of Medicine*, April 13, 1989. p. 1023.

drug users, officials said there were none in Cuba. I have been unable to find evidence to contradict these statements.

The smallest percentage of people with the HIV virus came from the category of pregnant women—.0037 percent. All women receive free prenatal care. If routine blood tests reveal the HIV virus, a woman may choose to have an abortion. As of 1990, only one child had died of AIDS. I have received one unconfirmed report that two HIV positive women chose to take the risk of giving birth.[37] If so, they are in a no-win dilemma. The mothers must take up life in one of the sanitoriums; if the babies do not carry the virus, they must be brought up by someone else, although there can be frequent visits between mother and child. Only if the child is also infected can it join its mother in the sanitorium.

Table 5.2 presents the incidence of AIDS in Caribbean countries with populations of more than 100,000. Table 5.3 presents the incidence of AIDS (rate per million) for selected countries. The data in this table and in Table 5.2 indicate that Cuba has one of the lowest AIDS incidence rates in the world. In April 1991, Dr. Hector Terry and Dr. Francisco Machado reported that the infection rate for all of Cuba is .06 percent. (9,771,691 tested; total population is over 10,000,000.) [38] Although I am critical of the HIV quarantine, a major feature of Cuban policy, the facts in Tables 5.1 and 5.2 are straightforward: Cuba has kept the AIDS epidemic under control and contained the spread of AIDS.

For patients in a hospital or a prenatal clinic, or anywhere else where blood samples are taken and tested, the test for HIV is now one of the

TABLE 5.2   Cumulative Incidence of AIDS in Caribbean Countries with Populations of More Than 100,000, October 1990

Country	Rate per Million
Bahamas	2,006
Guadaloupe	650
Trinidad and Tobago	540
Barbados	494
Martinique	409
Haiti	397
St. Vincent and the Grenadines	203
Dominican Republic	198
Grenada	170
Saint Lucia	120
Jamaica	66
Cuba	6.2

SOURCE: Jens J. Pindborg, Department of Oral Pathology, Royal Dental College, Copenhagen, Denmark, "Global Aspects of the AIDS Epidemic," *Oral Surgery, Oral Medicine, Oral Pathology*, 73 (1992): 139. Data in the table is based on the *WHO Weekly Epidemiological Record*, No. 40, October 5, 1990. Reprinted by permission.

TABLE 5.3   Cumulative Incidence of AIDS in Selected Countries, October 1990

Country	Rate per Million
Congo	1,021
Uganda	724
United States	589
Zaire	379
France	174
Canada	170
Spain	159
Australia	118
Brazil	77
U.K.	60
Mexico	53
Venezuela	46
Argentina	23
Cuba	6.2

SOURCE: Adapted from Jens J. Pindborg, Department of Oral Pathology, Royal Dental College, Copenhagen, Denmark, "Global Aspects of the AIDS Epidemic," *Oral Surgery, Oral Medicine, Oral Pathology*, 73 (1992): 139. Data in the table is based on the *WHO Weekly Epidemiological Record*, No. 40, October 5, 1990.

routine tests done in Cuba. Most people are probably not aware that their blood is being tested for the virus. Those who are screened in residential settings or at the workplace are aware only when the process is for the specific purpose of testing for the HIV virus. There have been reports of some people refusing to be tested.[39] These people are not forced to give a blood sample, but a great deal of peer pressure is put on them to do so from the mass organizations, the block committees, their family doctors and coworkers who believe strongly that cooperation with the testing program is for the common good.

Testing is supervised and checked by a national laboratory, although the administration and processing of the tests are carried out at the provincial level. If a sample tests positive, two or three additional tests are done to confirm the results. "Persons with borderline results are followed in the community under very strict confidentiality, providing them with intensive counseling and support, until a definitive diagnosis is reached."[40]

Research studies in the United States on the rate of false positives in testing procedures for HIV infection suggest that the data presented in Table 5.1 in all probability include false positives. Ronald Bayer and Cheryl Healton of the Columbia University School of Public Health believe they do: "With infection rates of .01 percent or less, even when stringent laboratory standards are maintained, one in 135,000 would be mistakenly designated as positive. More typical laboratory standards would produce much higher false positive rates. We estimate that among the seven low-infection groups tested in Cuba, between 21 and 53 persons may have been inaccurately considered positive as a result of testing."[41]

When Dr. Francisco Machado, head of Cuba's national laboratory conducting research on AIDS, was asked about the unjust quarantine of people, he responded, "I can publicly assure you that not a single person is unjustly quarantined in Cuba."[42] The reason he could be so categorical, he explained, was because in the last analysis of whether the diagnosis is negative, positive, or indeterminate, "we follow the criteria of the Center for Disease Control in Atlanta, Georgia, because we consider them as the best in the world."[43]

Public Fear and Ignorance

AIDS is not just an epidemic; it is also a social and political phenomenon. How an epidemic is understood in social and political terms, in turn, affects the disease's progress and its medical treatment. Thus, diseases are never simply medical problems. Epidemics, in particular, become the focus of social attitudes because they raise the spector of mass death.

In 1988 an article on AIDS in *Cuba International* began:

> Some months ago, the Buenos Aires magazine *Somos* told the story of an Argentine entrepeneur who went on a business trip to Brazil and who decided, before returning, to have a wild weekend. When he awoke on Monday morning, he found the girl he had spent the past two nights with gone. On the bathroom mirror he read with horror the following words written in lipstick: "Congratulations, you have just joined the AIDS brigade."
>
> Around the same time, the Madrid magazine *Tiempo* described in graphic detail the death of Tarim, a homosexual and make-up artist who had been a darling of the jet set.
>
> A Spanish writer, Sánchez Ocana, in his book *What Can I Do About AIDS?* has a whole chapter on the problems of homosexuality and drug addiction in Spanish jails, and says that the prison authorites now distribute condoms and hypodermic needles among the inmates to protect them from AIDS.
>
> Acquired Immune Deficiency Syndrome (AIDS) is both an individual and a collective issue. Thousands of scientists around the world are concentrating their energies on finding a cure for it. A U.S. doctor compared it to the "black plague" that killed a third of Europe's population in the 14th century.[44]

These few introductory paragraphs illustrate age-old attitudes common to many societies and many epidemics: that the disease is brought in by foreigners, that it is caused by moral corruption, that if no salvation is found total destruction will result.

Robert Swenson, an infectious disease specialist and immunologist with an interest in the history of epidemics, analyzed AIDS and other plagues in history with reference to what he calls the "internal anatomy of an epidemic"—that is, attitudes and behavior.[45] One of these identified attitudes is to place blame elsewhere for the epidemic.

> Once the epidemic is recognized, it follows quickly that someone (something else) is blamed for it. As bubonic plague swept through Europe in 1348, it was claimed that it was caused by Jews who had poisoned wells. As a result, thousands of Jews were burned at the stake. The cholera epidemics in the United States fell disproportionately on the poor. At that time, poverty was viewed as a consequence of idleness and intemperance. The latter was also clearly felt to make one more susceptible to cholera. Since new immigrants were often the most poor, they were blamed for their own susceptibility to cholera, as well as for bringing the disease into the country. Prostitutes were also blamed for the epidemic, even though cholera was not thought to be a venereal disease. Many felt that their "moral corruption" caused them, as well as their clients, to develop cholera.
>
> Blame would also be placed at a national level. After the initial outbreak of influenza in the United States, epidemics occurred in Spain, England, and France. In addition to attempting to deny their own epidemics, the countries blamed one another. The French referred to the epidemic as the Plague of the Spanish Lady, and the English called it the French Disease. (Even today we refer to the Asian Flu.)[46]

Fidel Castro himself followed this tradition in a September 1988 speech: "Who brought AIDS to Latin America? Who was the great AIDS vector in the Third World? Why are there countries like the Dominican Republic, with 40,000 carriers of the virus; and Haiti, and other countries of Central America and South America—high rates in Mexico, in Brazil and other countries? Who brought it? The United States, that's a fact."[47]

The foreign power that had militarily invaded Cuba in the past, that had made numerous assassination attempts on his life, that maintained hostile policies, could now easily be blamed for introducing the plague. This sense of an island under siege no doubt has contributed to the decision to control the disease through the drastic means of a quarantine.

The quarantine policy itself has contributed to the popular panic about AIDS. People feel, "We are all safe, as long as they are kept behind the sanitorium walls," and thus they support the quarantine policy. For example, when Alfaro Mendoza, a twenty-six-year-old graduate student, was told by his doctors that he should go to the sanitorium, a friend of his agreed: "It's too bad for him, but he got infected, and it's safer for everybody that he go; and it's safer for us."[48] Monika Krause notes that sanitorium isolation makes minimal educational campaigns even more difficult because the population now feels safe and no longer takes the threat of AIDS seriously.[49]

There is general ignorance about the difference between someone with AIDS and someone who has tested HIV-positive but is nevertheless a healthy person, who may never become ill with an AIDS-related disease. The quarantine does nothing to diminish this ignorance; in fact, the press often refers to sanitorium residents as "AIDS patients"—a phenomenon Susan Sontag has observed in the United States.

> The obvious consequence of believing that all those who "harbor" the virus will eventually come down with the illness is that those who test positive for it are regarded as people-with-AIDS, who just don't have it . . . yet. It is only a matter of time, like any death sentence. Less obviously, such people are often regarded as if they do have it. Testing positive for HIV, which usually means having been tested for the presence not of the virus but of antibodies to the virus, is increasingly being equated with being ill.[50]

Magic Johnson, one of the most accomplished players in basketball history, was aware of this when he announced publicly on November 7, 1991, that he had the HIV virus: "I want to make clear, first of all, that I do not have the AIDS disease, because a lot of you want to know that, but the HIV virus. . . . I plan on going on, living for a long time. . . . And I will now be a spokesman for the HIV virus because I want people, young people, to realize they can practice safe sex. . . . But I am going to deal with it and my life will go on."[51]

In 1986 most epidemologists estimated that the average period from infection to development of AIDS was between eight and nine years.[52] As noted above, in 1991, AIDS researchers such as Dr. Jerome Groopman of the New England Deaconess Hospital in Boston, reported that the median time is ten and one-half years, with some HIV positives not getting AIDS for fifteen to twenty years.

The question, however, is whether treatment requires quarantine. Using quarantine to deal with fear of an epidemic is not unique in public health history. Quarantining lepers is perhaps the oldest example and certainly the most well known.

By the thirteenth century in Europe, thousands of people diagnosed as lepers were being put in asylums located outside cities and towns. "The primary function of the leper house was to form a prison or, if we prefer the term, a compulsory isolation hospital, for the seclusion of the lepers from the general population."[53] In 1179, the Third Lateran Council not only called for living arrangements for lepers—which included provision for their own priest, cemetery, and chapel—but also spelled out rituals and ceremonies for the separation process. This church mandate updated the biblical passage in Leviticus, "The leper who has the disease shall wear torn clothes and let the hair of his head hang loose, and he shall cover his upper lip and cry, 'Unclean, unclean.' He shall remain unclean as long as he has the disease; he is unclean; he shall dwell alone in a habitation outside the camp."[54]

Leprosy was connected with sin and viewed as God's punishment for the leper's transgressions—including sexual promiscuity. "Leprosy in its early stages stirs the venereal appetite in a marked fashion."[55] As in Cuba today, medieval society emphasized both the mutual wisdom of the decision to quarantine and the community's promise to take care of the basic needs of those isolated people. It was a paternalistic policy for those who were being punished for their sins in a time when the causes of the disease were not known. People with leprosy were placed in quarantine in many countries well into the 20th century. Even now, at the end of the 20th century, some societies still isolate those with leprosy. And as Nancy Wexler explains in a study she calls "Learning to be a Leper," "A society's expectations for lepers, its beliefs about them, have a significant influence on their experiences as sick people. If we examine what a particular patient does when he discovers he has leprosy, we find that his response to leprosy is consistent with society's expecations for lepers. In fact, he learns to be a leper, the kind of leper his family and neighbors, even his doctors, expect him to be."[56]

There is a striking similarity in historical attitudes concerning syphilis, a disease which came to the notice of European physicians in the late fifteenth century. In 1909, Sir William Osler wrote that syphilis was seen in his day as: "a mysterious epidemic, hitherto unknown, which had struck terror into all hearts by the rapidity of its spread, the ravages it made, and the apparent helplessness of the physicians to cure it."[57]

Unlike leprosy, which actually spreads slowly and with difficulty, syphilis could spread quickly. While those who had it could be condemned as sinful and degenerate and considered outcasts and deviants, it was never possible anywhere to institute a quarantine for those with the disease. (Attempts were occasionally made, as when during the First World War "some thirty thousand American women—prostitutes, and women suspected of being prostitutes" were kept in detention camps behind barbed wire; the measure caused no drop in the military's rate of infection.)[58]

Machismo, the "Uncontrollable Force"

Two assumptions dominate the Cuban quarantine policy: First, people will always be irresponsible in terms of sex, and no policy of safe sex will work that relies on individual control. Second, education cannot change this behavior. Since, therefore, it is impossible to know which infected people can be trusted to behave responsibly, all must be treated as dangerous.

Both assumptions are rooted in macho mentality and have long been a barrier to controlling sexually transmitted diseases. Referring to nineteenth century England and venereal disease, Robert Swenson wrote:

> With the realization that these were sexually transmitted diseases with grave health consequences (mental illness and infertility, for example), it was recognized that there was a need for sex education; yet great obstacles existed to what became known as the social hygiene movement. First, the remaining tenets of Victorian respectability made it virtually impossible to discuss venereal diseases. The basic assumption was that men were driven by lust and that discussing sex with them would only make them more uncontrollable. The major question became, how can sex education be presented to men without their recognizing the subject? The answer was to include much talk about the plants, birds, bees, and little about sex. Given these subterfuges, there could be little effective sex education. Prince Morrow, a leader of the social hygiene movement, concluded, "Social sentiment holds that it is a greater violation of the properties of life publicly to mention venereal disease than privately to contract it."[59]

The idea that the male sexual urge is uncontrollable is shared by women, as well, where it prevails. This is why, in many societies, it has been the custom that an unmarried woman should never be alone with a man as he could not be expected to control himself. Speaking of a Cuban friend living in the Havana sanitorium, Bill Rowe, who served on the Emergency AIDS Task Force for the American Anthropological Association, discovered similar attitudes in Cuba regarding uncontrollable male sexual urges. His friend had tested HIV-positive but had no symptoms and reported "no negative health conditions." He was chaperoned by a medical student during his regular Sunday visits home. After speaking to the man's family and friends, Rowe reported that "the elderly ex-banker, heterosexual father of the household, his gay son, and his gay son's lover, all explained to me very forcefully that Cuban men would require that kind of chaperonage. That male sexuality was a totally uncontrollable force."[60]

Both the acceptance of irresponsible sex as a social norm and the limitations of the quarantine policy are painfully evident in interviews with some of the people confined to the sanitorium. A young man who is confined in the sanitorium, shares his experience.

> I think that the isolation is dreadful. It's dreadful. I understand it. There are cases where really I understand it because not everybody has "conciencia."

I say that, together with HIV, comes a heavy responsibility. There are people who simply do not have this "conciencia" and are really dangerous. I don't know; I have no idea how to solve this. I think it's difficult, but there must be a solution because we can't stay here all our lives. And, besides, nobody knows when people will get it, and so they can't spend their lives here. For example, the people who may live 10, 20 years . . . (Raúl, a resident in the Havana sanitorium, 1989)[61]

The assumption that male sexual behavior is unchangeable makes the quarantine policy, with its reliance on testing, seem the only solution. However, not only is it based on a false assumption about the accuracy of the "testing net," but recent research indicates new medical treatments that delay AIDS even further. On August 18, 1989, the director of the National Institute of Allergy and Infectious Diseases announced that a research study conducted by the Institute found that the drug AZT can delay the onset of AIDS in people who are infected with the virus but have no AIDS symptoms. The researchers reported that people taking the drug were half as likely to develop symptoms as those taking a dummy capsule.[62] These same researchers had earlier reported AZT success in delaying the onset of AIDS in people who already had mild symptoms of immune system damage.[63]

The research findings had exciting implications for HIV-positive people and health professionals working with the AIDS crisis. Jim Graham, an administrator of a large AIDS clinic in Washington, D.C., said that people had viewed HIV-positive results as a death sentence, but the new discovery showed that "with early diagnosis and treatment, there can be an extended life span at a quality level."[64] This data regarding the effectiveness of AZT in delaying symptoms in people such as those who are quarantined, (that is, asymptomatic HIV-positive people) further diminishes the logic behind the sanitorium.

In late 1984, the *Annals of Internal Medicine* reported that it can take more than three and one-half years before the body begins to produce antibodies detected by standard tests. This raises the specter of the HIV virus hiding in the body and evading easy detection longer than had been previously reported. The researchers, led by Dr. Steven Wolinsky of Northwestern University, said: The data from this study indicate that (the AIDS virus) can have a long and variable interval between virus infection and the manifestation of detectable immunological abnormalities.[65]

The accuracy of the Wolinsky report's findings for people who were found virus free has been questioned. Two and one-half years later, in the October 24, 1991, issue of the *New England Journal of Medicine*, the authors of the report have acknowledged that they have been unable to reproduce their results. Other researchers have found that the discovery of 23 percent error in gay men who tested positive is much too high. Analysis of available data suggests that most exposed individuals will develop antibody against the virus within a few months, and some as early as a few weeks after viral infection.[66]

Nevertheless, a person testing positive may remain without symptoms for years: Thus, there is no reason he or she cannot work. Thousands of such people throughout the world are working productively in their respective fields and, by adhering to safe health and sex practices, not infecting others. One young medical student who had chaperoned people to their homes on weekends told me that although sanitorium residents try to understand the logic behind the quarantine, they simply do not want to be there.

AIDS as a Homosexual Disease

In the Third World in general, AIDS is not primarily an epidemic within homosexual communities or among drug users. It is, by far, an epidemic spread through sexual contacts among heterosexuals—as in Cuba. In 1988 in Cuba almost half the people infected were heterosexual men, about a quarter were women, and another quarter were gay or bisexual men. However, by December 1, 1992, about 40 percent of HIV infections in Cuba were among gay men or bisexuals.

Reflecting these figures, the official position now is that AIDS cuts across gender, sexual preference, and age. Nonetheless, a strong popular view tends more often to associate homosexuality and AIDS. This perception grows out of pervasive homophobia but is encouraged by exposure to U.S. media reports, which often blame homosexuals for the AIDS epidemic. In the beginning, the Cuban press was not immune to this tendency.

In April 1986, the press reported that the first person to contract AIDS in Cuba was a homosexual theater producer who contracted the disease in New York City.[67] Also, in early educational programs on AIDS, the message was that if you were not gay, you had little to worry about. This position soon changed, and the emphasis has since been on AIDS as a disease, not a gay disease. As Lajonchere pointed out, even the first sex education video about AIDS carried the implicit message that if you were not gay, you were safe.[68] This opinion was supported by Dr. Juan Carlos Rexach, one of the physicians who is also an HIV-positive resident at the Havana sanitorium.[69] In 1988 when I asked several medical students what they thought the Cuban population perceived as the basis for AIDS, they responded that most people believe it stems from homosexual sex.

These Cuban attitudes are common worldwide. Just as in plagues and epidemics of old, foreigners and sex are blamed—in this case, homosexuality. During the 1980s, homosexuality and the United States were in first and second place in the blame campaign for AIDS. For example, in 1984, letters in the Australian press attacked American decadence as the source of AIDS and called for a ban on homosexuals traveling to the States. In Britain, AIDS was attributed to "homosexuals who have been on 'sex holidays' to America."[70] In Paris, the journal *Nouvel Observateur* had a headline on AIDS as the "curse which came from America."[71] In Arab countries, religious leaders and some governments portrayed AIDS as divine retribution for Western decadence. Presiding over police cadets at an AIDS Conference in February 1988, a health official in Kuwait, Ibrahim Al-Sayyad, offered a lurid description of gay bars in New York City and then quoted the prophet Muhammad: "When obscenity flourished among them, even in public, a plague appeared that their forefathers never knew."[72]

In the United States, the blame has been put on homosexuals, drug users, and Haitians.[73] Moreover, the U.S. government refuses to allow even temporary entry to foreigners infected with the virus on the grounds that letting them in would expose the country to public health risks and huge potential medical costs. Here the assumptions are that AIDS is a contagious disease, spread through casual contact, and that those infected become ill in a short period of time. The second and third assumptions are wrong. When the policy became an issue in May 1991, Dr. Jonathan Mann said, "a restriction on travel of people infected with the AIDS virus is inappropriate, unnecessary and unhelpful and would represent a clear victory for fear, misinformation and simplistic thinking over public health realities."[74] With the enormous number of AIDS cases in the United States at present, it is ludicrous to imagine that prohibiting a few foreigners will make any difference at all.

The obstacles to intelligent sex education are great enough in any modern society; they are even stronger in highly macho-oriented societies. Add to this the common heterosexual repression of homosexuals and homosexuality, and they are greater still. This is, I think, another important cause of the quarantine policy. AIDS is associated with homosexuality even in a country where the majority of virus carriers are heterosexual. The reality of the international spread of AIDS, especially AIDS in Central Africa, where the epidemic exists in proportionately large numbers, is that it is primarily found among heterosexuals. Even in the United States, "gays being first" with the disease is open to dispute and is connected to both class and racial issues and access to medical care. It is correct that American middle-class gay men were first observed as having AIDS and, of course, it has tragically affected large numbers of them. However, as Douglas Crimp, a gay activist and editor of *AIDS: Cultural Analysis/Cultural Activism*, points out:

Probably AIDS did not affect gay men first, even in the U.S. What is now called AIDS was seen in middle-class gay men in America, in part because of our access to medical care. Retrospectively, however, it apppears that IV drug users—whether gay or straight—were dying of AIDS in New York City throughout the 70s and 80s, but a class-based and racist health system failed to notice, and an epidemiology equally skewed by class and racial bias failed to begin to look until 1987.[75]

Like the Victorians' response to syphilis and gonorrhea, the Cubans are trying to deal with AIDS without having to talk publicly about sex. This massive avoidance culminates in a quarantine with people in isolation while state policy pronounces on the "common good." But the only way to control a sexually-transmitted virus is to educate people about it and its prevention—that is, "safe sex."

As the AIDS epidemic spread, so have public pronouncements on homosexual promiscuity and 'underground' meeting places for gay sex. This international phenomenon includes Cuba and is directly related to the oppression of gays. Historically, gays have had to express their sexual orientation covertly and to remain anonymous in respect to their real identity. Matthew Shebar, former legal director of the Gay Men's Health Crisis in New York, speaks about gay oppression and anonymity in the United States.

It must be recognized that there is a direct correlation between anonymity and oppression. When a parent discourages his gay son from being involved with another man, when a church refuses to accept gay congregants, when an employer says, "Just keep it out of the office," what they are really saying is, keep it in the bathhouses and backrooms, the places where one runs a higher risk of being infected. I think AIDS will lead gay people to rebel against this sort of oppression and to become more visibly committed to their gay identities and to their gay partners.[76]

Juan Carlos, at the Havana sanitorium, commented on being gay:

I think that, for example, heterosexuals have various opportunities and supportive surroundings in which to fulfill their sexuality. But the gays no. The gays do not have *posadas* [small hotels where a man and woman can rent a room for several hours]—for example, don't have other places to go—and this pushes gays to go into the underbrush, the public lavatories, and do a thousand other things that heterosexuals don't do. . . . How about the heterosexual *rascabuchadoras* [cruisers], the man in his car who drives around and meets a woman, who constantly is doing this—isn't this just as promiscuous? But the homosexual who has several relations is promiscuous because he is "always changing partners." Do you understand? It's simply a conceptual problem. It's the same.[77]

In the United States, education about AIDS and the whole safe sex campaign began within the gay community where there were already organized gay rights activists. Cindy Patton, in a striking and significant analysis of the AIDS epidemic, points out that it was the gay community that developed safe sex. The strategy came from both the feminist movement and gay liberation.

> At the 1987 lesbian and gay health conference in Los Angeles, many long-time AIDS activists were surprised by the extent to which safe sex education had become the province of high-level professionals. The fact that safe sex organizing began and is highly successful as a grassroots, community effort seemed to be forgotten. . . . Heterosexuals—and even gay people only beginning to confront AIDS—express panic about how to make appropriate and satisfying changes in their sex lives, as if no one had done this before them. It is a mark of the intransigence of homophobia that few look to the urban gay communities for advice, communities that have an infrastructure and a track record of highly succcessful behavior change.[78]

The gay community in the United States was able to use the experiences of the 1960s and 1970s, including the "sexual revolution," to save their lives. Douglas Crimp says:

> We were able to invent safe sex because we have always known that sex is not, in an epidemic, limited to penetrative sex. Our promiscuity taught us many things, not only about the pleasures of sex, but about the great multiplicity of those pleasures. It is that psychic preparation, that experimentation, that conscious work on our own sexualities that has allowed many of us to change our sexual behaviors—something that brutal "behavior therapies" tried unsuccessfully for over a century to force us to do—very quickly and dramatically.[79]

In fact, the education and preventative campaigns against AIDS in the United States seem to have resulted in a far greater degree of behavior change than any other health campaign ever documented in public health literature.[80]

Cuba's Authoritarian Government

Visitors to the Cuban sanitoriums report seeing healthy-looking people—in most cases asymptomatic—in a confined residence, not working at their trained occupation but "serving time," no matter how "pleasant" the surroundings. One report in *Granma* on the Havana sanitorium showed a picture of a man and woman walking on a road with the caption: "It's difficult to tell patients from workers because most seem strong and healthy."[81] But one of the "patients" revealed the difference.

At first it was rough; they didn't tell me I was sick until I got here. Now it's better. I share this house with my wife and work in the carpentry and refrigeration department when I feel like it. What I want most is for time to pass so I can go home (about 160 kilometers from Havana). I have nothing to complain about concerning the way I'm treated. There are a lot of people from my home town who joke and say I'm not sick, that I'm living off the government.[82]

The workers can go home at night. They have control over their own lives denied to the "patients." The possibility of the residents doing some kind of work within the sanitorium was one of the reforms instituted at Los Cocos by the new director who took over in early 1989. For four of the residents who are doctors, it meant they could at least continue to practice medicine within the sanitorium. One of them expressed what a vast improvement that was:

Something else I saw in the director, and it's very important. He believes in people. He believes in us. . . . One of the things I observed was that, from the moment we had AIDS (sic), we became "irresponsible" people, people who had no reason to be . . . we were completely nullified socially, intellectually; and he, he believes in us and gives us opportunities to grow, to do something useful. . . . when he called me to talk and see if I would like to work, I asked, "Is it true?" . . . at first I endeavored to see if it were true, if I really was going to be a doctor in this institution. They simply showed me that, yes, I have my own patients; I have everything, and I work as a doctor.

Now, the only thing that's missing is to demonstrate that we have "conciencia," that we are normal people equal to everyone else, that we can work, that we can lead a social life like other people and conduct ourselves as we have and as many people in the streets who don't have AIDS do.[83]

The physician, Juan Carlos, also prepared a written statement on the quarantine policy, parts of which I reproduce below. (Omitted are descriptions already incorporated in this chapter.) Following the statement is a transcript of part of a conversation between Juan Carlos and another young man confined to the sanitorium. The contrast is revealing. The statement is very careful and does not question policies. Not that he does not believe what he is writing, but unlike the conversation, his writing does not reflect his real anguish and awareness that an alternative is possible.

There is a great difference between the sanitorium's past and present from the point of view of isolation. At the beginning, we found ourselves almost totally isolated from society because the visits from relatives were restricted, because the means of transmission were not completely known.

This isolation lasted a few months, and a system of passes and structured leaves was estabished and perfected over time.

We must take into account that the population of the sanitorium is heterogeneous and constitutes a micro-society in which there are people fully aware of the situation—who feel a tremendous social responsibility. But, on the other hand, it is certain that we don't all think alike, and that is why any patient leaving the sanitorium is accompanied by health department personnel who will prevent sexual contact and foresee any possible incident. With experience, it has been decided to attempt to modify this system of leaves, taking into account individual character and the degree of social responsibility acquired for each one of the patients.

Inside the sanitorium, all the conditions exist to make possible a restful life. Participation in sports and adequate nutrition are provided. We go to the beach and the movies regularly as well as museums and recreational centers. But, of course, admission to the sanitorium is a radical change in our lives and in one aspect that I consider fundamental: It cuts us off from work. Although we can fill the free time with other activities, it just leaves a vacuum and longing for the work we were trained for. At present, this is a concern for everybody—patients, MINSAP, the government. There is an attempt at connecting patients with work so we can feel socially useful.

I must also say that the stay in the sanitorium permits better medical care, and I must emphasize that this is the only country in the world where detected HIV carriers are checked regularly whether they are healthy or sick. This makes greater survival possible. I think that, with the little I have explained, you can get a brief idea of our sanitorium from its beginnings— how it evolved in its efforts to improve and achieve its goal with a more humane perspective. In a certain way, it has protected us from rejection from society when it was believed that AIDS was a disease afflicting only homosexual and drug addicts or, to be more precise, people with an incorrect social conduct.[84]

Juan Carlos and his friend Raúl both advocate treating the problem of AIDS and HIV by keeping certain aspects of the sanitorium system, specifically as a center for HIV checkups and medical treatment of HIV-positive people. But they also want those who test HIV-positive to be treated with the same dignity as other people. They want to live normally. In this conversation, they debate the question of their rights and the ability of patients to leave the sanitorium—the problem of those who are irresponsible and therefore "dangerous to others":

Raúl: This behavior today (forming couples, avoiding bathrooms, etc.) is intelligent, and they must also contact the sanitorium to get treatment. But they must also be integrated into society, like a diabetic who works everyday, like someone with high blood pressure, like—I don't know—like any sick person, sensibly and simply.

I would agree that we are here for medical care ... but for me, on the human aspect I also think we need to be outside, go to the movies, and do other things. Do you want to have a mark on a part of your body?

Juan: But why not? Look, I was thinking ...

Raúl: So we can be outside and be free?

Juan: At some point I thought: "Look, put on my I.D. that I am an HIV CARRIER."

Rául: No, Chico, that's useless.

Juan: Wait a minute, let me explain. I would prefer to have a really big placard in front of me saying: "HIV POSITIVE" and be on the street than be confined. I don't care if I have AIDS and that people know that I have AIDS and want to look at me or not. I don't care about that because the people I'm interested in treat me according to my politics, my personality.

But my great anger is about all this effort I made to develop a career and that all of that was suddenly, completely destroyed. I have not been able to develop myself socially. If they want me to wear a big poster, right here in front. ...

It seems to me that you're exaggerating a little ... there are people who will never be able to leave this place. It's the same as the thief that spends his life stealing and, therefore, must be kept in jail. Please, that's evident. It's evident. It's his way.

Moreover, when you sit down to talk with people here, you can classify all those who should not leave this place. You're sure that they have to stay here. Unfortunately, it has to be so. If they're not here, they're going to be put in jail or be locked up somewhere else. You have to understand, they are people who socially contribute nothing. ... there's something else. Here there are many people whom I think ... it is a question of a psychological approach ... who just are not responsible, who think they are not sick, that they're not dangerous. But if these people were persuaded, were made sensitive to the problem they have, then I think they could be outside.[85]

Providing the possibility for work within the sanitorium was certainly an important advance in the patient's quality of life. Apparently there has been some further reform. Dr. Hector Terry was quoted in a *Granma International* article saying, "Several of our hospitalized AIDS patients go to their jobs daily and sleep in the sanitorium. As time goes by, the restrictions could become more flexible, but it will all depend on how responsible each patient proves to be. I reiterate that our responsibility as the government is to protect all citizens."[86]

But most of the 703 people confined to a sanitorium do not have the possibility of meaningful work and cannot go out to jobs. No matter how much institutional life is cloaked with a "children's camp" style of recreational activities, such as trips to the beach and the movies, the basic condition of life is confinement and enforced passivity—waiting for death or the Big Cure, being "saved by world science," in Dr. Terry's words. The extensive health care that prolongs the lives of people carrying HIV is commendable, but these are basically healthy people who are being treated by the medical establishment as though they were sick—patients who cannot be expected to exercise any control over their lives. Those who have succumbed to opportunistic cancers and infections because of their immune deficiency are certainly patients, but being the carrier of a virus does not make one so. Yet Dr. Terry himself refers to residents of a sanitorium, who have only tested HIV-positive, as "hospitalized AIDS patients."

Cuban government spokesmen perpetuate the myth that "there is no other alternative to quarantine." However, there is an alternative. Dr. Jonathan Mann, former director of the World Health Organization's program on AIDS said when asked about the Cuban quarantine program: "We don't think well of it. In fact, the World Health Organization has very strong policies, including a resolution passed by the latest world health assembly, that specifically state that discrimination against people who are infected should not be allowed . . . people lose confidence in the ability to educate and would rather have confidence in laws or in jails."[87]

In July 1989, at a meeting sponsored by WHO and the UN Commission on Human Rights, H. Daniel, a Brazilian revolutionary who spent seven years in political exile, made public a letter he had written to Fidel Castro. As a follower of Che Guevara and a person with AIDS, Daniel wrote that there were no possible arguments to defend Cuba's quarantine policies "except for those based on the most reactionary forms of prejudice against gays" that will, in the end, be "counterproductive." In his letter, he spoke first of Brazil, where,

> From the beginning, the AIDS epidemic was not taken seriously by our authorities. And, up to this day, there is nothing close to a national program to control the epidemic and assist those with AIDS, even though Brazil is one of the countries most affected by this illness in the world. Beyond this, old prejudices against gays are added to the new stigmas that mark this recent global epidemic, stigmas which marginalize the person with AIDS. Deprived of basic human rights, the person with AIDS experiences a de facto civil death.

H. Daniel then contrasted that with Cuba:

> I have followed with great sorrow the Cuban initiatives in relation to AIDS. From Cuba especially, I hoped for a great example in the search for solutions to this very grave public health problem. Cuba could take pride

in its health system. Could, if it weren't for the way it treats those who are HIV seropositive, whether sick or not, burying them in an isolation which has no technical justification, which goes against all scientific advice and which seriously infringes on human rights.

Cuba has used, in an abusive manner, compulsory HIV tests and has incarcerated those who test positively. Thus Cuba seeks to combat the virus by combating those people whom the virus attacked. In this way, Cuba is defeated by the HIV virus and by the ideological virus of prejudice and discrimination. There are no possible arguments to defend these positions, except for those based on the most reactionary forms of prejudice against gays.

Certainly Cuba will soon discover that these measures are counterproductive. People with AIDS will be placed in the position of enemies, even more difficult to locate, and the epidemic will *not* be overcome. The only result will be to impose absurd suffering on those who today could easily contribute to control of the epidemic, as has been happening in other countries of the world.

Daniel concludes his letter with a plea:

In my name, in the name of the 10 million people with AIDS across the world, of their families and friends, in the name of all who believe in life as an act of freedom, I ask you, compañero Fidel, to change the Cuban AIDS program. First, it is necessary to free those political prisoners. Second, it is necessary to implement a program based on the revolutionary principle of solidarity.

I sincerely hope that Cuba will not permit itself to be defeated by prejudice.

H. Daniel
Rio de Janeiro, Brazil[88]

The experience of people with AIDS in Brazil and many other countries is similar to that in the United States. Douglas Crimp expresses it so well:

Most people dying of AIDs are very young, and those of us coping with these deaths, ourselves also young, have confronted great loss entirely unprepared. The number of deaths are unthinkable: lovers, friends, acquaintances, and community members have fallen ill and died. Many have lost upwards of a hundred people. . . .

Through the turmoil imposed by illness and death, the rest of society offers little support or even acknowledgment. On the contrary, we are blamed, belittled, excluded, derided. We are discriminated against, we lose our housing and jobs and are denied medical and life insurance. Every public agency whose job it is to combat the epidemic has been slow to act, failed entirely, or been deliberately counterproductive. We have therefore had to provide our own centers for support, care, and education, and even fund our own treatment research. We have had to rebuild our devastated community and culture, reconstruct our sexual relationships, reinvent our sexual pleasure.[89]

In the United States the fight is against not only the sex and racial prejudices of society, but a government whose policies demonstrate deep disregard for those on the bottom. Thus, the Cuban officials argue that their policy is more just for all. When Vice-Minister Terry was asked about Cuba's position on human rights and AIDS, he defended it and juxtaposed the United States' neglect of people with AIDS:

To respond to this question, it seems very important to define our concepts of discrimination, exclusion, and human rights. . . .

In Cuba, nobody lacks economic resources because of being an AIDS carrier. In Cuba, no one dies abandoned on the streets for lack of access to a hospital. In Cuba, we haven't had to open hospices so that patients who have been abandoned have a place to die in peace. In Cuba, no one's house has been set on fire because its inhabitants are people with AIDS. In Cuba, no homosexual has been persecuted because he's assumed to be likely to spread the virus. In Cuba, we don't have the problem of national minorities or drug addicts with high rates of AIDS.

Our country has more than 10 million inhabitants, all of whom are guaranteed the right to health care, and that is why the immense majority of the population backs the AIDS Prevention and Control Program. Therefore, our concept of human rights is in no way incompatible with that of the WHO. We are convinced that we are respecting the rights of those who are ill with AIDS or carrying the virus, and we are protecting the rights of the immense majority of the population that is still healthy.[90]

The Cuban government claims great success for its quarantine policy—"the proportion of carriers to patients is 5.4 to 1, as compared to an estimated 60–100 to 1 in countries where no checks exist"[91]—and proudly acknowledges that the country stands alone with its AIDS policy.

No other country in the world is concerned with checking its seropositive patients. This is so because other countries are either unable to do it from the practical point of view or for economic or social reasons. The fact is that they don't know who the seropositive cases are and so the figures they report are estimates based on studies of representative groups. . . . As a result, no direct action is being taken to avoid the sexual transmission of the disease that, as we know, is the most common means and the one responsible for the pandemic dissemination the virus has acquired. The strategy of isolating patients and carriers under a sanitorium regime is justified from the epidemiological point of view, provided that it is possible to detect most of the cases; otherwise, the effect this would have on the sexual transmisssion of the HIV would be cancelled out by transmission among undetected cases.

The main usefulness of this measure is to slow down the epidemic progression of the disease to allow time for other measures of disease control to have a medium- or long-time effect.[92]

Four years later, on December 1, 1992, Dr. Terry underscored again that the six-year-old quarantine policy "has protected the vast majority of the Cuban people, including those with AIDS." The director of the AIDS Advice and Information Center in Havana, Dr. Giselle Sanabria, reported that 98 percent of the HIV-positive persons (the 703 people in the sanitoriums) contracted the virus through sexual relations. 41 percent were homosexual or bisexual while 57 percent were heterosexual. The other 2 percent were infected by blood transfusions, most of them in 1986 before the introduction of careful controls. There are no reports of any drug related cases.[93]

In their rush to quarantine, the Cubans have edited out one important, but crucial, point: *it is possible to prevent new infections.* Unlike epidemics in earlier historical periods, *we do know how AIDS is transmitted.* These behaviors are identifiable and recognizable. Because of this, it is possible to prevent the spread of the virus. It requires information and education programs in all countries.[94]

However, in most countries, including Cuba, the taboo subject of sexual practices—especially homosexual ones—is part of old inhibitions that have not been shed. The minimalist Cuban AIDS educational campaign is aimed entirely at heterosexuals and ignores the increase in HIV infections among homosexuals. Of course, behavioral change through education is not easy, especially when education means little more than advertising campaigns and catchy slogans. A follow-up study on one such campaign in the United States indicated that 60 percent of those originally influenced by the advertisements only occasionally used a condom.[95]

Role of Education

In the United States, there has been a strong reaction by people with AIDS to the media's use of the term "victim" to describe them. This reaction stems not from semantic quibbling but from the reality that, as with "victims" of rape, there is the public suspicion that people with AIDS were "asking for it." For them, the term victim brings with it emotions of fear and pity. These emotions in regard to AIDS imply a fatalism that almost nothing can be done about the epidemic and, therefore, no one is responsible for doing anything.[96]

The Cuban government must be, as Dr. Terry says, responsible for protecting all citizens as the greater good. In seeing the health of all citizens as a government responsibility, Cuba is far superior to most governments. Certainly it is lunatic to expect anywhere that there would never be conflicts between the good of particular individuals and the good of the whole society. But Cuba's benevolent, paternalistic, and authoritarian approach means that if the government starts out on a wrong path, it will continue down it. There is no ongoing correcting mechanism, except for great lurching changes made by the people at the top when they come to realize a terrible mistake has been made.

In the case of AIDS, which concerns people's intimate lives, it is crucial to put education at the center of all policies. Only through sex education can a primarily sexually-transmitted virus be controlled without having to resort to measures that deny basic human rights.

In Cuba, the best alternative to quarantine is *not* an advertising campaign but rather a full educational program within all sectors of the society involving schools, newspapers, television, all the mass organizations, and the armed forces—that is, within the entire political and cultural structure. It would use what Cubans call nonpejoratively "propaganda." The appeal would be equivalent to the "battle" focus of the literacy campaign. Pride in bringing down the infection rate would be dependent *not* on banning people to Los Cocos or one of the other sanitoriums, but rather on the very *conciencia* and revolutionary spirit that had been tapped since 1959 for other educational campaigns and emergencies.

The content of this campaign would have to include *human relations, love, and sexuality—including an awareness of homosexuality* that goes beyond the stereotypes perpetuated in Cuban society and other countries. My experience of Cuba's effective and highly organized education campaigns suggests that the country has the capacity and the history to effectively overcome this most difficult health problem without a barbaric quarantine—*if* the top leadership can put aside its own homophobia, machismo, and fear of losing control. The Cubans even have the embryo of organizational structure for this battle in GNTES with its dynamic, knowledgeable leaders.[97]

A most important first step would be to break the taboo on gays speaking publicly as gays. The experience of gay grass roots organizations in other countries could be an invaluable source in developing an educational campaign to combat AIDS.

Countering machismo and changing sexual behavior means explicit sex talk and promotion of condom use—a cultural revolution far more difficult than instituting a quarantine. Talking to teenagers about sex and sexual practices makes adults uncomfortable. This cultural revolution would have to confront the myth that men's sexual urge is uncontrollable and unable to change.

The frame of this analysis of Cuban policy is François Delaporte's bold statement based on his study of the cholera epidemic of 1832 and applied to the current epidemic. "I assert, to begin with, that 'disease' does not exist. It is therefore, illusory to think that one 'can develop' beliefs about it, to 'respond' to it. What does exist is not disease, but practices."[98] This does not mean that illness is a myth. We are all familiar with the suffering and death connected to disease. What the statement means in our context is that:

> AIDS does not exist apart from the practices that conceptualize it, represent it, and respond to it. We know AIDS only in and through these practices. This assertion does not contest the existence of viruses, antibodies, infections, or transmission routes. Least of all does it contest the reality of illness, suffering, and death. What it *does* contest is the notion that there is an underlying reality of AIDS, upon which are constructed the representations, or the culture, or the politics of AIDS. If we recognize that AIDS exists only in and through these constructions, then hopefully we can also recognize the imperative to know them, analyze them, and wrest control of them.[99]

The use of a quarantine prevents people with the virus from making tough choices about the remaining years of their lives. With such a horrifying diagnosis, what does one do? The Cuban government makes a paternalistic decision for its citizens who have tested HIV-positive. They go to a sanitorium for the rest of their lives. If they are deemed "responsible," furloughs will be extended.

The key to change is a combination of knowledge and empowerment. I am speaking of the psychological belief in one's ability to make necessary behavioral changes—in this case, to reduce the risk of getting AIDS. This ability has been called *self-efficacy* in recent literature in psychology. Knowledge about AIDS is important, but not enough. *Self-efficacy* has emerged as a crucial differentiating factor. In a study of AIDS among Black and Hispanic men, John Peterson and Gerardo Marín state that:

> Whether minority gay men consider themselves at risk for AIDS or not, they are still unlikely to engage in safe sexual activities unless they believe they are capable of making the necessary behavioral changes to reduce their risk for AIDS. In this view of self-efficacy, for homosexual men to engage in AIDS prevention, they must believe they are able to reduce their risk of exposure to the AIDS virus. Stated differently, if minority gay men do not feel that they have the ability to follow safe sex guidelines, then they will probably ignore those recommendations and continue with high-risk behaviors. Knowledge of AIDS and perceptions of susceptibility to AIDS

are insufficient to predict adoption of health behaviors unless gay men *believe*that they are able to perform these behaviors. [Italics mine][100]

Antihomosexual attitudes often prevent many men in the United States from either receiving AIDS information or accepting it if received. Also, those working with people with AIDS in Latino communities suggest that the best approaches are those emphasizing verbal communications, community-wide information campaigns, and messages from relatives and friends, instead of more anonymous media propaganda efforts.[101]

It has also been pointed out that a safe sex campaign would have to take into account that many men engage in sex with both male and female partners during relatively close periods of time. They do not see themselves as homosexuals.[102]

Among the determining factors of heterosexual and homosexual behavior are *community norms and normative behaviors*. Social scientists have documented that group norms affect individual behavior choices and thus can influence disease prevention, i.e., people conform to the social norms of their reference group or social network. Cubans who accent the "uncontrollable sexual urge" of Cuban men are, in essence, saying that the group norm of attitudes held by men, cannot be influenced or changed. Thus, in reference to AIDS, group norms may reject the use of condoms during sex, and individuals will conform to such group values because they fear social sanctions for non-conformity.[103]

Also, some research has indicated that general group norms and values such as machismo may affect risk-taking behavior. Appearing to be concerned about AIDS is inconsistent with "machismo" values.[104] This means that, for change to occur, there must be changes in social agreements among members of a society. Therefore, essential to AIDS prevention is *freedom to assemble* and form political and social organizations of choice.

One must remember that, for gays, "coming out" and gathering publicly as gays has historically been difficult, even in relatively more open societies. It is still inhibited by the reality of discrimination and prejudice, not only in social situations, but in employment, housing, health, the armed services, community, and family circles. Such discrimination continues to this day almost everywhere.[105]

Notes

1. Some people call AIDS "full blown AIDS"; in this text *HIV positive* will be used for people who have tested positive for the HIV virus. It is not only redundant to use language like "full blown AIDS" but such language implies that HIV positive tested people have AIDS, which is not true. If they come down with AIDS, then they will be people with AIDS.

2. *Primer Seminario Sobre Infección Por VIH y SIDA en Cuba, Octubre 30 y 31, 1992: Libro de Resumenes* (Havana: Sanitorio Santiago de Las Vegas, Ministerio de Salud Pública, 1992), 1; Reuters International Dispatch (Havana: Reuters, 14:42, December 1, 1992); Dr. Hector Terry, Vice Minister of Public Health, *Radio Havana Report on AIDS in Cuba*, February 28, 1993.

Also see: Carlos Cabrera, "Fight against Death," *International Granma*, April 7, 1991, 8. This is one of the lowest AIDS infection rates in the world and the lowest in Latin America. *Newsday*, "Cuba's AIDS Success," April 10, 1991; Robert Collier, "AIDS: Cuba's Quarantine," *Newsday*, May 2, 1989, Discovery section, 3; also see Ronald Bayer and Cheryl Healton, Special Report: "Controlling AIDS in Cuba: The Logic of the Quarantine," *The New England Journal of Medicine*, April 13, 1989, 1022–1024; Sarah Santana, "AIDS in Cuba," *Cuba Update*, Summer 1989: 23–25.

3. The Cuban Ministry of Health states that the special treatment and diets have extended the average survival rate to seven years. Dr. Hector Terry, public health deputy minister, as quoted in Carlos Cabrera, "Fight Against Death," 8; see Gina Kolata, "Studies Cite 10.5 Years From Infection to Illness," *New York Times*, November 8, 1991, B12.

4. "The AIDS Battle: Tempered by Experience," *Cuba Update*, Summer 1991: 23–24.

5. Bayer and Healton, "Controlling AIDS," 1023; Santana, "AIDS in Cuba," 23.

6. Carlos Cabrera, "On the Frontiers of AIDS," *Weekly Granma*, December 10, 1989, 12.

7. Interview with Cuban Ministry of Health (MINSAP) officials, February 1988.

8. Cabrera, "On the Frontiers of AIDS," 12.

9. Karen Wald, "Cuban Health Official Talks About AIDS Policy," *Cuba Update*, Summer 1989: 26.

10. Karen Wald, "Questions and Answers on AIDS in Cuba," (unpublished interview with Dr. Hector Terry, 1989).

11. Bayer and Healton, "Controlling AIDS," 1023; MINSAP, February 1988 interview; Cabrera, "On the Frontiers of AIDS," 12.

12. Santana, "AIDS in Cuba," 24. It appears very few people have earned this special privilege; for summaries of scientific papers presented at the October 1992 Havana "First Seminar on HIV Infections and AIDS in Cuba" see *Primer Seminario Sobre Infección Por VIH*, 1–45; see Robert Bazell, "Happy Campers," *The New Republic*, March 9, 1992, 12, 14.

In June, 1993 the Cuban government announced a further easing of its quarantine policy. After six months of quarantine and "political education" individuals deemed trustworthy will be allowed to live "freely as long as they behave properly." Those who cannot qualify will continue to stay in the sanitorium with weekend passes by chaperone "until they modify their conduct." Radio Havana Cuba, "Cuba's New AIDS Policy," June 21, 1993; Laurie Garrett, "Cuba Institutes a Freer AIDS Policy," *New York Newsday*, August 3, 1993, 53, 59.

13. "The AIDS Battle," *Cuba Update*, Summer 1991: 23–24; Garrett, "Cuba Institutes Freer AIDS Policy," 59.

14. Cabrera, "On the Frontiers of AIDS," 12.

15. *Sideroso:* a term taken from the Spanish word for AIDS—Sida.

16. Karen Wald, "Visits to the Sanitorium" (Los Cocos, Havana; unpublished interviews, July 1989).

17. Santana, "AIDS in Cuba," 23.

18. Ministry of Health Officials (MINSAP) interview, February 1988.

19. Ministry of Health (MINSAP) interview, 1988.

20. Cabrera, "On the Frontiers of AIDS," 12.

21. Hector Terry in Wald, "Questions and Answers."

22. Margaret Gilpin, "Cuba: On the Road to a Family Medicine NATION," *Family Medicine* 21 (November–December 1989): 405; Robert Ubell, "High Tech Medicine in the Caribbean," *New England Journal of Medicine* 309 (December 1983): 1468; Julie Feinsilver, "Cuba As a 'World Medical Power': The Politics of Symbolism," *Latin American Research Review* 24 (1989): 1–33.

23. Harry Nelson, "Overmedicated?: An Excess of Success May Ail Cuba's Top-Flight Health Care System," *Cuba Update*, November 1991: 33–34 (originally published in *Los Angeles Times*, July 22, 1991); also see Feinsilver, "Cuba As A World Medical Power."

24. Jeanne Smith and Sergio Piomelli, "Letters: The War on AIDS," *New York Times*, January 22, 1989, 24E.

25. Sarah Santana, "AIDS in Cuba: The AIDS Program," *Cuba Update*, Summer 1989: 23.

26. Paula A. Treichler, "AIDS and HIV Infection in the Third World: A First World Chronicle," in Elizabeth Fee and Daniel M. Fox, eds., *AIDS: The Making of a Chronic Disease* (Berkeley: University of California Press, 1992), 392; see also Hector Terry in Wald, "Questions and Answers"; see also Elizabeth Fee, "Sex Education in Cuba: An Interview With Dr. Celestino Lajonchere," *International Journal of Health Services*, 18, no. 2 (1988), 343–56; Nicholas Wade, "Cuba's Quarantine For AIDS: A Police State's Health Experiment," *New York Times*, editorial, February 6, 1989, A14.

27. Bruce Lambert, "The Best AIDS Programs Are Too Few for Too Many," *New York Times*, June 15, 1990, B4.

28. Lawrence K. Altman, "AIDS-Focused New Parties Are Proposed at Conference," *New York Times*, July 20, 1992, A2; "Health and Science: Troubling Dispatches From the AIDS Front," *TIME*, August 3, 1992, 28,30; also see Laurie Garrett, "AIDS Global Spread," *New York Newsday*, June 26, 1990, 4; "World HIV: 5,000 a Day, 75% Straight," *New York Newsday*, November 12, 1991, 13.

29. Jonathan Mann, Daniel J. M. Tarantola, and Thomas W. Netter, eds., *AIDS in the World 1992* (Cambridge: Harvard University Press, 1992), 2–3, 5–6; also see: Jonathan Mann, "Detecting the Next Pandemic," *Scientific American*, March 1991; Masha Gessen, "Mann the Torpedoes," *The Advocate*, July 30, 1992, 42–43; also see Laurie Garrett, "Report from the AIDS Front," *New York Newsday*, July 28, 1992, 51, 56–58; Philip Shenon, "After Years of Denial, Asia Faces Scourge of AIDS," *New York Times*, November 8, 1992, 1, 12; James Sterngold, "Japan Confronts Sudden Rise in AIDS," *New York Times*, November 8, 1992, 13.

The current head of WHO's global AIDS program, Dr. Michael Merson, is more conservative in his estimate of the spread of the AIDS epidemic. He predicts 40 million people will be HIV infected in the year 2000 instead of the 40 to 110 million predicted by Jonathan Mann and his colleagues of the AIDS Center at Harvard and authors of *AIDS in the World 1992;* see Lawrence K. Altman, "Researchers Report Much Grimmer AIDS Outlook," *New York Times,* June 4, 1992, A1.

30. "Symposium," *Postgraduate Medicine/HIV Worldwide,* 91, no. 8, June 1992, 99–100; Jonathan Mann, "AIDS: The Second Decade: A Global Perspective," *Journal of Infectious Diseases,* 1992; 165 (2), 245–50; John Gallagher, "In the Dark About AIDS," *The Advocate,* July 30, 1992, 37–41; for earliest citations of what is now called AIDS: see Centers for Disease Control, "Kaposi's Sarcoma and *Pneumocystis* Pneumonia Among Homosexual Men: New York City and California," MMWR, 1981:30 (25), 305–8.

For strong reaction from Third World delegates to the 1992 Amsterdam International Conference on AIDS, see Laurie Garrett, "Global Actions Urged to Contain Aids 'Volcano'," *New York Newsday,* June 17, 1991, 6; also see *Lancet,* July 1990; *In These Times,* May 29–June 11, 1991.

31. "Symposium," *HIV WORLDWIDE,* 100; Gina Kolata, "For Heterosexuals, Diagnosis of AIDS is Often Unmercifully Late," *New York Times,* 32; see table in same article entitled "Risk Patterns for AIDS: An Emerging Picture" (Sources of data: Centers for Disease Control and the New York City Department of Health); Gallagher, "In the Dark about AIDS," 39; *New England Journal of Medicine,* January 1992.

32. Lambert, "Best Aids Programs,"*New York Times,* June 15, 1990, B4.

33. In New York City, the scope of AIDS is staggering. If there is no cure in the near future, epidemiologists predict that the total AIDS cases in that city will reach 64,000 by 1994. AIDS activists think that this figure is an understatement.

On February 4, 1991, the Citizen's Commission on AIDS estimated that 130,000 to 170,000 people have the HIV virus in New York City. Catherine Woodward, "Panel Warns of Apathy About AIDS," *New York Newsday,* February 5, 1991, 21; Bruce Lambert, "Koch's Record on AIDS: Fighting a Battle Without a Precedent," *New York Times,* August 27, 1989, 30.

34. Carlos Cabrera, "AIDS: Fight Against Death," *International Granma,* April 7, 1991, 8.

35. Marlise Simons, "A Latin AIDS Meeting Opens its Ears to What Was Once Unmentionable," *New York Times,* January 16, 1989, A6; Collier, "Cuba's Quarantine," 3.

36. Santana, "AIDS in Cuba," 23.

37. Karen Wald, "AIDS in Cuba: A Dream or a Nightmare?" *Z Magazine,* December 1990, 104–109.

38. Carlos Cabrera, "Fight Against Death," 8; Dr. Abelardo Martínez, Prof. Hector de Arazoza, Dr. José Joanes, Dr. Rigoberto Torres, Dr. Jorge Pérez, "*Comportamiento del SIDA en Cuba Hasta 30–de Septiembre, 1992,"* in *Primer Seminario Sobre Infección por VIH y SIDA en Cuba,* 1.

39. Santana, "AIDS in Cuba," 23.

40. Ibid.

41. Bayer and Healton, "Controlling AIDS in Cuba," 1023.

42. Cabrera, "Fight Against Death," 8.

43. The respect for the capacity of the United States to offer high standards in technology and the sciences went beyond Dr. Machado's statement about the Center for Disease Control being the "best in the world." In spite of the blockade, but with much hardship (sometimes getting materials via Canada and Europe) Cuban educators did learn about some of the curriculum changes in U.S. public schools. For example, I was surprised in 1969 when I interviewed Dr. María de Carmen Nuñoz Berro. In charge of introducing a modern mathematics program from kindergarten through senior high school, she was familiar with and favorably impressed by such U.S. mathematics programs as the Greater Cleveland Program and the Madison Program. And, as indicated earlier, the sex educators in GNTES were familiar and articulate about John Money, Helen Singer Kaplan, and other U.S. experts on sex education.

44. Ciro Bianchi Ross, "To Contain AIDS," *Cuba International*, January 1988, 8.

45. Robert Swenson, "Plagues, History, and AIDS," *The American Scholar* 57 (Spring 1988): 188.

46. Ibid.

47. Fidel speech in *Granma*, September 1988.

48. Collier, "Cuba's Quarantine," 3; Dr. Hector Terry, Vice Minister of Public Health "admitted that AIDS education has been one of weakest links in the island's AIDS program. There is still much to be done, he said, to get the message across to people by making more effective use of the mass media." Dr. Hector Terry, *Radio Havana Report on AIDS*, February 28, 1993.

49. Wald, "A Dream or a Nightmare," 106.

50. Susan Sontag, *AIDS and Its Metaphors* (New York: Farrar, Strauss and Giroux, 1989), 32.

51. Laurie Garrett, "'It Can Happen To Anybody, Even Me': Opening Eyes to the Risks," *Newsday*, November 8, 1991, 4; Richard Stevenson, "Magic Johnson Ends His Career, Saying He Has AIDS Infection," *New York Times*, November 8, 1991, 1.

52. Jonathan M. Mann et al., "The International Epidemiology of AIDS," *Scientific American* 259 (October 1986): 88, Gina Kolata, "Studies Cite 10.5 Years From Infection to Illness;" also see Harold Burger et al., "Long HIV-1 Incubation Periods and Dynamics of Transmission within a Family," *The Lancet*, July 21, 1991, 134–136, for the documentation of incubation periods of longer than 12 years in a mother and daughter with HIV-1 in one family. "Although neither has symptoms, both are definitely infected," 134. The longest study of people with HIV-positive, the eleven—year follow-up of gay men in San Francisco, shows that of the 341 men infected with HIV before 1980, 19 percent have no clinical symptoms. Ann Guidici Fettner, "Tend the Healthy," *The Village Voice*, January 15, 1991, 16.

53. Charles A. Mercier, *Leper Houses and Medieval Hospitals* (London: Lewis, 1915), 7; cited in Saul Nathaniel Brody, *The Disease of the Soul: Leprosy in Medieval Literature* (Ithaca: Cornell University Press, 1954) 74–75.

54. Lev. 13:45–46; *The Holy Bible*, Authorized (King James) Version; David F.

Musto, "Quarantine and the Problem of AIDS, in Elizabeth Fee and Daniel Fox eds., *AIDS: The Burden of History* (Berkeley: University of California Press, 1988), 69.

55. Paolo Zappa, *Unclean! Unclean!* trans. Edward Storer (London: L. Dickson, Ltd., 1933) 97–98.

56. Nancy E. Waxler, "Learning to Be a Leper: A Case Study in the Social Construction of Illness," in Elliot G. Mishler, *Social Contexts of Health, Illness, and Patient Care* (Cambridge: Cambridge University Press, 1981), 169–194.

57. Sir William Osler in Theodore Rosebury, *Microbes and Morals* (New York: Viking Press, 1971), 31.

58. Sontag, *AIDS and Its Metaphors*, 81.

59. Swenson, "Plagues, History and AIDS," 189.

60. Karen Wald, "Interview with Bill Rowe, National AIDS Task Force of the American Anthropological Association," September 1988.

61. Karen Wald, "Conversations in Sanitorium" (Los Cocos, Havana; unpublished interviews, September 1989).

62. Philip J. Hilts, "Drug Said To Help AIDS Cases With Virus But No Symptoms," *New York Times*, August 18, 1989, A1.

63. Gina Kolata, "Strong Evidence Discovered That AZT Holds Off AIDS," *New York Times*, August 4, 1989, A1, B6.

64. Philip J. Hilts, "Major Changes for Health System Seen in Wake of the AIDS Finding," *New York Times*, August 19, 1989, 8; also see Philip J. Hilts, "Drug Said To Help AIDS Cases With Virus But No Symptoms," *New York Times*, August 18, 1989, A1.

65. Steven M. Wolinsky, et al., "Human Immunodeficiency Virus Type 1 (HIV-1) Infection a Median of 18 Months Before a Diagnostic Western Blot," *Annals of Internal Medicine* 3, no. 12 (December 15, 1989): 971; see "AIDS Can Hide From Tests for Years," *New York Post*, December 15, 1984, 14R.

66. Richard T. Davey, Jr., M. B. Vasudevachari, H. Clifford Lane, "Serologic Tests for Human Immunodeficiency Virus Infection," in Vincent T. DeVita, Jr., M.D., et al., eds., *AIDS: Etiology, Diagnosis, Treatment, and Prevention* 3rd ed. (Philadelphia: J. B. Lippincott Company, 1992): 142; C. Robert H. Horsburgh, Jr., et al., "Duration of Human Immunodeficiency Virus Infection Before Detection of Antibody," *The Lancet*, September 16, 1989, 637–640; also see David T. Imagawa and Roger Detels, "HIV-1 in Seronegative Homosexual Men," (letter to the editor) *New England Journal Of Medicine* 325 no. 17 (October 24, 1991): 1250–1251; also see Lawrence K. Altman, M.D. "Researchers in Furor Over AIDS Say They Can't Reproduce Results," *New York Times*, November 5, 1991, C3.

67. *Cuba Business*, 10.

68. Elizabeth Fee, "Sex Education in Cuba: An Interview with Dr. Celestino Alvarez Lajonchere," *Journal of Health Services* 18, no. 2 (November 2, 1988): 354.

69. Dr. Juan Carlos Rex, in Wald, "Conversations in the Sanitorium."

70. Dennis Altman, *AIDS in the Mind of America* (New York: Anchor Press, 1986).

71. Ibid., 15.

72. Christian Huxley, *Middle East Report*, November–December 1989, 24. Libya's official news agency JANA reported that Moamar Khadafy accused U.S.

intelligence services of creating the AIDS virus and spreading it throughout the world. "Khadafy: U.S. Made AIDS Germ," *New York Post*, July 21, 1990.

73. Altman, "AIDS," 175.

74. Robert Pear, "Health Department Loses AIDS Rule Dispute," *New York Times*, May 28, 1991, 18.

75. Douglas Crimp, "How to Have Promiscuity in an Epidemic," in Douglas Crimp, ed., *AIDS: Cultural Analysis/Cultural Activism* (Cambridge: MIT Press, 1988), 249; also see Ronald Sullivan, "Aids in New York City Killing More Drug Users," *New York Times*, October 22, 1987, B1.

76. Matthew G. Shebar in *Harper's*, October 1985, by Lieberson, et al., 52. Matthew Shebar is the former director of the Gay Men's Health Crisis.

77. Wald, "Conversations in Sanitorium."

78. Cindy Patton, "Resistance and the Erotic: Reclaiming History, Setting Strategy as we Face AIDS," *Radical America* 20, no. 6 (Facing AIDS: A Special Issue); studies of gays in the United States demonstrate the success of grass roots safe sex education efforts. The rate of infection among gays declined five to tenfold during the 1980s. Geoffrey Cowley, "The Future of AIDS," *Newsweek*, March 22, 1993, 51.

79. Crimp, *AIDS: Cultural Analysis/Cultural Activism*, 253; see Cindy Patton, *Sex and Germs: The Politics of AIDS* (Boston: South End Press, 1985); also see Cindy Patton and Janis Kelly, *Making It: A Woman's Guide In the Age of AIDS* (Ithaca: Firebrand Books, 1987).

80. Ron D. Stall, Thomas J. Coates, and Colleen Hoff, "Behavioral Risk Reduction for HIV Infection Among Gay and Bisexual Men: A Review Of Results from the United States," *American Psychologist* 43 no. 11 (1988): 878.

81. Cabrera, "On the Frontiers of AIDS," 12.

82. Ibid.

83. Wald, "Conversations in Sanitorium."

84. Ibid.

85. Ibid.

86. Dr. Hector Terry as quoted in Cabrera, "Fight Against Death," 8.

87. Jonathan Mann, in interview on PBS' AIDS Quarterly, April 25, interviewed by Peter Jennings.

88. "Letters: AIDS in Cuba," *New York Review of Books*, October 26, 1989, 68–69.

89. Douglas Crimp, "Mourning and Militancy," *October* 51 (Winter 1989): 15.

90. Hector Terry in Wald, "Questions and Answers."

91. Editorial, "Cuban Strategy in the Struggle Against AIDS," *Weekly Granma*, September 18, 1988.

92. Ibid.

93. Reuters International Dispatch, December 1, 1992; Bazell, "Happy Camper," 14.

Recent reports from health officials on the AIDS epidemic in Latin America indicate an alarming increase in the rate of HIV infection and AIDS. Cuba is the one exception in the region. "Latin America's most successful effort in limiting the spread of the infection has apparently been in Cuba," James Brooke, "In Deception and Denial, an Epidemic Looms," *New York Times*, January 25, 1993, A6.

94. Mann, "The International Epidemiology of AIDS," 89.

95. Harvey V. Fineberg, "The Social Dimensions of AIDS," *Scientific American* 259, no. 4 (October 1988): 130; Bazell, "Happy Camper," 14.

96. Jan Zita Grover, "AIDS: Keywords," in Douglas Crimp, ed., *AIDS: Cultural Analysis/Cultural Activism* (Cambridge: MIT Press, 1988), 29.

97. This is different from Sontag's warnings about the game of talk about emergency mobilizations, which end up being ad nauseum appeals about a nation's survival. In mass societies, the mobilization is usually kept general and loaded with rhetoric, and "the reality of the response falls well short of what seems to be demanded to meet the challenge of the nation-endangering menace." Sontag, *AIDS and Its Metaphors*, 85.

98. François Delaporte, *Disease and Civilization: The Cholera in Paris, 1832,* trans. Arthur Goldhammer (Cambridge: MIT Press, 1986), 6.

99. Douglas Crimp, "AIDS: Cultural Analysis/Cultural Activism," in Douglas Crimp, ed., *AIDS: Cultural Analysis/Cultural Activism* (Cambridge: MIT Press, 1988), 3.

100. John L. Peterson and Gerardo Marín, "Issues in the Prevention of AIDS Among Black and Hispanic Men," *American Psychologist* 43 (1988): 872; Catania, et al., 1988; also see Albert Bandura, "Self-Efficacy: Toward a Unifying Theory of Behavioral Change," *Psychological Review* 84, no. 2 (1977): 191–215 for a discussion of an integrative theoretical framework to explain behavioral change. "Expectations of personal efficacy determine whether coping behavior will be initiated, how much effort will be expended, and how long it will be sustained in the face of obstacles and aversive experience." (Bandura, 191)

101. J. M. Carrier, "Cultural Factors Affecting Urban Mexican Male Homosexual Behavior," *Archives of Sexual Behavior* 5 (1976): 103–124, as cited in Peterson and Marín, "Issues in the Prevention of AIDS," 872; B. V. Marín, G. Marín, and R. Juarez, "Strategies for Enhancing the Cultural Appropriateness of AIDS Prevention Campaigns," paper presented at the Annual Meeting of the Western Psychological Association, Burlingame, California, April 1988, as cited in Peterson and Marín, "Issues in the Prevention of AIDS," 872.

102. J. P. Paul, "The Bisexual Identity: An Idea Without Social Recognition," *Journal of Homosexuality* 9:45–63 (1984); Peterson and Marín, "Issues in the Prevention of AIDS," 873.

103. Peterson and Marín, "Issues in the Prevention of AIDS," 873; Jeffrey D. Fisher, "Possible Effects of Reference Group Based Social Influence on AIDS-Risk Behavior and AIDS Prevention," *American Psychologist* 43, no. 11 (1988), 914. Interviews with primarily heterosexual college students suggested that they found it "easier to have (unprotected) sex than to discuss STD prevention." Also see Fisher, "Reference Group Based on Social Influence," 915. Both males and females feared rejection by their sex partner (sanctions) if they failed to conform to group norms and raised the question before sex about STD.

104. "Hispanic Culture and HIV Infection," in Culturelinc Corporation, *Cultural Factors Among Hispanics: Perception and Prevention of HIV Infection,* (New York: Culturelinc Corporation, 1991), 14–21; also see Fisher, "Reference Group Based Social Influence," 915; E. Vasquez-Nuttall, Z. Avila-Vivas, and G. Morales-Barreto, "Working With Latin American Families," *Family Therapy Collections* 9 (1984): 74–90.

105. Peterson and Marín, "Issues in the Prevention of AIDS," 873–875; also, see Fabio Sabogal, Regina Otero-Sabogal, Barbara Vanoss Marín, Gerardo Marín, and Eliseo J. Pérez-Stable, "Perceived Self-efficacy to Avoid Smoking Among Hispanic and White Nonhispanic Smokers" (Technical Report no. 8) *Hispanic Smoking Cessation Research Report*, University of California, 1986.

6

The Cuban Revolution in Crisis

It has often been said that a society is judged by how well it responds in times of greatest need. A tragedy such as the HIV epidemic brings a society face to face with the core of its established values and offers an opportunity for the reaffirmation of compassion, justice, and human dignity.

—Admiral James Watkins

In 1987 the socialist leader Michael Harrington told the following parable: "In a desert society where water is scarce, everyone knows it's human to covet water. Wars are fought over water. People kill over water. If you bring someone to this meeting from the desert, and he sees one can freely get a glass of water, he will say 'It's impossible. People will come back at night to take buckets of water. We have learned that it's human nature to covet water.'"[1]

He went on to say that we have learned to socialize water, to make it universally, freely available to people. For a socialist society, the concept is extended: We learn that not only is it not "human nature" for people to go without water, it is also not human nature for them to go without education, food, shelter, and medical care. Having free access to all these is a basic socialist ideal.

This has been a fundamental belief of the Cuban Revolution. When, however, it comes to machismo and the fear of losing "control" to nonauthorized groups, Castro and others in power do not live up to their faith in education and the "capacity to change" thesis. When the socialist message of the power of education comes up against machismo and male sexual habits, it is greeted with a Pavlovian shrug and the repeated response, "It's Cuban male human nature." This conviction that people can not change, and its corollary, "education won't work," are then rationalized to support the quarantine because "one has to bite the bullet and take hard measures during a plague." In today's world, gay rights and AIDS are a society's litmus test of its social values, of their strengths and weaknesses. Cuba has been a case study.

In differing economic and political systems, there are different standards of human rights. In the United States, with its exaggerated emphasis on private profit, a basic standard of living for those who do not work is not considered a human right. And yet, it has long been recognized in theory, if not always in practice, that all citizens have the right to vote and organize politically. In Cuba, recognized human rights such as shelter, adequate food, employment, health care, and free education through university are counterbalanced by the absence of equally vital political rights.

It is not a recognized human right in either the United States or Cuba for people to openly express their sexual preference without discrimination. In the United States, a gay rights movement struggles toward that goal, has achieved some successes, but still has a long way to go. In Cuba, while there have been significant improvements since the 1960s, gays do not have the right of assembly, the right to hold any job or political office they choose, or to organize politically or support particular candidates in elections. With greater guaranteed political rights, it is unlikely the Military Units to Aid Production (UMAP) tragedy would have happened at all.

All of these rights can be summed up in one: the right to dissent. These rights would also include a press that would enable gay dissenters to express their views—publicly opposing or advocating views that are different. For example, during the 1971 Educational and Cultural Congress when the anti-gay positions were unanimously adopted and published, opposition to these positions could have been publicized with a free press. In a public debate, views of the minority would have allowed discussion of the rights of gays, not only by gays but by anyone who challenged the homophobic platform adopted under the banner of what's good for Cuban children and country.[2]

In this book, I have used gays as a barometer, as both image and touchstone. The freedom to dissent, to express views that are not popular, to oppose bureaucratic and arbitrary policies, are all-important questions not only in terms of gays, but throughout the society.[3] Thus, in the United States, we hear, "Yes, you can have freedom of assembly—but, 'we're sorry.' When it comes to 'social' rights such as medical care, jobs, housing, and education through the university level. These are not really rights at all. If you don't have them, you simply didn't work hard enough to get them."

And in Cuba we hear, "Yes, we see housing, education, jobs, and medical care as basic rights of men and women—but, "'we're sorry.'" We have to have necessary controls. We are a controlled society for the common good, which means you cannot travel outside the country, join together as gays, or, speak your alternative views, and publish your alternative, even dissenting newspapers."

When questioned whether interning people in a sanitorium is a violation of human rights, Juan Carlos, the interned physician, summarized the official Cuban position with a passionate defense of the treatment they are receiving. He compared it to AIDS care in other countries.

> You ask me if I think being here violates my human rights. Now I ask you, all those people with AIDS who have no option, who don't have the option of receiving medical care, of seeing a doctor, of receiving the few medicines that are available—aren't their human rights being violated?
>
> I don't think any human rights are being violated. On the contrary, I think what they're doing is trying to help us live a little longer, while the majority in most countries—I'm not just talking about the U.S. because it happens in a lot more countries—are struggling to get maybe a third of what I have.[4]

Cuban social policies express views held by particular political and religious groups found in every country—those who usually take extreme conservative positions on sexuality. For them, sexual disease is tied to sin, which must be "controlled" (also a favorite word of those forces opposing change in Cuba). Social construction of AIDS has led to abuse of the rights of people with AIDS and of people who have tested HIV-positive; it is contrary to the spirit of science and enlightened social policy.

As Allan M. Brandt, professor of the history of medicine and science at Harvard Medical School, has eloquently pointed out, "So long as disease is equated with sin, there can be no 'magic bullet,'—that is, a biomedical solution. We need to recognize that 'behavioral change' does not mean celibacy, heterosexuality, or morality; it means avoiding contact with a pathogen."[5]

When a society concludes that the costs of explicit sexual education are too high—that is, when AIDS education is interpreted as encouraging homosexuality, the result is victimization of people with AIDS and people testing HIV-positive, whether because of the influence of the Catholic hierarchy or homophobics in government positions or the political leadership in Havana. It is no different than the opposition to educational approaches in Victorian England when legislators opposed public health education as equivalent to "condoning" vice.[6]

What has been common in Cuba has been what Susan Sontag describes in her book *AIDS and Its Metaphors:* the disease becomes a metaphor for the morally corrupt, the bad and sinful. Sontag had previously analyzed the ways in which "illnesses have always been used as metaphors to enliven charges that a society was corrupt or unjust."[7] She observed that diseases such as cancer and tuberculosis came to be viewed not as fundamentally medical concerns, but as issues tied to personality traits, thus perpetuating a myth that makes character type a cause of illness. When Sontag met cancer patients who felt a "kind of shame" at their disease,

> it occurred to me that some of these notions were the converse of now thoroughly discredited beliefs about tuberculosis. As tuberculosis had been often regarded sentimentally, as an enhancement of identity, cancer was regarded with irrational revulsion, as a diminution of the self. There were also similar fictions of a characterological predispositon to the illness: cancer is regarded as a disease to which the psychically defeated, the inexpressive, the repressed—especially those who have repressed anger or sexual feelings—are particularly prone, as tuberculosis was regarded throughout the nineteenth and twentieth centuries (indeed, until it was discovered how to cure it) as a disease apt to strike the hypersensitive, the talented, the passionate.[8]

The themes of normal and pathological—good and evil—have influenced humankind throughout history. Foucault writes:

> Every society establishes a whole series of systems of oppositions between good and evil, permitted and prohibited, lawful and elicit, criminal and noncriminal, etc. All of these oppositions which are constitutive of society today . . . are being reduced to the simple opposition between normal and pathological. This opposition not only is simpler than the others but also has the advantage of letting us believe there is a technique to bring the pathological back to normal.[9]

In many countries, including the United States, the right-wing has used AIDS as proof that the wrath of God has come down on people, especially homosexuals, because of their "perverted" and sinful behavior. Jerry Falwell calls it, "God's judgment on a society that does not live by His rules." Patrick Buchanan, in the *New York Post*, defined AIDS as tied to immoral, unnatural acts and ignored the fact that AIDS is not only a worldwide epidemic but predominantly one of heterosexual transmission.[10]

People with AIDS are no longer people who are ill; rather they are immoral people who have committed wrongs and been stricken down as punishment. In writing *AIDS and Its Metaphors*, Sontag wanted AIDS to be regarded "as if it were just a disease—a very serious one, but just a disease. Not a curse, not a punishment, not an embarrassment."[11] The associations people have with AIDS are not favorable associations as with tuberculosis or with polio, whose victims were mostly innocent children. With AIDS, they are outcasts and untouchables. Sontag's brilliant contribution is to make us remember that AIDS is a disease—not bad behavior.

Prescription for Change

Cuba's leaders either cannot or refuse to hear that people under socialism genuinely want and are entitled to political rights and freedoms in spite of their having other human rights. These rights are loudly missing in Cuba. The historic treatment of homosexuals in the 1960s and the current quarantine of HIV-positive people both represent a lack of basic freedoms—such as those of press, speech, and assembly.

Instead of hearing calls for *greater freedoms*, Castro sees the undermining effects of U.S. *imperialism* and blames it for having "accelerated the destabilizing process in Eastern Europe." He also defends Cuba's August 1989 censorship of the Soviet publications *Sputnik* and *Moscow News* because the magazines "are full of poison against the U.S.S.R. itself and socialism. You can see that imperialism and reactionary forces and the counterrevolution are responsible for the tone."[12]

An example of the Cuban people's exposure to rhetoric and double-speak occurred when three months earlier Castro—at the opening of the school year (September 1989)—called on schools to emphasize the development of thinking skills.[13] Censorship continues to prevent access to information—a crucial necessity for critical thinking skills. Whatever the risks, people have to be able to make up their own minds about issues—whether something is "decadent" (*Sputnik* and *Moscow News*, according to Castro) or not.

Of course, some of the opposition to Communist governments in Eastern Europe has come from those who hope to restore pure capitalism, from advocates of fascism and other reactionary programs one would have thought died out long ago. Virulent racism and anti-Semitism also seem to have burst forth from dormancy. And there is no doubt that the CIA and extreme right-wing forces have long worked to destroy any kind of socialism. But it is simplistic and ignorant to assume that the massive popular uprisings against these governments and Communist parties were not grounded in widespread, deeply-felt rejection of narrow-minded authoritarian rule—deeply felt by socialists as well.

Castro's view that the Cubans are not able to decide for themselves about Soviet publications or *The New York Times*, that the government must make that decision for them to protect against such "poison," has the same effect, of course, as did the banning of Henry Miller's *Tropic of Cancer* in Boston in the 1920s. Thus, Radio Martí ("The Unmentionable Station") previously thought to be boring North American propaganda by most Cubans, was drawing new listeners by reading excerpts from *Moscow News* and *Sputnik*.[14]

Castro does not think socialism can exist "without a strong, disciplined and respected Party. Such a process cannot be advanced by slandering socialism, destroying its values, casting slurs on the Party, demoralizing its vanguard, abandoning the Party's guiding role, eliminating social discipline, and sowing chaos and anarchy everywhere. This may foster a counterrevolution, but not revolutionary change."[15]

Control, Conformity, Centralization, and the Revolution in Crisis

One example of the invidious effect of one-party rule and the failure to allow political diversity over the years can be seen in teaching styles and curriculum content. Teachers and administrators worry lest they fail to promote the "correct line" in their classrooms and in overall school policy. They worry lest they are guilty of what Prieto called "ideological dependency" or "extravagances." This anxiety and the pressure to increase percentages of promotion make for a hidden curriculum. Teachers and paraprofessionals often "hand down" knowledge to students, and this "handing down" neither stresses nor encourages individual critical thinking.[16] The historian and vice dean of the University of Havana, María del Carmen Barcia, maintains that history is not taught effectively in her country. She has urged teachers "to let go of the habits of memorizing, of learning unconnected dates, and happenings of no importance."[17] The word of the educator can become more important than what's happening to the student. Thus, Cuba's quest for quality is undermined by the lack of interaction within the classroom, by its failure to recognize that the heart of education remains the interaction between student and teacher.

When teachers and principals are insecure and unable to resist the pressures of test mania or are concerned about adhering to the Party line, rigidity often sets in as a defense. They easily revert to a lecture format, the methodology and philosophy that they received as youngsters— whether it be in a capitalist or socialist environment—even though they often acknowledge having been bored out of their minds as youngsters by the pedantic reading of teacher notes. Elsewhere I have referred to the Cuban blue book syndrome, where students simply copy teacher lectures in blue notebooks in elementary and secondary level classes, with minimal student-teacher interaction. Veteran Cuban educators such as Garcia Gallo have criticized what he calls this "formalismo." At the beginning of the twentieth century in the United States, John Dewey challenged just this traditional format. A leader in the progressive education movement, he urged education by doing. Today Dewey's voice is again being heard in many countries.[18]

In a creative, progressive learning environment, classroom students should not be passive blobs absorbing (or resisting) what teachers say. One should be learning not merely facts but higher-order thinking skills—how to acquire and organize knowledge, to formulate questions, and to figure out the strategies necessary to answer them. From my observation, 80 percent of questions in Cuban classrooms are factual: teaching usually consists of asking a factual question that requires a correct answer. The students ask few questions, and it is usually the same few students who do so. This situation, of course, is by no means unique to Cuba.

One creative program that fell victim to overcentralization was the *jardines infantiles*, (literally "kindergarten"), an alternative day care system, which Jorge Domínguez called "the longest lasting instance of citizen initiative" in the Revolution.[19] Organized by Haydee Salas and Lela Sánchez in 1964, it lasted seven years, growing from 20 jardines to 178 in 1971. Salas and Sánchez tried to build a program after Scandinavian models and emphasized free play, inter-age groupings, flexibility in schedules—exploration, and spontaneity as opposed to the mainstream day care (*círculos infantiles*) which focused very heavily on cleanlinesss, structured learning, achievement, and fixed schedules.

In 1971 the day care programs were unified, with all day care centralized under the *círculos infantiles* administration. Sánchez and Salas were removed and given other positions in housing. What had been a decentralized effort was now replaced by strong central control. The focus on centralization, discipline, and authority blurs ideological and educational differences in the service of conformity and prevents the healthy emergence of creative, educational approaches.

Overcentralization often leads to rigid curriculum, with an overreliance on test scores as the only measure of the student. On numerous occasions during almost a quarter of a century of observing Cuban classrooms, I have been shown the bulletin board or chart that indicates the percentage of promotion—the statistic of pride. This percentage, closely related to system-wide test scores, has come to represent improvement in education. Also, high test and promotion percentages have become the measure of a teacher's "revolutionary attitude" and individual as well as collective accomplishment. Veteran teachers everywhere know that this inevitably leads to "teaching for the exam" and to cheating. Indeed, this was a source of scandal in the summer of 1986 when the minister of education revealed that 30 percent of junior high school students and 24 percent of senior high school students in Havana had failed to pass their annual exams.[20] There were reports of cheating and of teachers selling answers to the final exams.

Allowing teachers to make creative curriculum innovations is one of the major hopes for lasting, effective educational change. The opportunity for real changes in the schools comes about when teachers (and students too) are *involved* in the process. This is the unharnessed power, the unignited dynamite, of schools and learning in the cities of the most developed countries and in the most remote, isolated areas of the world. This was true when I started teaching in the ghetto schools as an elementary teacher 40 years ago. It holds true today and will for the twenty-first century.[21]

The late Myles Horton, radical educator and guiding light of the adult Highlander Folk School in Tennessee, emphasized the crucial relationship between good teaching and democracy. "Education is what happens to the other person, not what comes out of the mouth of the educator . . . what people need are experiences in democracy, in making decisions that affect their lives and communities."[22]

In Cuba, genuine participatory involvement by non-Party community organizations and newspapers not only could enable the quarantine to be challenged, but could, on a much broader scale, energize and motivate Cubans to work toward much-needed changes in the economy, the schools, and other areas within socialist society. As a result, changes could be generated both from the top, as in sex education or the extension of women's rights, and from below by a renewed commitment to people's power—a concept dreamed of by the early socialist theorists sometimes cited in Cuban classrooms.

Those who support a one-party government in Cuba also point to the fact that the island is still threatened by an aggressive superpower, and there are strong nationalist feelings throughout Cuba. Any notion on the part of United States politicians that an invasion would be welcomed by the masses of Cubans is wishful thinking indicating ignorance of the paradox that is Cuba. In his March 23, 1990 column for the Gannett newspapers, the black writer William Raspberry wrote: "Any attempt to invade Cuba would be an all-out disaster . . . not because black Cubans are necessarily pro-Communist, but because they are nationalist and optimistic regarding their prospects under the present regime."[23]

A leading dissident in Cuba, Gustavo Arcos, who spent ten years in jail and heads the Cuban Committee for Human Rights, acknowledges that a considerable part of the Cuban people "support the Cuban government and its leaders" and states that labeling everyone "revolutionary and counterrevolutionary" is "ambiguous and useless." He calls for a dialogue among all sectors, including the Cuban government.[24]

In private, Cubans say that changes have to take place. The long lines for food and gasoline, and the long wait for delayed or unavailable public buses, overcrowded when they do arrive, irritate and demoralize even the most ardent revolutionary by the time she or he gets to work. People are dissatisfied with delay in more than transportation: There

have been years and years of *talk* about improving the availability of food
and consumer goods, about improving the quality of goods, and about
improving a great variety of services.[25] Young adults wanting to get married or live alone are faced with a severe housing shortage, and the subsequent stress and anxiety within families is a serious problem. Some
citizens in their forties and fifties, who are "dedicated to the Revolution,"
told me of their bitterness when they realized that they may never see the
dream of having their own house or a larger apartment. They also realize
that sometimes it's not *socialismo* that works but *sociolismo*, "socio" being
slang for one's pal or buddy. *Sociolismo* means resolving problems not by
an "impartial, fair socialist process" but by "who you know." "It's good
to have pull" whether to get your child into a preferred school or to get a
plumber for repairs or food that is not available.

Young Cubans are also weary of having a rigid correct line prescribed
for almost all aspects of social as well as political life. As one teenager put
it recently to a *Village Voice* reporter,

> We are a generation that is really tired of repeating 30-year-old slogans. . . .
> But it seems like Fidel forgets who he is. He is not an art critic, not a food
> critic, not a historian, not an entertainer, not a storyteller. Fidel is *theoreti-
> cally* the elected political representative of the Cuban people. We want an-
> swers, not speeches. We want explanations, not rhetoric. If someone in-
> vades our island we don't need him to tell us to fight. In the meantime,
> we'd like to know what, if anything, Fidel has planned to turn things
> around? We are all old enough now to no longer take orders. We want to
> discuss things, debate them and decide together.[26]

The *Village Voice* reporter spent most of his time in Havana talking to
teenage males who were not opposed to socialism but simply wanted to
grow their hair long and listen to hard rock. Other Cubans want to read
without censor, to travel, to break the stagnant political structure. They
want to freely and publicly debate how to develop socialism and democracy without being ostracized or endangering advancement in their
careers. If they are gay or lesbian, they want also to live without harassment and discrimination. If they test HIV-positive, they want the right to
work and live their own lives with dignity, as they cannot do in the
"golden cages" of the sanitoriums. They want to pursue and enjoy the
fruits of socialism. Yet Fidel Castro and the Communist Party remain rig-
idly opposed to giving up any social control and persist in labeling anyone who questions authority as antirevolutionary.

There is no guarantee, of course, that an open environment and democratic process produces the best solutions and approaches, as is all too
clear in the experiences of other countries. However, it would increase
the odds, especially in Cuba, precisely because of past achievements of

the Revolution. In particular, the Cuban population as a whole is highly educated by any standards, and especially in comparison to other non-industrial countries. This is important to finding new and creative solutions to the problems of underdevelopment. An educated public is the essential prerequisite of a democratic process. And, at the local level, Cubans already have working structures for political democracy.

It is unclear what the full effects of the October 1991 Fourth Congress of the Communist Party will be. Over half the 225 members of the Central Committee are now new and younger. Thirty of them are women.[27] The Congress also called for the first direct elections for members of the National Assembly and provincial assemblies rather than the customary election of delegates who then choose the National Assembly.

The elections were held in February 1993 with one candidate running for each of 589 parliamentary seats and nominated by the municipal assemblies elected the previous December. Nominations were based on proposals from slate-making commissions, whose members came from the largest national organizations, such as the federations of trade unions, of students, and of women. There were no independent candidates; voters could vote yes or vote a blank ballot for all, some, or none of the candidates nominated. To win, a candidate had to receive over 50 percent of the votes cast.

Candidates could not campaign around any specific issues. There was no acceptance of a loyal opposition, or for organized groups that would pressure all candidates for any particular legislation, for instance, making it illegal to discriminate on the basis of sexual orientation. Final tallies showed 99.6 percent of registered voters cast ballots with only 7.2 percent of these blank or spoiled, in spite of a strong campaign by Miami-based groups urging voters to leave ballots blank.[28]

Cuba is now suffering from a convergence of serious problems, some cumulative internal conditions and some shocks from outside. The United States government has maintained its hostility through a trade embargo that has recently become even more severe. Rapid changes in Eastern Europe and Russia have drastically diminished Cuba's most essential trade relations. Cuba has failed to sufficiently diversify its economy and achieve necessary levels of productivity in the production and distribution of goods. Over the years, its political leadership has refused to significantly loosen its control over all aspects of the economy and society.

There is no way to predict how the political forces will play themselves out. The U.S. government has, especially since 1980, nurtured the power of an organized extreme right-wing Cuban-American network. On the other hand, one great strength of the Cuban government is the unity of the population against U.S. intervention, a unity that includes those who are apathetic toward the government and even the small number of active dissidents. Meanwhile, the successful social programs of the Revolution that have brought a better life to millions are in danger of beginning to erode under pressure. Drastic change is inevitable, especially the need to open both the politics and the economy.[29]

The quarantine policy is representative of the crisis in Cuba today. Whatever solutions become possible, they preclude a political leadership that is so afraid of losing macho control that it hides its head in the sand and waits for the storm to pass.

Notes

1. Michael Harrington's sixtieth birthday party, Roseland Ballroom, New York, 1989.

2. I'm indebted to I. F. Stone's lucid discussion of human rights in the USSR. See I. F. Stone, "The Rights of Gorbachev," *N.Y. Review of Books*, February 16, 1989, 3–4, 6,7.

3. The U.S. blockade certainly did not help with access to alternative educational or psychological approaches. Educators in MINED such as Abel Prieto, Max Figueroa, Raúl Ferrer, and Lydia Turner would urge me to bring them professional journals on new curriculum developments. They were eager to learn about new trends and approaches "in the States."

4. Karen Wald, "AIDS in Cuba: A Dream or a Nightmare?" *Z Magazine*, December 1990, 109.

In a letter to the *New York Times* on February 23, 1993, Juan Carlos de la Concepcion and Raúl Llanos, residents in Cuba's Havana sanitorium for people infected with HIV, defend the accomplishment of Cuba's AIDS policy, underscoring that Cuba has indeed contained the spread of AIDS: "Cuba has the same population as New York City. Visiting and exchanging experiences with AIDS care providers in your city and around your country, we have learned that New York has had 42,737 reported cases of full-blown AIDS. Cuba has 159." Juan Carlos de la Concepcion, M.D., and Raúl Llanos (letter translated by Karen Wald), "U.S. Can Learn from Cuba's AIDS Program," *New York Times*, February 16, 1993, A16.

5. Allan M. Brandt, "AIDS, From Social History to Social Policy," in Elizabeth Fee and Daniel M. Fox, eds., *AIDS: The Burdens of History* (Berkeley: University of California Press, 1988), 167.

6. Dorothy and Roy Porter, "The Enforcement of Health: The British Debate," in Fee and Fox, eds., *AIDS: The Burdens of History*, 97–116.

7. Susan Sontag, *Illness as Metaphor* (New York: Farrar, Straus and Giroux, 1978), 71; Susan Sontag, *AIDS and Its Metaphors* (New York: Farrar, Straus, and Giroux, 1989).

8. Sontag, *AIDS and Its Metaphors*, 12; for a critique of Susan Sontag's work on *AIDS and Its Metaphors*, see Tim Dean, "The Psychoanalysis of AIDS," *October* 63 (Winter 1993): 93–94; D. A. Miller, "Sontag's Urbanity," *October* 49 (Summer 1989): 91–101.

9. Michel Foucault, *Madness and Civilization: A History of Insanity in the Age of Reason* (New York: Random House, 1973), 73.

10. Gregory M. Herk and Eric K. Glunt, "An Epidemic of Stigma: Public Reactions To AIDS," *American Psychologist* 43, no. 11. (November 1988): 888.

11. Sontag, *AIDS and Its Metaphors*, 14.

12. Fidel Castro, *Weekly Granma*, December 17, 1989, 3.

13. Fidel Castro, speech delivered on September 6, 1989, *Granma*. Castro speaks about the need to emphasize *thinking* in the Cuban curriculum. See Lauren B. Resnick and Leopold E. Klopfer, "Toward the Thinking Curriculum: Concluding Remarks," in Lauren B. Resnick and Leopold E. Klopfer, eds., *Toward the Thinking Curriculum: Current Cognitive Research, 1989 ASCD Yearbook,* (Alexandria: Association for Supervision and Curriculum Development, 1989), 207–211.

14. Pat Aufderheide, "Cuba's Conundrum," *In These Times*, January 10, 1990, 24.

15. Speech given by Fidel Castro, at the Memorial Ceremony in El Cacahual, *Weekly Granma*, December 7, 1989, 3.

Almost a century ago theorists like Rosa Luxemburg, a principal founder of the Communist party of Germany, criticized Vladimir Lenin's advocacy of one-party rule under socialism. She wrote that the job of the proletariat is "to replace bourgeois democracy with socialist power, not to abolish democracy itself." Rosa Luxemburg, *Gesammelte Werke*, Berlin: Dietz Verlag, 1947, vol. 1–2, 440, cited in Michael Harrington, *Socialism: Past and Future*, (New York: Arcade Publishing, Inc., 1989), 68.

16. Educators, critical of the emphasis on testing in their own countries, have called those practices an educational mania.

In 1984 the Supreme Soviet in the USSR passed a reform statement entitled "Guidelines for the Reform of General and Vocational Education," which sounded warnings about the state of Soviet Education. The call was for reforms in textbooks, curriculum, and accountability.

Soviet educators decried what they called the danger of "percentage mania," because of the use of tests to foster accountability and an "overly academic direction" and infatuation with test scores. "School Reform, Soviet Style," *ASCD Update* 31, no. 3 (May 1989), 1, 4; National Commission on Excellence in Education, *A Nation At Risk: The Imperative for Educational Reform* (Washington, D.C.: U.S. Government Printing Office, 1983). Nikolai Nikandrov, Deputy Director of the Institute of General Pedagogics of the USSR, expressed concern about didactic instruction and humanities textbooks that spent "too much time on theorizing . . . and paid too little attention to emotional understanding."

In the United States, teachers' unions have been in the forefront of similar criticisms. They use the same word as the Soviets, referring to *the test mania* in many communities in the United States. It is interesting that these unions also find support from libertarians who are concerned about the dangers of centralization and national testing. William Safire states: "Libertarians like me are suspicious of national testing of children because it leads to national teaching standards, centralized curriculums and, ultimately, a regimented population. While striving for fairness, national exams would endanger democracy and diversity. Create a supertest and teachers will teach to it and students will study to it. The hand that writes the test molds the mind, and we do not want that hand in Washington, D.C." William Safire, "Abandon the Pony Express," *New York Times*, April 25, 1991.

17. *Bohemia*, May 8, 1987, 58.

18. "Get Ready for the New Math,"*Washington Post*, May 28, 1989, B3.

19. Jorge I. Domínguez, *Cuba: Order and Revolution* (Cambridge: Harvard University Press, 1978), 410.

20. *Granma Weekly Review*, December 14, 1986, 6; *Diario Las Americas*, July 30, 1986, 15A; Alfred Padula and Lois M. Smith, "The Revolutionary Transformation of Cuban Education, 1959–1987," in Edgar B. Gumbert, ed., *Making the Future: Politics and Educational Reform in the United States, England, the Soviet Union, and Cuba* (Atlanta: Center for Cross-cultural Education, Georgia State University, 1988), 133–134.

21. Marvin Leiner, ed., *Children of the Cities: Education of the Powerless* (New York: New American Library, 1975), 16; Charles Silberman, "Change and Teacher Centers," *Notes from Workshop Center for Open Education* 11, no. 2 (June 1973), 9; Vicki I. Karant, "Supervision in the Age of Teacher Empowerment," *Educational Leadership* 46, no. 8 (May 1989): 27–29; Jane I. David, "Synthesis of Research on School-Based Management," *Educational Leadership* 46, no. 8 (May 1989): 45–53.

22. Maurice Isserman, "Experiences in Democracy," review of *The Long Haul: An Autobiography*, by Myles Horton, with Judith Kohl and Herbert Kohl, *The Nation*, November 12, 1990, 569.

23. William Raspberry, March 23, 1990, cited in Sweezy, *Monthly Review*, July–August 1989, 21.

24. Medea Benjamin, *NACLA*, "Soul Searching," August 1990, 26; see also, *Miami Herald*, June 12, 1990; NY *Diario/La Prensa*, July 22, 1990; Tim Golden, "Cuban Rights Advocate Beaten and Detained," *New York Times*, December 13, 1992, 8; Tim Golden, " 'Down with Fidel!' Is Heard in Cuba, But There Is No Sign Yet of His Fall," *New York Times*, January 13, 1993, A10.

25. Tim Golden, "Castro's People Try to Absorb 'Terrible Blows'," *New York Times*, January 11, 1993, A1, A6; Tim Golden, "Cuba's Economy, Cast Adrift, Grasps at Capitalist Solutions," *New York Times*, January 12, 1993, A1, A6.

26. Marc Cooper, *Village Voice*, "Roll Over Che Guevara: Cuba's Got Those Rock and Roll Blues," July 16, 1991, 33. For a discusssion of *socialismo* and *sociolismo* see Julie Feinsilver, "*Socialismo* or *Sociolismo*? The Case of Cuba," paper presented at the XVII International Congress, Latin American Studies Congress, September 25, 1992, Los Angeles.

Guillermo Fernández, a 34-year-old civil engineer and a member of two dissident political groups in Cuba (the Democratic Socialists and the Civic Current), says: "I am one of those who doesn't want to leave . . . I have a position that's both open and moral, and I will never go. I am a patriot. I'm against the Americans. I'm against the United States blockade against the Cubans." He wants a chance to ask questions, to disagree with the government, and wants a "better future." Jo Thomas, "The Last Days of Castro's Cuba," *New York Times Magazine*, March 14, 1993, 37; also see Rolando Prats Paez, "Hard Line, Hard Luck for Cuba," *New York Times*,May 10, 1993, A19.

27. At the first meeting of the Central Committee at the Fourth Congress of

the Communist Party (October 10–14, 1991) Fidel Castro and Raúl Castro were elected First and Second Secretaries of the Communist Party. Twenty-five members of the Political Bureau were elected. Only two are women. "New Central Committee Reelects Fidel and Raúl as First and Second Secretaries of the Party," *Granma International*, Special Supplement on the Fourth Party Congress, October 20, 1991.

28. National Electoral Commission, Havana: "Final Results of Cuba's February 24, 1993, Parliamentary Elections," *Radio Havana Cuba's International Short-wave Service*, March 1, 1993.

29. See Saul Landau, "Your Special Island," *The Nation*, December 7, 1992, 710–713; William Rhoden, "17 Hours Across Rural Cuba: A Living Revolution," *New York Times*, August 18, 1991, 1, 14; Andrew Zimbalist, "Teetering on the Brink: Cuba's Current Economic and Political Crisis," *Journal of Latin American Studies*, vol. 24, no. 2 (May 1992): 407–418; Isel Rivero Y Méndez, "Cuban Women: Back to the Future?" *Ms.* May/June 1993, 15–17. Rivero y Méndez, whose great-grandfather was a "founding father" of Cuba's independence movement in the nineteenth century, is strongly critical of the 1992 incarceration of the outspoken human rights leader and poet, María Elena Cruz Varela; also see Tom Miller, *Trading with the Enemy: A Yankee Travels Through Castro's Cuba* (New York: Atheneum, 1992), for a portrait of contemporary Cuba that captures both the economic and political erosion, and also the national pride in the accomplishments of the revolution.

Series in Political Economy
and Economic Development in Latin America

Series Editor
Andrew Zimbalist
Smith College

Through country case studies and regional analyses this series will contribute to a deeper understanding of development issues in Latin America. Shifting political environments, increasing economic interdependence, and the difficulties with regard to debt, foreign investment, and trade policy demand novel conceptualizations of development strategies and potentials for the region. Individual volumes in this series will explore the deficiencies in conventional formulations of the Latin American development experience by examining new evidence and material. Topics will include, among others, women and development in Latin America; the impact of IMF interventions; the effects of redemocratization on development; Cubanology and Cuban political economy; Nicaraguan political economy; and individual case studies on development and debt policy in various countries in the region.

About the Book and Author

Cuba is the only country in the world that quarantines people who test positive for the HIV virus. In this book, Marvin Leiner analyzes the practice of quarantine in the context of the Cuban Revolution, which has otherwise brought significant advances in social programs, such as free universal education and comprehensive health care for all. He also focuses on efforts by Cuban educators to introduce sex education in the schools and to change sexist and homophobic attitudes, discussing their successes and failures with candor and examining the explicit and implicit linkages between machismo and homophobia.

Drawing on interviews, diaries, and techniques of participant observation, Dr. Leiner shows how the HIV sanitorium and earlier oppressive treatment of gays and lesbians serve as a barometer for contemporary Cuban society. Despite the impressive achievements of the Revolution, Cuba remains a society lacking political rights, in particular the right to dissent.

Marvin Leiner is emeritus professor of education at Queens College of the City University of New York. He is author of *Children Are the Revolution: Day Care in Cuba* and editor of *Children of the Cities: Education of the Powerless*. An internationally known scholar on Cuban schools, he has made frequent research trips to Cuba over the past twenty-five years.

Index